BIBLIOTHECA JAINICA

THE SACRED BOOKS OF THE JAINAS

VOLUME 11

AMS PRESS
NEW YORK

THE SACRED BOOKS OF THE JAINAS

Edited

WITH CO-OPERATION OF VARIOUS SCHOLARS

By

S. C. GHOSHAL, M. A., B. L.

Sarasvatī, Kāvyatirtha, Vidyābhūṣaṇa, Bhāratī.

Sometime Professor of Sanskrit, Edward College, Pabna (Bengal), and Professor of English and Philosophy, Hindu College, Delhi (Punjab), Member, Legislative Council, District Magistrate, Cooch Behar.

Volume XI

PARĪKṢĀMUKHAṂ

PRINTED BY
KIRAN KUMAR ROY,
AT METROPOLITAN PRINTING & PUBLISHING HOUSE, LTD.
90, LOWER CIRCULAR ROAD, CALCUTTA.

PARĪKṢĀMUKHAM

By

MĀṆIKYANANDĪ

(WITH PRAMEYA-RATNAMĀLĀ BY ANANTAVĪRYA)

EDITED WITH TRANSLATION, INTRODUCTION, NOTES AND AN ORIGINAL COMMENTARY IN ENGLISH

By

SARAT CHANDRA GHOSHAL, M. A., B. L.

Sarasvatī, Kāvyatīrtha, Vidyābhūṣaṇa, Bhāratī.

Jubilee Post Graduate Scholar, Bankim Chandra Gold Medallist and Jyotish Chandra Medallist (University of Calcutta) ; Ewart Prizeman, Scottish Church College ; Author of "The Digamvara Saints of India", "Vāruṇi", "Yautuk", "Vairāgyer Pathe", Editor of "Kriyāyogasāra", "Upakathā", "Gītāvalī", "Sundarakānda Rāmāyaṇa", "Dravya-saṃgraha", "Vedanta Paribhāṣā" etc.

PUBLISHED BY

THE CENTRAL JAINA PUBLISHING HOUSE,

AJITASRAM, LUCKNOW.

1940

Library of Congress Cataloging in Publication Data

Māṇikyanandī.
Parīkṣāmukham.
English and Prakrit, with each śloka of the original text rendered into Sanskrit.
Original ed. issued as v. 11 of the Sacred books of the Jainas.
Bibliography: p.
1. Jainism. I. Ghoshal, Sarat Chandra, ed. II. Anantavīrya. Prameya-ratna-mālā. 1974. III. Title. IV. Series: the Sacred books of the Jainas, v. 11.
BL1311.P34M3613 1974 294.4'8'2 73-3845
ISBN 0-404-57711-3

Original pagination has been maintained.

Reprinted from the edition of 1940, Lucknow
First AMS edition published, 1974
Manufactured in the United States of America

International Standard Book Number:
Complete Set: 0-404-57700-8
Volume 11: 0-404-57711-3

AMS PRESS, INC.
NEW YORK, N.Y. 10003

TO

PANDIT AJIT PRASAD, M. A., LL.B.

WITH

DEEPEST LOVE AND AFFECTION.

INTRODUCTION

Earlier writers on Jaina Nyāya.

Parīkṣāmukhaṃ is a standard work on Jaina Nyāya philosophy. The earliest writers on this subject were Kundakundāchārya and Umāsvāmi or Umāsvāti (1st century A. D.). Umāsvāmi wrote his work Tattvārthādhigama Sūtra in the form of aphorisms. Parīkṣāmukhaṃ is also written in the same style. Commentators to Tattvārthādhigama Sūtra were many and the most famous of them developed this subject in their commentaries. The following among them are worthy of special mention: (1) Pujyapāda Devanandi, a Digamvara, the writer of Sarvārtha-siddhi (5th century A. D.); (2) author of Gandhahasti Mahābhāṣya (Samantabhadra according to the Digamvara view, or Siddhasena Divākara according to the Śvetāmvara view or Siddhasena Gaṇi according to another view); (3) Akalaṅka, a Digamvara, the writer of Tattvārtha-rāja-vārttika (7th century A. D.); and (4) Vidyānandi or Vidyānanda, a Digamvara, author of Tattvārtha-śloka-vārttika (9th century A. D.).

Umāsvāmi.

Kundakundāchārya.

Kundakundāchārya is the author of many works the most famous of them being Pravachanasāra, Pañchāstikāya-samayasāra, Samayasāra and Niyamasāra.

Samantabhadra.

Samantabhadra (2nd century A. D. ?) a Digamvara scholar-saint whose date has not been definitely ascertained) was the author of the famous work Āpta-mimāṃsā. Akalaṅka Deva wrote a commentary on this work entitled Aṣṭa-śati. Vidyānanda or Vidyānandi wrote a commentary on Aṣṭa-śati entitled Aṣṭa-sahasrī. Yuktyanuśāsana is another important work of Samanta-bhadra among his voluminous writings.

Siddhasena Divākara.

Siddhasena Divākara, a Śvetāmvara (6th or 7th century A. D.) wrote Nyāyāvatāra a short treatise in verse on Jaina Nyāya. A commentary on this was written by Siddharṣi (10th century A. D.) and Chandraprabha Sūri (12th century A. D.). Siddhasena's other works are Dvātriṅśikā and Sammati Tarka the latter commented on by Abhayadeva Sūri (10th century A. D.).

Haribhadra.

Haribhadra Sūri the author of Ṣaḍdarśana-samuchchaya lived about 700—770 A. D.* Guṇa-ratna (15th century A. D.) wrote a commentary of this work.

Akalaṅka.

Akalaṅka Deva the great Digamvara writer developed in elaborate treatises the subject of Jaina Nyāya philosophy. His Tattvārtha-rāja-vārttika, Aṣṭaśati, Nyāya-viniśchaya, Laghīya-straya, Pramāṇa-saṅgraha etc. show the masterly way in which he handled this subject and all writers who followed him, modelled their writings on his treatises.

Māṇikyanandī.

Māṇikyanandī the author of Parīkṣāmukhaṃ was the first writer who condensed the subject in the form of aphorisms taking materials from Akalaṅka's works. Many commentaries of Parīkṣāmukhaṃ the most famous among them being Prameya-kamala-mārtaṇḍa by Prabhāchandra and Prameya-ratna-mālā by Ananta-vīrya came to be written and a large number of commentaries on Prameya-ratna-mālā exist in manuscript form in many Jain libraries scattered throughout India. The work Parīkṣā-

---

* "हरिभद्र सूरि का समय निर्णय" an article in Hindi published in Jain Sāhitya Sāṅśodhaka, Bhāga 1, Aṅka I.

Deva-Sūri

mukhaṃ received such a celebrity that Deva-sūri (11th century A. D.) wrote Pramāṇa-naya-tattvālokālaṅkāra with its commentary Syādvāda-ratnākara closely imitating the aphorisms of Parīkṣāmukhaṃ and substituting merely synonyms in many of the aphorisms. Ratnaprabha-sūri (12th century A. D.) wrote a commentary Syādvāda-ratnākarāvatārika to Syādvāda-ratnākara. Rājaśekhara (14th century A. D.) wrote a Pañjikā on Ratnaprabha's work and Jñānachandra (14th century A. D.) wrote a Tippaṇa to the same.

Hemachandra.

The next great writer was Hemachandra who wrote voluminous works on almost every subject. His celebrated work Dvātriṅśikā on the model of Siddhasena's work has been commented on in detail by Malliṣena (13th century) in a commentary entitled Syādvādamañjari in which different systems of Hindu, Bauddha, Chārvāka and other systems of philosophy have been reviewed and criticised. His famous work on Jaina Nyāya is Pramāṇamīmāṃsa a portion only of which has up to this date been discovered.

Later works on Jaina Nyāya.

Many other more or less important works on Jaina Nyāya such as Nyāya-dīpikā of Dharmabhūṣaṇa, Saptabhaṅgitaraṅginī of Vimala-dāsa, Patraparīkṣā and Āpta-parīkṣā of Vidyānanda, Pramālakṣma and Pramāṇa-parīkṣā of Vidyānandi, Jaina-tarka-bhāṣā, Jaina-tarka-vārttika, Naya-chakraṃ, Naya-pradīpaṃ, Naya-rahasyaṃ, Nayopadeśaḥ, Pramāṇa-nirṇayaḥ and innumerable glosses on the standard works and their commentaries already mentioned came to be written, but no new view-point was adopted by any of these later writers whose main object was to explain or amplify the view of older writers.

The goal of Nyāya philosophy.

The real object of the Nyāya philosophy in the Hindu śāstras was propounded as attainment of liberation[1]. In Brihadāraṇyaka Upaniṣad, the sage Yājñavalkya told his wife Maitreyī that we should learn about the soul, understand it and meditate on it[2]. For proper understanding of the nature of a thing, help of the Nyāya philosophy is essential. It is said that we suffer misery because we have false knowledge regarding the soul, such as considering the body as soul. When we perceive the error of such a wrong belief, we get true knowledge[3]. The Jain view also is that the Nyāya philosophy leads to right faith, right knowledge and right conduct which produce liberation[4].

Difference in philosophical views is based on different kinds and methods of appreciation of the one eternal truth All Indian philosophies aim at

---

1. "निःश्रेयसाधिगमः।" Gautama Nyāya Sūtra I. 1.

"प्रमाणादि-पदार्थ-तत्वज्ञानान्निःश्रेयसं दृष्टं, नहि कश्चित् पदार्थो ज्ञायमानो हानोपादानोपेक्षाबुद्धिनिमित्तं न भवतीति। एवञ्च कृत्वा सर्वे पदार्थो ज्ञेयतया उपक्षिप्यन्ते इति। परन्तु निःश्रेयसमत्यादेस्तत्वज्ञानाद् भवति।"

Nyāya-vārttika by Udyotkara.

2. "आत्मा वा अरे द्रष्टव्यः श्रोतव्यो मन्तव्यो निदिध्यासितव्यो मैत्रेय्यात्मनो वा अरे दर्शनेन श्रवणेन मत्या वा विज्ञानेनेदं सर्वं विदितम्।" Brihadāraṇyaka Upaniṣad. 4. 4. 5. Śaṅkarāchārya has mentioned that Manana as laid down in the word "Mantavya" is to be made by Tarka "पश्चान्मन्तव्यस्तर्कतः।" This gives rise to the development of the Nyāya philosophy.

3. "दोषनिमित्तानां तत्वज्ञानादहंकारनिवृत्तिः।" Nyāya Sūtra, 4. 2. 1.

"मिथ्योपलब्धिविनाशस्तत्वज्ञानात्॥" Ibid. 4. 2. 35.

4. See Pages 3 and 4.

the attainment of real happiness and destruction of misery. In Yogavāśiṣṭha Rāmāyaṇa it is mentioned: "O Rāma! the idea of creation consisting of Ahaṃkāra, Manas, Buddhi etc. which have been described by me as modification of one, are differently described by the authors of Nyāya philosophy. The Sāṅkhya and Chārvāka philosophies have described the same differently. The followers of Jaimini (Mimāṃsā philosophy), Arhats (Jainas), Bauddhas, Vaiśeṣikas and others of peculiar views like Pancharātras have described the same in different manner. All of them however will go to the same eternal goal as passengers from different places travelling at different times reach a particular city".[1]

The great masters of philosophy knew this truth and in ancient times though each propounded his own theory and even criticised the views of others, intolerance was absolutely absent. All great teachers and writers were always eager to learn what others have thought and said on a particular question and an attempt was always made to discuss a particular point from different aspects. There is indisputable

---

1. "अहंकारमनोबुद्धिदृष्टयः सृष्टिकल्पनाः ।
एकरूपतया प्रोक्ता या मया रघुनन्दन ।।
नैयायिकैरितरथा तादृशै परिकल्पिताः ।
अन्यथा कल्पितैः सांख्यैश्चार्वाकैरपि चान्यथा ।।
जैमिनीयैश्चार्हतैश्च बौद्धैर्वैशेषिकैस्तथा ।
अन्यैरपि विचित्रैस्तैः पाञ्चरात्रादिभिस्तथा ।।
सर्वैरपि च गन्तव्यं तैः पदं पारमार्थिकम् ।
विचित्रं देशकालोत्थैः पुरमेकमिवाध्वगैः ।।"

Utpatti Prakaraṇa 96. 48-51.

evidence that Buddha discussed the views of the Jainas as well as of other sects in his time. There is evidencc of such discussions by Sri Mahāvira the twenty fourth Tirthaṅkara of the Jainas.

Different systems of Indian philosophy.

The first attempt to give a concise view of the different systems of philosophy was made by Jain sage Haribhadra Sūri in his Saḍdarśana-samuchchaya. In this work he has described (1) Bauddha (2) Nyāya (3) Sāṅkhya (4) Jaina (5) Vaiśeṣika and (6) Mimāṃsā systems of philosophy.[1] We find that within Sāṅkhya, he has also described Pātañjala philosophy and within Mimāṃsā, he has dealt with Pūrva-mimāṃsā as well as Uttara-mimāṃsā or Vedānta. Thus though Haribhadra's work is named "A compendium of six philosophies", in reality it treats of eight systems of philosophy. In Viveka-vilāsa by Jinadatta Sūri (13th century) the same enumeration has been followed. Rajaśekhara Sūri (13th century) mentioning these six (really eight) systems of philosophy has stated that the Nāstika views cannot be accepted as philosophies.[2]

Astika and Nāstika philosophies.

It is necessary to understand the difference of Āstika and Nāstika philosophies. Though Mādha-vāchārya in his Sarvadarśana-saṅgraha has described sixteen systems of philosophy viz. (1) Chārvāka

---

1. "बौद्धं नैयायिकं सांख्यं जैनं वैशेषिकं तथा ।
जैमिनीयञ्च षड्विधानि दर्शनानाममून्यहो ॥"

Ṣaḍdarśana-samuchchaya 3.

2. "जैनं सांख्यं जैमिनीयं योगं वैशेषिकं तथा ।
सौगतं दर्शनान्येवं नास्तिकं न तु दर्शनम् ॥"

Ṣaḍdarśanasamuchchaya Page 1
(Yaśovijaya series, Benares)

(2) Bauddha (3) Ārhata (4) Rāmānuja (5) Mādhava (6) Pāśupata (7) Śaiva (8) Pratyavijñā (9) Raseśvara (10) Pāṇiṇiya (11) Nyāya (12) Vaiśeṣika (13) Sāṅkhya (14) Yoga (15) Pūrva-mīmāṃsā (16) Uttara-mīmāṃsā, it is on the basis of the distinction of the Āstika and Nāstika philosophies that the so-called Nāstika philosophies came to be excluded in the subsequent list of approved philosophies. By six systems of Indian philosophy, according to current acceptance Nyāya, Vaiśeṣika, Sāṅkhya, Pātañjala (Yoga), Mīmāṃsā and Vedānta are understood. The Jaina and Bauddha philosophies were excluded from this list by later writers on the ground that these systems are Nāstika philosophies. Raghunandan has quoted a verse from Hayaśīrṣa-pañcharātra that the philosophies of Gautama, Kāṇada, Kapila, Patañjali, Vyāsa and Jaimini are the only six systems of philosophy[1].

The word Nāstika is differently interpreted. The derivative meaning from the Sūtra of Pāṇiṇi[2] is taken to be "he who does not accept Paraloka or existence after death"[3] The second interpretation is that by Nāstika we mean the person who does not accept the existence of Īśvara[4] and the third

---

1. "गौतमस्य कणादस्य कपिलस्य पतञ्चलेः ।
व्यासस्य जैमिनेश्चापि दर्शनानि षडेव हि ॥" Devapratiṣṭhātattva.

2. "अस्ति नास्ति दिष्टं मतिः ।" Aṣṭādhyāyi of Pāṇiṇi. 4.4.60.

3. "परलोकः अस्तीति यस्य मतिरस्ति स आस्तिकः ।
तद्विपरीतो नास्तिकः ॥" Kāśikā.

4. "नास्तिकः परलोकतत्साधनाद्यभाववादी ।
तत्साक्षिण ईश्वरस्य असत्यवादी च ॥" Nyāyakoṣa.

meaning is that Nāstika indicates the man who denies the authority of the Vedas[1].

Now, if we accept the meaning of Nāstika as one who does not accept Paraloka (existence after death), Karma and the fruits of Karma, we cannot say that Jaina and Baudha philosophies are Nāstika philosophies for both of these systems of philosophy accept these.

Again, if we interpret 'Nāstika' to mean 'denying the existence of Īśvara', the Sāṅkhya as well as Mīmāṃsā systems of philosophy should be taken as Nāstika philosophies as neither Kapila nor Jaimini has accepted the existence of a creator (Īśvara). But we have shown above that these two systems of philosophy have not been excluded from the list of six philosophies on such a ground.

The conclusion is therefore inevitable that to call Bauddha and Jaina philosophies "Nāstika", the third interpretation of the word "Nāstika" viz. denying the authority of the Vedas, must be accepted, for these philosophies do not accept the Vedas as eternal or as infallible. The Bauddhas accept two Pramāṇas, Pratyakṣa and Anumāna and do not accept the authority of the Vedas. [2] In Jain

---

1. "नास्तिको वेदनिन्दकः ।" Institutes of Manu.

2. "ये तु सौगतसंसारमोचकागमाः कस्तेषु प्रामाण्यमार्योऽनुमोदते,
बौद्धशास्त्रे हि विशिष्टा दृश्यते वेदवाह्यता ।
जातिधर्मोदिताचार-परिहारावधारणात् ॥" Nyāyamañjarī.

"महाजनश्च वेदानां वेदार्थानुगामिनां च पुराणधर्मशास्त्राणां वेदाविरोधिनाञ्च केषाञ्चिदागमानां प्रामाण्यमनुमन्यते, न वेदविरुद्धानां बौद्धाद्यागमानाम् ॥"

Nyāyamañjarī.

For a full discussion vide a Bengali article "Āstika and Nāstika Darśana" by Dr. Ashutosh Śāstri.

philosophy Āgama (words, signs etc. of an Āpta or reliable person), has been accepted as a variety of Pramāṇa but the authority of the Vedas has not been accepted[1].

But this exclusion of Jain philosophy was effected at a very late stage. We find that its doctrines were attempted to be refuted in the Vedānta-sūtras, and Kumārila and Śaṅkarāchārya levelled their arguments against certain Jain views such as existence of omniscient beings. There cannot be any doubt that all the different systems of philosophy whether the same were Āstika or Nāstika according to different interpretations were thoroughly studied and in conferences before saints, kings and scholars, discussions and refutations of various doctrines were of very frequent occurrence. We find in Śaktisaṅgama Tantra [between 1555 to 1604 A. D.] that Jaina philosophy was taken as one of Kāli Darśanas[2] Even Jayanta Bhatta the celebrated Hindu author of Nyāya mañjarī [9th century] accepted Jaina philosophy to be authoritative[3].

---

1. Vide Pages 44 to 49 of Prameya-ratnamālā appended to this work in which the view that Āgama can include the Vedas is refuted whether it be accepted that the Vedas are Pauruṣeya (produced by human beings) or Apauruṣeya (not produced by human beings and eternal).

2. Śaktisaṅgamatantra edited by Binayatosh Bhattacharya M.A. Ph. D. (Gaekwad Oriental Series).

3. Jayanta Bhatta began his argument that others can be Āpta like the author of the Vedas, saying "अन्ये सर्वागमानान्तु प्रामाण्यं प्रतिपेदिरे". His conclusion is exemplified in the verse :—

"नानाविधैरागममार्गभेदैरादिश्यमाना वह्वोऽभ्युपायाः ।
एकत्र ते श्रेयसि संपतन्ति सिन्धौ प्रवाहा इव जाह्नवीयाः ॥"

Nomenclature of Nyāya.

The name "Nyāya" came to be applied later to a system of philosophy which dealt with logic. The original name was "Ānvīkṣikī" from Anvīkṣā (discussion). Fruitless Tarka Vidyā was always discouraged[1] but that Ānvīkṣikī which will lead to the attainment of a knowledge of self was always regarded as a subject to be learnt. In Manu-samhitā we find that a King should learn Ānvīkṣikī[2]. Rājaśekhara in his Kāvya-mīmāṃsā has mentioned that Ānvīkṣikī knowledge is of two kinds, being of the nature of Pūrvapakṣa and Uttarapakṣa and that Jaina, Bauddha and Chārvāka systems are of the former and Sāṅkhya, Nyāya and Vaiśeṣika systems are of the latter kind[3].

In Chhāndogya Upaniṣad (VII-1) and in Mahābhāṣya of Patañjali, we find Nyāya philosophy named as "Vāko-vākya." Vātsyāyana mentioned the five-limbed syllogism (for Parārthānumāna) as Nyāya.

After describing persecution of persons who set up new sects for worldly enjoyment and profligacy, by king Śankaravarmā of Kashmir, Jayanta Bhatta says that the doctrines of the Jains etc. are not such :

"तदपूर्वमिति विदित्वा निवारयामास धर्मतत्त्वज्ञः ।
राजा शंकरवर्म्मा न पुनर्जैनादिमतमेवम् ॥"

1. Vide : "आन्वीक्षिकीं तर्कविद्यामनुरक्तो निरर्थिकाम् ।" Mahābhārata Śāntiparva 180. 47. To what extent such wrong arguments can proceed will appear from the attempt of sage Jābāli to dissuade Rāma from going to the forest to fulfil the vow of his father. Rāmāyana. Ayodhyākānda. Canto 109.

2. "आन्वीक्षिकीञ्चात्मविद्याम् ।" Manu-saṃhitā, 7.43.

3. Kāvyamimāṃsā. Chapter II.

From analogy the science propounding this has also been called Nyāya[1].

Essence of Nyāya-Vaiśeṣika principles of reasoning.

The Hindu Nyāya and Vaiśeṣika philosophies are mentioned as Yauga by Jain logicians. The Vaiśeṣika system is earlier than the Nyāya philosophy and its logical principles are accepted by the latter. "The Nyāya analyses the different ways in which our knowledge is acquired. They are said to be intuition (Pratyakṣa), inference (Anumāna), comparison (Upamāna), and verbal testimony (Śabda). Though Pratyakṣa originally meant sense-perception, it soon came to cover all immediate apprehension whether through the aid of senses or otherwise. It is knowledge whose instrumental cause is not knowledge (Jñānākaraṇakaṃ jñānaṃ). In inference comparison etc. we require a knowledge of premises or of similarity, but such knowledge is not an antecedent condition of intuition. The word is used for the result or the apprehension of the truth as well as the process or the operation which leads to the result.

Sense-perception follows on the modification of the self produced by the contact of the senses with their objects. Two kinds of perception are distinguished, determinate (Savikalpaka) and indeterminate (Nirvikalpaka) which correspond roughly to knowledge about and acquaintance with an object.

Inference operates neither with regard to things unknown nor with regard to that known

---

1. In Subalopaniṣad we find : "न्यायो मीमांसा धर्मशास्त्राणि।" In Yājñavalkya Saṃhitā we read : "पुराणन्यायमीमांसा।" Some also use the word Nīti to mean Nyāya e.g. "सांख्ययोगा नीतिविसेसिका" Miliṅda-pañha.

definitely for certain; it functions only with regard to things that are doubtful.' (N. B. I. I. i.). It derives a conclusion from the ascertained fact of the subject possessing a property which is constantly accompanied by another. We ascertain that the hill is on fire from the fact that the hill has smoke and smoke is universally accompanied by fire. Inferential reasoning is stated in the form of a syllogism of which the five members are: 1. Proposition (Pratijñā): the hill is on fire; 2. Reason (Hetu): because it smokes; 3. Example (Udāharaṇa): whatever shows smoke shows fire *e. g.* a kitchen; 4. Application (Upanaya): So is this hill, and 5. Conclusion (Nigamana): therefore, the hill is on fire. The first member states the thesis to be established. It is only a suggestion. It contains a subject of what is observed, which is generally an individual or a class, and a predicate, which is to be proved. The subject is the minor term (Pakṣa, Dharmin) and the predicate the major (Sādhya, Dharma). The second member of the syllogism states the presence in the minor of the middle term called ground (Hetu). The third takes us to the basis of inference, the major premise. Though Gautama and Vātsyāyana may not have regarded the example as the illustration of a general rule later Nyāya looks upon it as the statement of an invariable concomitance between the mark and the character inferred (Vyāpti-prati-pādakam Vākyam). The conclusion re-states the proposition as grounded. Nāgārjuna is given the credit for dispensing with the last two members of the syllogism as superfluous.

Universal propositions are reached through enumeration, intuition and indirect proof. Uninterrupted agreement (Niyata Sāhacharya) reinforced by absence of exceptions (Avinābhāva-rūpa-sambandha) leads to unconditional concomitances. Nature does not always supply us with positive and negative instances of the necessary type. In such cases indirect proof (Tarka) may be used. By pointing out the absurdities in which we are landed, if we deny a suggested hypothesis, we indirectly prove its validity. Even when we observe all possible cases and strengthen our conclusion by indirect proof we cannot reach absolute certainty. Experience of sensible particulars, however thorough and exhaustive, cannot give rise to universal relations. Gangeśa recognises the non-sensuous (Alaukika) activity involved in the apprehension of universals (Sāmānyalakṣaṇa)[1]."

In my commentary on the Parīkṣāmukhaṃ, I have pointed out in detail where and in what manner Jain logicians differ from the above views of Hindu Nyāya and Vaiśeṣika Philosophies.

Pramāṇas.

Pramāṇa is the main theme of all Nyāya philosophies. Different systems admit different number of Pramāṇas In Tārkika-rakṣā (11th century) we find; "The Chārvākas accept only one Pramāṇa viz. Pratyakṣa ; Kaṇāda and Buddha accept two Pramāṇas Pratyakṣa and Anumāna; the Sāṇkhya system and some sects of Nyāya philosophy acknowledge three Pramāṇas viz, Pratyakṣa, Anumāna and Śabda; some followers of the Nyāya philosophy accept four Pramāṇas, Pratyakṣa, Anumāna, Śabda and Upumāna; Prabhākara (one school of Mimāṃsā philosophy) accept five Pramāṇas, Pratyakṣa, Anu-

1. S. Radhakrishnan : Indian Philosophy Encyclo. Britt. Vol. 12. Page 250.

māna, Upumāna, Śabda and Arthāpatti; the Bhāttas (followers of Kumārila Bhatta, another school of Mīmāṃsā philosophy) as well as the followers of the Vedānta philosophy accept six Pramāṇas viz. Pratyakṣa, Anumāna, Upamāna, Śabda, Arthāpatti and Abhāva."[1]

Jain Nyāya before Māṇikya-nandi.

The earliest detailed reference to the subject of Pramāṇa in Jain Nyāya is found in the Tattvārthādhigama Sūtra of Umāsvāmi. The twelve Aṅgas of the Jainas prevalent at the time of Śrī Mahāvīra only give a hint of Anekāntavāda but no specific reference of Pramāṇa, Naya or Sapta-Bhaṅgi is found in the same.

Kunda-kunda.

Kundakunda in his Pravachanasāra has mentioned the two kinds of Pramāṇa viz Pra-

(1) "प्रत्यक्षमेकं चार्वाकाः कणादसुगतौ पुनः ।
प्रत्यक्षमनुमानञ्च सांख्याः शब्दञ्च ते अपि ।।
न्यायैकदेशिनोऽप्येवमुपमानं च केचन ।
अर्थापत्त्या सहैतानि चत्वार्याह प्रभाकरः ।।
अभावषष्ठान्येतानि भाट्टा वेदान्तिनस्तथा ।"
Tārkika rakṣā by Varadarāja

Writers like Varadarāja as above have termed scholars who have formulated different views from the same of Gautama as "Nyāyaika-deśins". Mallinātha in his commentary on Tārkika-rakṣā has explained Nyāyaikadeśins as Bhūṣaṇa and others ("न्यायैकदेशिनो भूषणीयाः ।") The Jain scholor Guṇaratna in his commentary on Saḍdarśanasamuchchaya (Haribhadra Sūri) has mentioned a commentary called Nyāya-bhuṣaṇa among the eighteen commentaries of the work Nyāya-sāra by Bhā-sarvajña ("भासर्वज्ञप्रणीते न्यायसारेऽष्टादशटीकाः तासु मुख्या टीका न्यायभूषणाख्या ।") Some infer that the view of Bhūṣaṇa is novel and opposed to Nyāya-sūtras of Gautama on some points which include the number of Pramāṇas, Bhūṣaṇa accepting only three (Pratyakṣa, Anumāna and Śabda) though Gautama admits four (Prayakṣa, Anumāna, Upamāna and Śabda).

tyakṣa and Parokṣa and the Sapta-bhaṅgi. But these references give only the barest outlines without any definite details. For example, Kundakunda says :

"The knowledge of him who beholds the immaterial, the supra-sensorial in material objects (mūrtāni), and the hidden, complete (embracing) the self and the other, is called Pratyakṣa (immediate)" [1]

---

1. Pravachanasāra. Śruta-skandha I. 54 Trans. by Barrend Faddegon.

Amritachandra in his commentary thus explains this verse : "Supra-sensorial knowledge beholds the immaterial, the supra-sensorial even in material objects, and the hidden complete, whether included in own as in other. Such knowledge surely is a seer, owing to its immediateness, with reference to (a) immaterial (a-mūrta) substances such as the principles of motion and stationariness (b) immaterial, but supra-sensorial substances, such as the ultimate atom, (c) that which is hidden in respect of substance e. g. time: that which is hidden in respect of place e. g. the Pradeśas of space located outside the world ; that which is hidden in time, e. g. in non-present modifications ; that which is hidden in respect of forms-of-being, namely five (Sukṣma) modifications latent within gross (Sthūla) modifications: thus with reference to all things, distinguished as own and other.

Immediate knowledge indeed, bound to a single self, called the Akṣa and having the immediacy of its manifested infinite purity and beginning-less connection with the generality of perfect intelligence (Siddha-Chaitanya Sāmānya) does not search for exterior means, enjoys infinity, because of its possession of infinite energies. Knowledge enjoying such prestige, seeing that the knowable appearances no more outgo knowledge than combustible appearances the fire, what can resist such knowledge ? Therefore it is acceptable." Ibid p. 35.

Here Akṣa is taken as synonym of Ātman. This is to be remembered to contrast the interpretation of Akṣa as Indriya (senses) by other Naiyāyikas.

"The soul, in itself immaterial, goes into materiality (mūrti) and then apprehending with this material (body) the material (world), sometimes knows and sometimes does not know that—which-is-fit-for-knowledge (yogya)."

"Touch, taste, smell, colour and sound are the material objects (pudgalas) for the sense-organs ; the sense organs do not grasp them simultaneously."

"The sense-organs are called an exterior (para) substance, and not an innate nature of the self; how then could that which is reached by them be an immediate perception for the self ?"

"Knowledge of objects from another is called indirect ; but if knowledge is acquired by the soul alone (Kevala Jñāna) then it is direct." [1]

Kundakunda describes the sensorial joy ; not supremely real of those who possess indirect knowledge (Parokṣa-Jñāna) thus :

"The lords of men, demons and Gods, oppressed by their natural (sahaja) organs of sense, unable to withstand that misery, find pleasure in satisfying objects"[2].

---

1. Pravachana-sāra. I. 55-58 Trans by Barend Faddegon.

2. Ibid I-63. Amritachandra explains this verse thus : "Those creatures who through lack of immediate knowledge take refuge in indirect knowledge have a congenial affection for their organs of sense, which are the equipment therefor. So in these persons having this affection for their sense-organs and, while devoured by the flaring *Kāla*-fire of great infatuation, utterly longing and thirsty, like heated balls of iron, and unable to withstand the vehemence of this misery, there arises a satisfaction (rati) with these satisfying (ramya) objects, which serve to soothe their disease. Hence since the sense-organs must be compared to a disease and the objects to means for soothing the disease, no really-true joy exists for those who have a limited knowledge."Ibid. pp. 41-42.

Kundakunda lays down that a soul in its perfect condition has omniscience knowing by direct intuition (pratyakṣa) substances, states etc. in all times and places without operation of senses. Parokṣa (indirect) knowledge is sense-knowledge, the senses being a material accretion to the soul.

Saptabhaṅgi is briefly described in Pravachana-sāra II.23. As this matter is not dealt with in Parīkṣāmukhaṃ, we do not dilate upon this subject here.

Umāsvāmi.

Umāsvāmi in the Tattvārthādhigama Sūtra made a more detailed reference to Pramāṇas and its sub-divisions. Laying down the utility of Pramāṇas and Nayas as means of instruction for attaining right faith[1], Umāsvāmi has mentioned that "Mati, Śruta, Avadhi, Manaḥparyaya and Kevala are right knowledge"[2] and these also consist of two Pramāṇas.[3] Mati and Śruta are taken to be Parokṣa[4] and Avadhi, Manaḥparyaya and Kevala as Pratyakṣa[5]. We find in Kundakunda's Pravachana-sāra the idea of Mati, Śruta, Avadhi and Manaḥparyaya in the following verse :

"The saint (Sādhu) has the scripture for eye; all creatures have their sense-organs for eyes; the Devas have eyes which see the remote (avadhi); but the liberated souls (siddhas) have eyes which see everywhere."[6]

1. "प्रमाणनयैरधिगमः ।" Tattvārthādhigama Sūtra, I. 6.
2. "मतिश्रुतावधिमनःपर्ययकेवलानि ज्ञानम् ।" Ibid I. 9.
3. "तत् प्रमाणे ।" Ibid I. 10.
4. "आद्ये परोक्षम् ।" Ibid I. 11.
5. "प्रत्यक्षमन्यत् ।" Ibid I. 12.
6. Pravachana-sāra III. 34. Trans. by Barend Faddegon p. 177.

Kundakunda's description of Kevala knowledge has already been quoted.

The oldest idea of Pramāṇā in Jainism as expounded by Umāsvāmi and as already described is that the knowledge which is derived without the help of the senses or mind is Pratyakṣa and the knowledge derived from the help of the senses or mind is Parokṣa. Among the three varieties of Pratyakṣa Avadhi, Manaḥparyaya and Kevala, the first two cognise only objects having form. For this reason knowledge derived from these two kinds of Pratyakṣa Pramāṇa are called Vikala Pratyakṣa, but Kevala knowledge cognises all objects with or without form in the past, present or future and is therefore known as Sakala Pratyakṣa. Mati and Śruta are the two varieties of Paroakṣa and Umāsvāmi has mentioned that Smriti, Sañjñā (Pratyabhijñāna), Chintā (Tarka), and Abhinibodha (Anumāna) are within Mati Jñāna (the first variety of Parokṣa)[1].

Samantabhadra.

Samantabhadra first used the nomenclature "Nyāya" and in this respect he inaugurated a separate subject. He however did not compose any special work in Jain Nyāya. He mentions that Pramāṇa illuminates itself as well as other objects[2] and states that the result of Pramāṇa is acceptance of desirable things, leaving undesirable things or indifference [3] He has also mentioned Śruta Pra-

---

1. "मतिः स्मृतिः संज्ञा चिन्ताभिनिबोध इत्यनर्थान्तरम् ।"

Tattvārthādhigama Sūtra.

See Parikṣāmukhaṃ page 80. Aphorism 2.

2. "स्वपरावभासकं यथा प्रमाणं भुवि बुद्धिलक्षणम् ।"

Svayambhū Stotra. Verse 63.

3. "उपेक्षा फलमाद्यस्य शेषस्यादानहानधीः ।"

Āpta-mīmāṃsā Verse 102.

māṇa as Syādvāda and has stated Naya to be its part[1].

Siddhasena.

Siddhasena Divākara added the word "Bādhavivarjjita" (without any obstruction) to the definition of Pramāṇa by Samanta-bhadra viz. that it illuminates itself as well as other objects[2]. Though Samantabhadra used inference to establish an omniscient being in his Āpta-mīmāṃsā, yet we find the definition of Anumāna with its subdivisions Svārtha and Parārtha for the first time in the Nyāyāvatāra of Siddhasena. In this work also we get definitions of limbs of Parārthānumāna such as Pakṣa, Hetu and Driṣṭānta. The fallacies also have been described in the aforesaid treatise[3].

Akalaṅka.

It is of the utmost importance to remember that except in the Jaina Nyāya, we nowhere find knowledge derived from the senses being called Parokṣa Pramāṇa. In Hindu Nyāya philosophy [4] and in all other Hindu Śāstras, knowledge derived from the senses is known as Pratyakṣa Pramāṇa. Akalaṅka the greatest of Jain logicians attempted to reconcile this in the following way. He accepted Pratyakṣa and Parokṣa as two Pramāṇas but instead of dividing Pratyakṣa into Śakala and Vikala, he laid down two hitherto unknown divisions viz.

---

1. "स्याद्वाद-प्रविभक्तार्थे विशेषव्यंजको नयः।"

Āpta-mīmāṃsā. Verse 106.

2. Vide Parikṣāmukhaṃ p. 20 Note 9.

3. Verses from Nyāyāvatāra on all these matters have been quoted in footnotes in Parīkṣāmukhaṃ in appropriate places.

4. "इन्द्रियार्थसन्निकर्षोत्पन्नं ज्ञानमव्यपदेश्यमव्यभिचारि-व्यवसायात्मकं प्रत्यक्षम् ॥" Nyāya Sūtra (Gautama) I. 1. 4.

Sāṅvyavahārika and Mukhya Pratyakṣa[1]. He further laid down that Mati Jñāna derived through the senses and mind is not Parokṣa but Sāṅvyavahārika Pratyakṣa[2]. As Mati came to be recognised as Sāṅvyavahārika Pratyakṣa, its corelated Smriti, Saṅjñā, Chintā and Ābhinibodha as mentioned by Umāsvāmi also came under the same head. But a subtle distinction was made by Akalaṅka. He subdivided Sāṅvyavahārika Pratyakṣa into two heads (a) Indriya-pratyakṣa (knowledge derived through the senses) under which came Mati and (b) Anindriya-pratyakṣa (knowledge derived through mind)[3] under which came Smriti, Saṅjñā, Chintā and Abhinibodha[4] as mind is prevalent in these four. This change necessitated a change of definition of Pratyakṣa and Akalaṅka accordingly defined Pratyakṣa as "clear knowledge." ("Pratyakṣam viśadaṃ jñānaṃ.")

Now, to meet the argument that if we take Mati as Pratyakṣa we must say that the traditional acceptance of the view that it is Parokṣa is denied undermining the oldest authorities like Umāsvāmi, Akalaṅka has written that Mati, Smriti, Saṅjñā, Chintā and Abhinibodha will be Pratyakṣa so long as these

1. "प्रत्यक्षं विशदं ज्ञानं मुख्यसांव्यवहारिकम् ।
परोक्षं शेषविज्ञानं प्रमाणमिति संग्रहः ॥" Laghīyastraya Verse 1.

2. "आद्ये परोक्षमपरं प्रत्यक्षं प्राहुरंजसा ।
केवलं लोकबुद्धैथव मतेर्लक्षणसंग्रहः ॥" Nyāya-viniśchaya Verse 93.

3. 'तत्र सांव्यवहारिकं इन्द्रियानिन्द्रियप्रत्यक्षम् ।"
Vivriti on Laghīyastraya. Verse 4.

4. "अनिन्द्रियप्रत्यक्षं स्मृतिसंज्ञाचिन्ताभिनिवोधात्मकम् ।"
Vivriti on Laghīyastraya. Verse 61.

remain in the mental state. The moment these are connected with words i.e. are expressed in words they will become Parokṣa[1]. Thus, Akalaṅka has accepted Mati etc, as Pratyakṣa in one sense and Parokṣa in another sense. According to Akalaṅka Śruta is what is heard and so the knowledge derived through words is Śruta and the knowledge having no connection with words is Sāṅvyavahārika Pratyakṣa.

The peculiarity of Akalaṅka is that under Śruta in Parokṣa Pramāṇa he has two subdivisions Akṣarātmaka and Anakṣarātmaka. Other Jain logicians have mentioned that Anumāna (inference) is of two kinds Svārthānumāna (inference for one's own self) and Parārthānumāna (inference for the sake of others). Akalaṅka says that it is not inference alone that has these two subdivisions but other Pramāṇas also may be for Svārtha and Parārtha. Svārthānumāna is accepted by Akalaṅka to be included in Anakṣarātmaka Śruta Pramāṇa as no help of words is necessary for its acceptance and Parārthānumāna according to Akalaṅka comes within Akṣarātmaka Anumāna as this cannot arise without help of words. The Pramāṇas Arthāpatti, Āgama etc are all recognised by Akalaṅka to be varieties of Śruta Pramāṇa.

The following tables will illustrate the difference between the divisions of Pramāṇa by the oldest writers such as Umāsvāmi and Akalaṅka.

---

1. "ज्ञानमाद्यं मतिः संज्ञा चिन्ता चाभिनिबोधनम् ।
प्राङ्नामयोजनाच्छेषं श्रुतं शब्दानुयोजनात् ॥" Laghiyastraya.

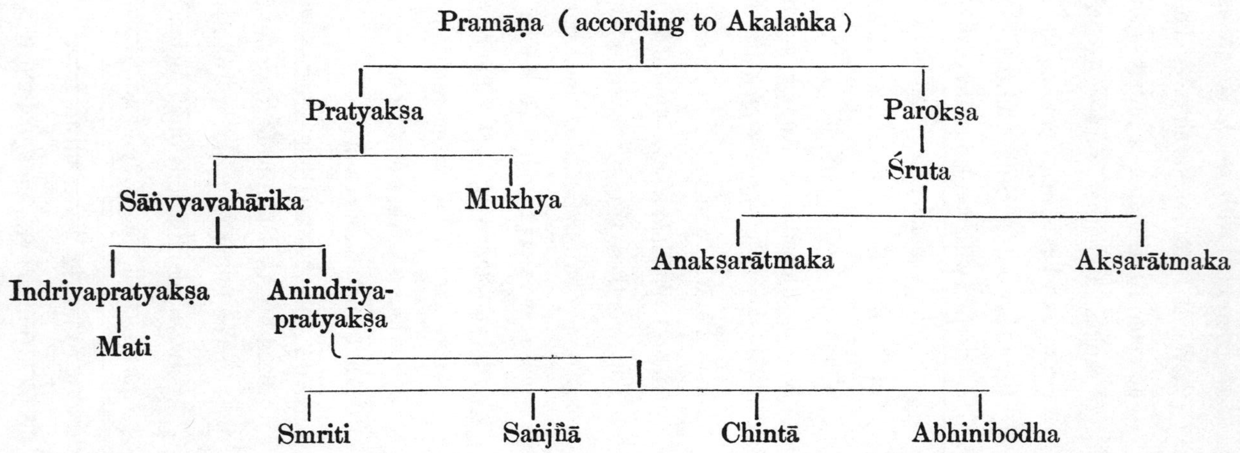
Pramāṇa (according to Akalaṅka)
Pratyakṣa
Parokṣa
Sāṅvyavahārika
Mukhya
Śruta
Indriyapratyakṣa
Anindriya-pratyakṣa
Mati
Anakṣarātmaka
Akṣarātmaka
Smriti
Sañjñā
Chintā
Abhinibodha

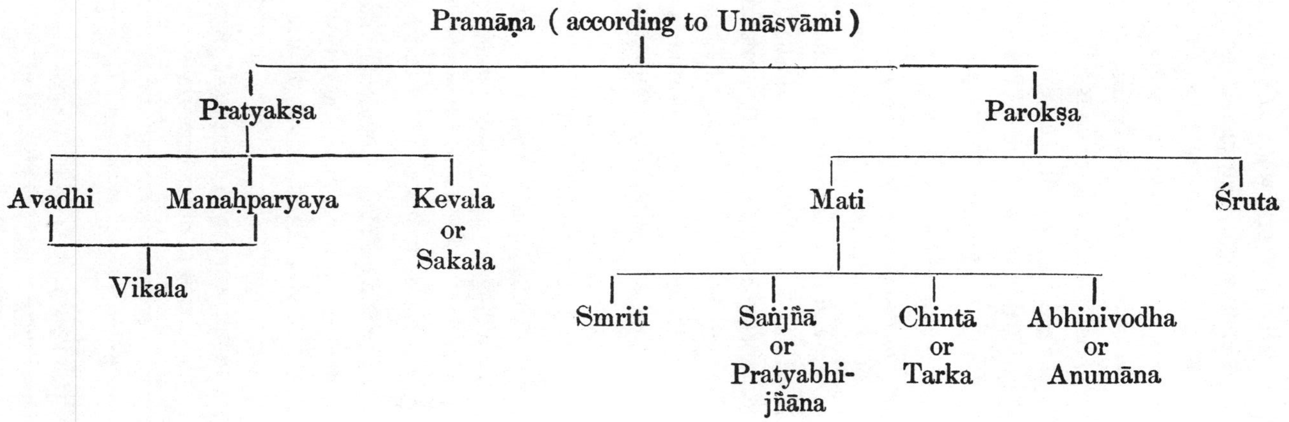
Pramāṇa (according to Umāsvāmi)
Pratyakṣa
Parokṣa
Avadhi
Manaḥparyaya
Kevala or Sakala
Vikala
Mati
Śruta
Smriti
Sañjñā or Pratyabhi-jñāna
Chintā or Tarka
Abhinivodha or Anumāna

The writers who followed Akalaṅka (such as Ananta-vīrya, Vidyānanda etc.) did not accept Smriti etc. as Anindriya-pratyakṣa though in one sense they were ready to accept knowledge derived through the senses to be Sāṅvyavahārika Pratyakṣa. The views of later writers have been fully discussed by me in the commentary of Parīkṣāmukhaṃ and the charts printed in Pages 76 and 77 of the work might be compared with the charts printed above.

Later Writers.

Māṇikyanandi in his Parīkṣāmukhaṃ has closely followed the views of Akalaṅka. Before the time of Māṇikyanandi, Pramāṇa was defined as "Svapara-vyavasāyi jñāna" (valid knowledge of itself and other). Māṇikyanandi added the word "Apūrva" (not proved before) in the definition. Akalaṅka has mentioned the same thing by the word "Anadhigatārthagrāhi"[1]. A verse (the author of which has not been identified) in Mīmāṃsā philosophy shows that the element "Apūrva" was also accepted as essential to Pramāṇa in that philosophy also[2].

Māṇikyanandi has not followed Jaināgama by including Avagraha etc. within knowledge. He has mentioned Āgama in place of Śruta Pramāṇa and has placed it under Parokṣa Pramāṇa.

Subsequent developments and detailed definitions and discussions have been investigated in my commentary on Parīkṣāmukhaṃ where in all cases the original authority has been quoted to give the readers an opportunity to form their own opinions in case they wish to differ from the same of my own.

---

1. "प्रमाणमविसंवादि ज्ञानम् अनधिगतार्थाधिगमलक्षणत्वात् ।" Aṣṭa-śatī
2. "तत्रापूर्वार्थविज्ञानं निश्चितं बाधवर्जितम् ।
अदुष्टकारणारब्धं प्रमाणं लोकसम्मतम् ।।"

The use of 'Vyavasāya' or "Niśchaya" in the definition of Pramāṇa as used by Māṇikyanandi is to differentiate the Jain view from that of the Buddhists who do not accept this to be essential in Pramāṇa. Some Buddhist philosophers also deny the existence of external objects. To differentiate the Jain view the word "Artha" has been introduced in the definition of Pramāṇa by Māṇikyanandi (see page 29).

The Buddhist views.

There are four sects of Buddhist philosophers : 1 Mādhyamika 2 Yogāchāra 3 Sautrāntika and 4 Baibhāsika.[1] Those who maintain that everything is void are Mādhyamikas or Śūnyavādins or Nihilists. Those who maintain the reality of everything are known as Sarvāstitvavādin or Realists divided into two groups (a) Sautrāntikas and (b) Baibhāsikas. Those who maintain that thought only is real are known as Vijñānavādins or Idealists.

Śaṅkarāchārya in his Bhāṣya an Vedānta Sūtra II. 2-18 writes that the difference of views arose either from expounding different views at different times by Buddha or from the different views adopted by the disciples of Buddha[2]. Śaṅkarāchārya mentions that there are three kinds of disciples known as Sarvāstitvavādins, Vijñānavādins and Sarvaśūnyatāvādins [3]Bāchaspati Miśra in his commentary Bhāmati on the same Sūtra says "Disciples have great, medium or little intelligence. Those who have little

---

1. "बुद्धस्य हि माध्यमिक-योगाचार-सौत्रान्तिक-वैभाषिक-संज्ञकाश्चत्वारः शिष्याः ।" Brahmavidyābharaṇa

2. "स च बहुप्रकारः प्रतिपत्तिभेदाद्विनेयभेदाद् वा ।"
Śaṅkarabhāṣya to Vedānta Sūtra II. 2. 18

3. "तत्रैते त्रयो वादिनो भवन्ति । केचित् सर्वास्तित्ववादिनः, केचिद्विज्ञानास्तित्वमात्रवादिनः, अन्ये पुनः सर्वशून्यत्ववादिन इति ।" Ibid.

intelligence descend into Nihilism following the existence of everything. Those who have medium intellect descend into Nihilism following the view that thought only is real. Those who have great intellectual capacity grasp Nihilism without any intermediate hold of anything"[1]. The following verses from Bodhicharyāvatāra are quoted in the Bhamatī :

"The instructions of the preceptors of people follow the inclination of their souls and so differ in many ways by various means. Sometimes the instructions are deep, and sometimes superficial. Sometimes these are of both the above kinds. Though these are different, really they are not different being characterised by Śūnyatā (Nihilism)[2].

The view of Sarvāstitvavādins (Realists) who maintain that everything whether external or internal is real is thus described by Śaṅkarāchārya. "What is external is either element (Bhūta) or elementary (Bhautika); What is internal is either mind (Chitta) or mental (Chaitta). The elements are earth, water and so on; elementals are colour etc.

---

1. In explaining "Vineyabhedāt vā" in the Śāṅkara Bhāṣya, Bāchaspati Miśra says :

"हीनमध्यमोत्कृष्टधियो हि शिष्या भवन्ति। तत्र ये हीनमतयस्ते सर्वास्तित्ववादेन तदाशयानुरोधाद् शून्यतायामवतार्यन्ते। ये तु मध्यमास्ते ज्ञानमात्रास्तित्वेन शून्यताया—मवतार्यन्ते। ये तु प्रकृष्टमतयस्तेभ्यः साक्षादेव शून्यतातत्वं प्रतिपाद्यते।"

Bhāmatī on Vedānta Sūtra II. 2. 18

2. "देशना लोकनाथानां सत्वाशयवशानुगाः।
भिद्यन्ते बहुधा लोक उपायैर्बहुभिः पुनः॥
गंभीरोत्तानभेदेन क्वचिच्चोभयलक्षणा।
भिन्नापि देशनाभिन्ना शून्यताद्वयलक्षणा॥" Bodhichittavivaraṇa.

on the one hand, and the eye and the other sense-organs on the other hand. Earth and the other three elements arise from the aggregation of the four different kinds of atoms; the atoms of earth being hard, those of water viscid, those of fire hot, those of air mobile.

The inward world consists of the five so-called 'groups' (skandha), the group of sensation (rupas-kandha), the group of knowledge (vijñānaskandha), the group of feeling (vedanā-skandha) the group of verbal knowledge (sañjāskandha) and the group of impressions (samskāraskandha); which taken together constitute the basis of all personal existence"[1]. (Dr. Thibaut's translation. Sacred Books of the East. Vol. XXXIV Page 403).

The Skandhas are thus described in the following Note of Dr. Thibaut to the above. This will explain the Ālayavijñāna and Pravrittivijñāna mentioned in Page 29.

"The rūpaskandha comprises the senses and their objects, colour etc.; the sense-organs were above called Bhautika, they here reappear as Chaittika on account of their connection with thought. Their objects likewise are classed as Chaittika in so far as they are perceived by the senses. The vijñāna-skandha comprises the series of self-cognitions (ahamaham ityālayavijñānapravavaḥ) according to

1. "सर्वास्तित्ववादिनो वाह्यमान्तरञ्च वस्त्वभ्युपगच्छन्ति, भूतं भौतिकं चित्तं चैत्तञ्च। तत्र भूतं पृथिवीधात्वादयः, भौतिकं रुपादयश्चक्षुरादयश्च। चतुष्टये च पृथिव्यादिपरमाणवः खरस्नेहोष्णेरणस्वभावास्ते पृथिव्यादिभावेन संहन्यन्त इति मन्यन्ते। तथा रुपविज्ञानवेदनासंज्ञासंस्कारसंज्ञकाः पंच स्कन्धाः, तेऽप्याध्यात्मं सर्वव्यवहारास्पदभावेन संहन्यन्त इति मन्यन्ते।" Śāṇkarabhāṣya to Vedānta Sūtra II. 2. 18

all commentators; and in addition according to Brahmavidyābharaṇa, the knowledge determinate and indeterminate of external things (savikalpakaṃ nirvikalpakañcha pravrittivijñānasaṅgitaṃ). The vedanāskandha comprises pleasure, pain etc. The saṅjāskandha comprises the cognition of things by their names (Gauraśva ityādi-śabda-saṅjalpita-pratyayaḥ, Ānanda Giri; Gauraśva ityevaṃ nāma-viśiṣṭa-savikalpaḥ pratyayaḥ, Go. Au; Saṅjñā Yajnadattādipada-tadullekhi savikalpapratyayo vā dvitīyapakṣe vijñānapadena savikalpapratyayo na grāhyaḥ. Brahmavidyābharaṇa) The Saṃskāra-skandha comprises passion, aversion etc. dharma and adharma...The Vijñānaskandha is Chitta, the other skandhas Chaitta."

Similarities between the aphorisms in Parīkṣā-mukhaṃ and the same in Nyāya-prabeśa and Nyāyavindu of Dharma-kīrti have been shown by Pandit Kailās Chandra Śāstrī[1].

	Nyāya-praveśa		Parīkṣāmukhaṃ
1.	शुचि नरःशिरःकपालं प्राण्यङ्गत्वात् शंखशुक्तिवत् ।	....	VI. 19
2.	माता मे वन्ध्या ।	....	VI. 20
3.	वाष्पादिभावेन संदिह्यमानो भूतसंघातोग्निसिद्धावुपदिश्यमानः संदिग्धासिद्धः ।	...	VI. 25, 26
4.	तत्र पक्षः प्रसिद्धो धर्मी ।	....	III. 26, 27
	Nyāya-vindu		
1.	अनुमानं द्विधा ।	....	III. 52
2.	स्वार्थं परार्थं च ।	....	III. 53
3.	नेहाप्रतिवद्धसामर्थ्यानि धूमकारणानि सन्ति, धूमाभावात् ।	....	III. 81
4.	नात्र शिंशपा वृक्षाभावात् ।	....	III. 80
5.	नास्त्यत्र शीतस्पर्शः धूमात् ।	....	III. 73

Meaning of the title "Parīkṣāmukhaṃ."

The title of the work Parīkṣāmukhaṃ is thus derived according to the author of Nyāyamaṇi-dīpikā : Parīkṣa or Tarka is the discussion used in finding out the strength or weakness of various arguments which are opposed to one another. 'Pari' means 'full' and 'Īkṣaṇam' means 'discussion' (of subjects). 'Āmukha' means 'the entrance' to those who want to understand this subject. This work (Parīkṣāmukhaṃ) is like such a door."[1]

Another derivation is also suggested by the same writer as follows : "As examination of all objects is made by Pramāṇa so Pramāṇa is the first thing (Āmukha) in Parīkṣa (discussion). Here the work itself describing Pramāṇa (which is Parīkṣāmukhaṃ) is also titled in the same name. As ascertainment is made by Pramāṇas leaving aside fallacies, discussion goes on with the help of Pramāṇas by those engaged in arguments. So the name 'Parīkṣāmukhaṃ' of this work is justified.[2]

Māṇikyanandi.

Nothing in detail is known about Māṇikyanandi the author of Parīkṣāmukhaṃ. In the Visvakoṣa

---

1. "अन्योन्यविरुद्ध-नानायुक्तिप्रावल्यदौर्वल्यावधारणाय प्रवर्त्तमानो विचारः परीक्षा तर्क इति यावत्। 'परि' समन्तादशेष निःशेषत 'ईक्षणं' विचारणं यत्र अर्थानाम् इति व्युत्पत्तेः। तस्य 'आमुखं' तद्व्युत्पत्तौ प्रवेशार्थिनां प्रवेशद्वारमिदं प्रकरणम्।"

2. "अथवा समस्तप्रमेयजालपरीक्षायाः प्रमाणपूर्वकत्वात् प्रमाणं परीक्षामुखम्। अत्र मुखशब्दस्य प्रथमार्थवाचित्वात् प्रमाणप्रतिपादकं प्रकरणमपि परीक्षामुखमित्युच्यते। प्रमाणनिश्चयस्यापि एतत् प्रकरणपूर्वकत्वात् तदाभासव्यावृत्त्या निश्चितं हि प्रमाणं पुरस्कृत्य परीक्षा क्रियते प्रेक्षापूर्वकारिभिरिति प्रकरणस्य परीक्षामुखनामधेयमनुपचरितम्॥"

Nyāyamaṇi-dīpikā, a commentary on Prameya-ratna-mālā. [From a Manuscript preserved in Jain Siddhānta Bhavan, ARRAH].

(a Bengali encyclopaedia) it is mentioned "According to the Pattāvali of the Sarasvatī Gachcha of the Digamvaras, Māṇikyanandi became Pattadhara in 585 Vikrama Samvat (523 A. D.) Before be became a Pattadhara that is to say, in the beginning of the 6th century, Māṇikyanandi wrote Parīkṣāmukhaṃ.

Māṇikyanandi was later than Akalaṅka.

This view is untenable. It is accepted by everyone that Māṇikyanandi was later than Akalaṅka and that he based his work or Akalaṅka's writings. Anantavīrya, the author of Prameya-ratna-mālā a commentary on Parīkṣāmukhaṃ begins his work by saluting Māṇikayanandi in this manner :

Salutation to that Māṇikyanandi who has churned the nectar of the knowledge of Nyāya from the ocean of the words of Akalaṅka[1].

In Nyāyamaṇi-dīpikā a commentary on Prameya-ratna-mālā we find :

"Bhatta Akalaṅka Deva promulgated the influence of the true religion by the weapon of arguments delighting the hearts of all scholars of the world in the court of King Hima-śītala....Afterwards the great sage Māṇikyanandi wrote the Prakaraṇa Parīkṣāmukhaṃ culling the subject matter from the ocean of the śāstra written by him (Akalaṅka). This work (of Māṇikyanandi) is like a vessel to cross the ocean (of the work of Akalaṅka.)"[2]

---

1. "अकलंकवचोऽम्भोधेरुद्दध्रे येन धीमता ।
न्यायविद्यामृतं तस्मै नमो माणिक्यनन्दिने ॥" Prameyaratnamālā.

2. "सकलराजाधिराजपरमेश्वरस्य हिमशीतलस्य महाराजस्य महास्थानमध्ये ···भगवान् भट्टाकलंकदेवो विश्वविद्वन्मण्डलहृदयाह्लादियुक्तिशस्त्रेण जगत्सद्धर्मप्रभावमवूबुधत्तमाम् । तदनु···माणिक्यनंदिमुनिवृन्दारकस्तत्प्रकाशितशास्त्रमहोदधेरुद्धृत्य तदवगाहनाय पोतोपमं 'परीक्षामुख' नामधेयमन्वर्थमुद्वहत्प्रकरणमारचयन् मुदा ।"
Nyāyamaṇidīpikā (A Mss.).

Prabhāchandra the author of Prameyakamala-mārtaṇḍa has written: "As the subject as laid down by Akalaṅka could be understood only by the wise, the Āchārya (Māṇikyanandi) composed this Prakaraṇa to explain that subject quoting the same with the object of laying down the same and wishing to explain the same (to all)[1].

Time of Akalaṅka.

There are differences of opinion as to the time during which Akalaṅka flourished. In Ārādhanā-kathā-koṣa (15th or 16th century A.D.), Akalaṅka is described as the son of the minister of Śubhatuṅga the King of Mānyakheta. It is also mentioned that there was a discussion in the court of King Hima-śītala between him and the Buddhists. In the Malliṣeṇa Praśasti in Sravana Belgola the latter incident is supported. It is also mentioned there-in that Akalaṅka visited the court of King Sāhasa-tuṅga. Dr. Satish Chandra Vidyābhūṣana has taken Subhatuṅga or Sāhasatuṅga as Kriśṇarāja I of the Rashtrakuta dynasty[2]. Pandit Nathuram Premi following this view has mentioned that the time of Akalaṅka was from Vikram Samvat 810 to 832 (753 to 775 A.D.)[3] Dr. K. B. Pathak holds the view

---

1. "श्रीमदकलंकार्थोऽव्युत्पन्नप्रज्ञैरवगन्तुं न शक्यत इति तद्व्युत्पादनाय करतलामलकवत् तदर्थमुद्धृत्य प्रतिपादयितुकामस्तत्परिज्ञानानुग्रहेच्छाप्रेरितस्तदर्थ-प्रतिपादनप्रवणं प्रकरणमिदमाचार्यः प्राह।" Prameya-kamala-mārtaṇḍa.

2. "Māṇikyanandi was a Digamvara author...As his work is based on that of Akalaṅka, he must have lived after 750 A. D.... Māṇikyanandi seems to have lived about 800 A.D." History of the Medieval School of Indian Logic. Page 28.

3. Jain Hitaishi Bhāga 11. Page 428. Vide "अकलंकदेव ८१० से ८३२ तक के किसी समय में जीवित थे।"

that Akalaṅka was a contemporary of Sāhasatuṅga Dantidurga. B. Kamta Prasad Jain criticising the view of Mr. Premi, has accepted the view that Sāhasatuṅga was none other than Dantidurga who reigned from 744 to 759 A.D. and has suggested that the time of Akalaṅka was from 744 to 782 A. D. B. Kamata Prasad has given arguments to support his view in his article in Hindi entitled "Sree Bhattākalaṅka Deva" published in Jain Siddhānta Bhāskar Bhāga 3, Kiraṇ 4. This view has however been ably refuted by Pandit Kailās Chandra Śāstrī in his article "Bhattākalaṅka kā Samaya" printed in the same journal (Bhāga 4 Kiraṇ 3).

The first argument of B. Kamtaprasad is that Akalaṅka has been mentioned by Jinasena in his Harivaṃśapurāṇa and two verses have been quoted in support of this view[1] and it is also mentioned that Dr. R. G. Bhandarkar has also mentioned this fact[2]. It has however been pointed out by Pandit Kailās Chandra Śāstrī that it is not correct to interpret the word 'Deva' in the first verse to mean Akalaṅka. It really refers to Devanandi alias Pūjyapāda the author of Jainendra Vyākaraṇa. In the second verse it is merely mentioned that the fame of Vīrasena is 'akalaṅka' ('free from any flaw'). It has no

---

1. "इन्द्रचन्द्रार्कजैनेन्द्रव्याडिव्याकरणेक्षिणः ।
देवस्य देवसंघस्य न वन्दूयन्ते गिरः कथम् ।।"

Verse 31. Harivaṃśa Purāṇa.

"वीरसेनगुरोः कीर्त्तिरकलंकावभासते ।"

Verse 39. Harivaṃśa Purāṇa.

2. Principal Results of my last two years studies in Sanskrit Mss. Literature by R. G. Bhandarkar (Wier, 1889) Page 31.

connection with the author 'Akalaṅka'. Had Jinasena any desire to eulogise Akalaṅka, he would have done this in an un-ambiguous manner.

It is however not disputed by Pandit Śāstrī that Jinasena was a writer later than Akalaṅka. Vidyānanda in his Aṣṭasahasrī a commentary on Akalaṅka's Aṣṭaśatī has mentioned Kumārasena. This Kumārasena has also been mentioned in Harivaṃśapurāṇa of Jinasena. Prabhāchandra a commentator on Parīkṣāmukhaṃ who was undoutedly later than Māṇikyanandi who followed Akalaṅka is mentioned in the Ādipurāṇa of Jinasena. The next argument of B. Kamtaprasad is that Akalaṅka was later than Dharmakīrti, the Buddhist philosopher who flourished in the beginning of the seventh century (635 to 650 A.D. approximately) Pandit Śāstrī admits this and gives examples showing that Akalaṅka has quoted and refuted the views of Dharma-kīrti[1]. Pandit Śāstrī however

---

1. The following instances are given : (a) The Kārikā in Akalaṅka's Laghīya-straya beginning with "स्वसंवेद्यविकल्पानां" mentions "सर्वतः संहृत्य चिन्तास्तिमितान्तरात्मना" found in kārikā 124 Chapter III of Pramāṇa-vārttika written by Dharma-kīrti.

Vide also "Dharmakīrti who is not referred to by Hieun Thsang but is referred to by I-Tsing very probably belonged to a period between 600-650 A.D." Introduction to Sādhana-mālā Page XXVII by B. Bhattacharya M.A. (Gaekwad's Oriental Series).

(b) The argument "भेदानां बहुभेदानां तत्रैकस्मिन्नयोगतः ।" mentioned in Pramāṇa-vārttika I. 91 has been met by Akalaṅka in his Nyāyaviniśchaya in the verse beginning with "भेदानां बहुभेदानां तत्रैकत्रापि संभवात् ।"

(c) In Aṣṭa-śatī of Akalaṅka on Āptamīmāṃsā verse 53 we

is unable to accept the conclusion of B. Kamtaprasad from this fact that Akalaṅka was at least hundred years later than Dharmakīrti, for it is urged that even contemporary writers can quote and refute each other's views and many examples can be given of such refutations.

Dr. K. B. Pathak has mentioned that as Kumārila Bhatta has attacked some of the views of Samantabhadra and Akalaṅka, it must be supposed that he was a contemporary of those writers and lived even after the death of Akalaṅka. In his article discussing the date of Samanta-bhadra[1] he has mentioned that the refutations of each other's views by Kumārila and Akalaṅka took place at the latter half of the eighth century A.D. B. Kamtaprasad has accepted this view and lays down that the time of Kumārila is 700 to 760 A. D. Pandit Śāstrī points out that as B. Kamtaprasad accepts the time of Akalaṅka to be 744 to 782 A.D., how can it be possible that Kumārila lived even after the death of Akalaṅka as Kumārila according to B. Kamtaprasad (following Dr. K. B. Pathak) lived only up to 760 A. D.? Further, Pandit Śāstrī is unable to accept this date of Kumārila without satisfactory proof, but is willing to accept that Kumārila

---

find "न तस्य किंचिद् भवति न भवत्येव केवलम्". This is exactly the second half of verse 279, Chapter I of Pramāṇa-vārttika.

(d) The view of Akalaṅka expressed in the sentence beginning with "मतान्तरप्रतिक्षेपार्थं वा" mentioned in Aṣṭasahasrī Page 81 discussing the Nigraha-sthānas of the Buddhist philosophers is a refutation of the Vāda-nyāya of Dharmakīrti.

1. Annals of the Bhandarkar Oriental Research Institute Vol. II. p. 141.

existed during the latter part of the seventh century refuting the view of Dr. K. B. Pathak that Kumārila flourished in the 8th century[1].

In the work 'Akalaṅka-charitra' it is mentioned that in 700 Vikrama Samvat (643 A.D.) there was a great discussion between Akalaṅka and the Buddhists[2]. Pandit Śāstrī points out that B. Kamta Prasad has taken the date as saka 700 but it is clear from the Sanskrit verse that Vikram Samvat is referred herein.

Pandit Śāstrī holds the view that Akalaṅka flourished in the middle of the 7th century. After criticising the views of B. Kamtaprasad, Dr. Pathak, Dr. Bhandarkar, and Dr. S. C. Vidyābhūṣaṇa as mentioned above, he mentions the following evidence regarding the time of Akalaṅka.

Siddhasena Gaṇi has written a commentary on the Tattvārtha Bhāṣya. Siddhasena has mentioned Dharmakīrti (7th century). Silāṅka (9th century) has mentioned Siddhasena as Gandhahasti. The date of Siddhasena therefore lies between these broad periods. Siddhasena has mentioned the work

---

1. Annals of the Bhandarkar Oriental Research Institute Vol. XIII. P. 157.

2. "विक्रमार्कशताब्दीयशतसप्तप्रमाजुषि ।
कालेऽकलंकपतिनो बौद्धैर्वादो महानभूत् ॥"

Epigraphia Carnatika II. Introduction.

Pandit Jugalkishore Mukhtar in his article "समन्तभद्र का समय और डा० के० वि० पाठक" (Jaina Jagat. Year IX. Vol. 15 Page 16) has given the reading "विक्रमार्कशकाब्दीय" which appears to be the correct one.

'Siddhi-viniśchaya', of Akalaṅka in his Tattvārtha Bhāṣya Tīkā[1].

Jinadāsa Gaṇi Mahottar composed a Chūrṇi on Niśītha-sūtra. In a Mss. of this work, the date of its composition is mentioned as Śaka Samvat 598 (676 A.D.) Jinadāsa has mentioned the work Siddhi-viniśchaya of Akalaṅka[2]. So Akalaṅka cannot have flourished later than 676 A.D.

Pandit Śāstrī quotes the following internal evidence from Akalaṅka's works which may be valuable to ascertain his date.

Dignāga the celebrated Buddhist philosopher in laying down the definition of Pratyakṣa Pramāṇa has mentioned that Pratyakṣa is 'Kalpanāpoḍha' Dharmakīrti who was later than Dignāga added 'Abhrānta' to it in defining Pratyakṣa. Akalaṅka in his Tattvārtha-rājavārttika has criticised the definition of Pratyakṣa Pramāṇa as laid down by Dignāga. A verse from Dignāga's Pramāṇa-samuchchaya has also been quoted by Akalaṅka[3].

Pandit Śāstrī is of opinion that as Akalaṅka has not criticised Dharmakīrti's definition of Pramāṇa in his Tattvārtha-rāja-vārttika, though he criticised views of Dharmakīrti in his other works, we may infer that Dharmakīrti's works Pramāṇa-

---

1. "एवं कार्यकारणसम्बन्धः समवायपरिणामनिमित्तनिर्वर्त्तकादिरूपः सिद्धिविनिश्चयसृष्टिपरीक्षातो योजनीयो विशेषार्थिना दूषणद्वारेण।" Page 37.

2. "दंसणगाही—दंसणणाणप्यभावगाणि सत्थाणि सिद्धिविनिच्छयसंमदिमादि गेण्हंतो असंथरमाणे जं अकप्पियं पडिसेवति जयनाथे तत्थ से सुद्धो अप्रायश्चित्ती भवतीत्यर्थः।"

3. "प्रत्यक्षं कल्पनापोढं नामजात्यादियोजना।
असाधारणहेतुत्वादक्षैस्तद्व्यपदिश्यते॥"

Pramāṇa-samuchchaya by Dignāga.

vārttika, Pramāṇa-viniśchaya etc. were composed later than Tattvārtha-rāja-vārttika. In Tattvārtha-rāja-vārttika, Akalaṅka has quoted a verse which is said to be the first verse of the Prakaraṇa entitled 'Santānantara-siddhi' of Dharmakīrti[1]. Pandit Śāstrī holds the view that as Dharmakīrti flourished from 635 to 650 A. D. Akalaṅka's date can be ascertained from this.

Akalaṅka has also quoted from the work 'Abhidharmakoṣa' of Vasubandhu[2].

Pandit Śāstrī concludes from the above that Dharmakīrti flourished from 635 to 650 A. D. and that Akalaṅka lived in the middle of the 7th century A. D.

In my opinion, no great help is derived from the internal evidence namely that Akalaṅka has mentioned Dharmakīrti, Vasubandhu or Dignāga. There is a view that Vasubandhu and Dignāga were contemporaries[3]. Udyotakara in his Nyāyavārttika refuted the views of Dignāga while discussing Prameya of Anumāna Pramāṇa. Udyotakara has also mentioned Dharmakīrti and Vinīta-deva in Nyāyavārttika. This Udyotakara has been men-

---

1. "बुद्धिपूर्वां क्रियां दृष्ट्वा स्वदेहेऽन्यत्र तद्ग्रहात् ।
मन्यते बुद्धिसद्भावं सा न येषु न तेषु धीः ॥"

Tattvārtharāja vārttika. P. 19.

[Sanātana Jaina Granthamālā]

2. "सवितर्कविचारा हि पञ्च विज्ञानधातवः ।
निरूपणानुस्मरणविकल्पनविकल्पकाः ॥"

Abhidharma-koṣa of Vasubandhu.

We find the reading "विकल्पादविकल्पकाः" in Abhidharma-koṣa.

3. Nyāyadarśana by Mahamahopādhyāya Phanibhūṣaṇa Tarkabāgis Vol. I. (first edition) Page 39.

tioned by Subandhu the author of Vāsavadattā[1]. Subandhu was earlier than Bāṇabhatta who lived in the court of king Harshavardhana of Kanauj (beginning of the 7th century). Bāṇabhatta has praised the work Vāsavadattā in his work Harṣacharita[2]. Thus only this much can be mentioned with certainty that Dignāga, Dharmakīrti and Vasubandhu could not have flourished later than the sixth century. Dr. Jacobi says "He (Udyotakara) may therefore have flourished in the early part of the sixth century or still earlier"[3].

But Vasubandhu and Dignāga might have lived long before the 6th century A. D. Yuan Chwang who came to Nālandā Vihāra in 637 A. D. has written that within a thousand years from the death or the Nirvāṇa of Buddha, Monaratha and his disciple Vasubandhu lived[4]. Samuel Beal in his note to the above passage has written that at that time the Chinese Buddhists, accepted the date of Nirvāṇa of Buddha as 850 B. C. On this calculation

---

1. "न्यायस्थितिमिव उद्योतकर-स्वरूपाम् ।" Vāsavadattā.

2. "कवीनामगलद्दर्पो नूनं वासवदत्तया ।" Harṣa-charitam.

3. The Dates of the Philosophical Sūtras of the Brahmaṇas by Hermann Jacobi [Journal of the American Oriental Society Vol. 31, 1911].

4. "This Master (Manoratha) made his auspicious advent within the 1000 years after the Buddha's decease···Manoratha··· sent an account of the circumstances to his disciple Vasubandhu and died." (Ta-T'ang-Hsi-yü-chi by Yuan Chwang).

Thomas Watters writes : "According to Yuan-Chwang Manoratha flourished···within 1000 years after the decease of Buddha. This, taking the Chinese reckoning would place the date of the Śāstra-master before A.D. 150".

the date of Vasubandhu will fall in the 2nd century B. C.[1] Dignāga accordingly will be of the same date.

The commentator Mallinātha has mentioned while explaining a verse in Kalidāsa's Meghadūta[2] that Dignāga was a contemporary of Kalidāsa. This view has however been not generally accepted.

It is difficult to lay down definitely as has been done by Pandit Śāstrī that because Akalaṅka has criticised the definition of only Dignāga and not that of Dharmakīrti in his Tattvartharājavārttika, we should conclude that the work 'Pramāṇa-viniśchaya' of Dharmakīrti was not then written. In our opinion, it is very unsafe to draw such a conclusion from only this material specially as Pandit Śāstrī himself shows that Akalaṅka named his work 'Nyāya-viniśchaya' on the line of Dharmakīrti's 'Pramāṇa-viniśchaya' and the views of Dharmakīrti have been refuted in other works of Akalaṅka.

Kumārila Bhatta was not referred to in the Nyāya Vārttika of Udyotakara[3]. This may sup-

---

1. But see: "Asaṅga brother of Vasubandhu (280-360) must have flourished in the first half of the fourth century". Introduction to Sādhana-mālā (Geakwad's Oriental Series) Page XXVII by B. Bhattacharya M.A.

2. "दिङ्नागानां पथि परिहरण् स्थूलहस्तावलेपान् ॥" Meghadūtaṃ. Pūrva-meghaḥ verse 14.

"दिङ्नागाचार्यस्य कालिदासप्रतिपक्षस्य हस्तावलेपान् हस्तविन्यासपूर्वकदूषणानि अद्रेरद्रिकल्पस्य दिङ्नागाचार्यस्य श्रृंगं प्राधान्यं हरति ।"

Sañjīvanī (commentary by Mallinātha).

3. Nyāyadarśana by Mahāmohopādhyāya Phaṇibhūṣaṇa Tarkabagis Vol. 1 (first edition P. 37-38).

port the view of Pandit Śāstrī that Kumārila Bhatta was not at least earlier than the 7th century A. D.

A. B. Keith in his Karma-Mimāṃsā Pages 10-11 writes : "Kumārila's date is determinable within defiinite limits ; he used the Vākyapadīya of Bhartrihari ; neither Hieun-Thsang nor It-sing mentions him ; he was before Śaṅkara ; he attacked the Jain theory of an omniscient being as propounded in the Āpta-mīmāṃsā of Samanta-bhadra, but is not answered by Akalaṅka in his Aṣṭaśatī which comments on the Āpta-mīmāṃsā. On the other hand he is freely attacked by Vidyānanda and Prabhāchandra who both lived before 838 A. D. Vidyānanda assures us, doubtless correctly, that he criticised the Buddhist Dharmakīrti and Prabhākara, on the latter point agreeing with the result above arrived from internal evidence. The upper limit is therefore, not earlier than 700 A. D. The lower limit depends on his precise chronological relation to Śaṅkara and the latter's exact date. Later tradition, the Śaṅkara-vijayas of Mādhava and the pseudo-Ānandagiri would make him an older contemporary, but the interval may have been considerably longer."

We agree with the views of Pandit Śāstrī regarding his conclusion about the time of Akalaṅka so far as materials are available up to the present.

We have dealt with the date af Akalaṅka in detail as we have no other data for fixing the date of Māṇikyanandi who we only know flourished later than Akalaṅka and based his work on Akalaṅka's writings. From what have already been discussed, we may infer that Māṇikyanandi flourished during

Commentaries on Parīkṣā-mukhaṃ.

the end of the 7th or the beginning of the 8th century A. D. He has mentioned the Chārvāka school of philosophy[1] as well as the Buddhist, Sāṅkhya and Nyāya-vaiśeṣika systems of philosophy and Prabhākara and Jaimini[2]. Prabhāchandra was the most celebrated commentator of Parīkṣā-mukhaṃ.

I. Prameya-kamala-mārtaṇḍa by Prabhāchandra.

His work is entitled "Prameya-kamala-mārtaṇḍa". This Prabhāchandra has been mentioned (with his work Nyāya-kumuda-chandrodaya) by Jinasena in Ādipurāṇa (838 A. D.) in the following verse :

"I praise Prabhāchandra the poet whose fame is white as the rays of the moon and who has encompassed the whole world by making 'Chandrodaya' ('rising 'of the moon' ; another meaning 'the work entitled Kumudachandrodaya')"[3].

Prabhāchandra saluted Māṇikyanandi at the beginning of Prameya-kamala-mārtaṇḍa[4].

---

1. "लौकायतिकस्य प्रत्यक्षत: परलोकादिनिषेधस्य परबुद्धयादेश्चासिद्धेरतद्विषयत्वात् ॥" Parīkṣāmukhaṃ VI. 56.

2. "सौगतसांख्ययौगप्रभाकरजैमिनीयानां प्रत्यक्षानुमानागमोपमानार्थापत्त्यभावैरेकैकाधिकैर्व्याप्तिवत् ॥" Ibid VI. 57.

3. "चन्द्रांशुशुभ्रयशसं प्रभाचन्द्रं कविं स्तुवे ।
कृत्वा चन्द्रोदयं येन शश्वदाच्छादितं जगत् ॥" Ādi-purāṇa.

Jinasena lived in the court of Amoghavarṣa I who reigned according to Vincent Smith from 8I5 to 877 A.D. (Early History of India P. 328).

4. "शास्त्रं करोमि वरमल्पतरावबोधो
माणिक्यनन्दिपदपंकजसत्प्रसादात् ।
अर्थं किं न स्फुटयति प्रकृतं लधीयां-
ल्लोकस्य भानुकरविस्फुरिताद् गवाक्ष: ॥"

Prameyakamala-mārtaṇḍa.

Prabhāchandra's commentary is specially valuable as it quotes the views of various Hindu and Buddhist writers on Nyāya philosophy and criticising the same establishes the Jain view.

The view of Dr. K. B. Pathak that Prabhāchandra was a disciple of Akalaṅka is erroneous[1].

II. Prameya-ratnamālā by Anantavīrya.

The most widely read commentary of Parīkṣāmukhaṃ is Prameya-ratnamālā. We have published the full text of it in this edition. The writer of this is Ananta-vīrya who also wrote commentaries of Akalaṅka's works. Prabhāchandra has mentioned at the beginning of the fourth Chapter of his Nyāya-kumudachandra that he has been able to study and discuss many times through the writings of Ananta-vīrya, the difficult expositions of Akalaṅka imparting a knowledge of all objects in the three worlds[2]. Vādirāja Sūri in his Nyāya-viniśchaya-vivaraṇa writes that at every step the deep meaning of Akalaṅka's writing has been illuminated by the writings of Anantavīrya like a lamp[3].

---

1. Dr. Pathak has taken the following verse of Prabhāchandra in his work Nyāyakumudachandrodaya to mean that Prabhāchandra was a disciple of Akalaṅka, but no such interpretation is possible (Vide article by Pandit Jugalkisor published in Anekānta Vol. I. Page I30).

"वोधः कोऽप्यसमः समस्तविषयं प्राप्याकलंकं पदम्
जातस्तेन समस्तवस्तुविषयं व्याख्यायते तत्पदम् ।
किं न श्रीगणभृज्जिनेन्द्रपदतः प्राप्तप्रभावः स्वयं
व्यारव्यात्यप्रतिमं वचो जिनपतेः सर्वात्मभाषात्मकम् ॥"

2. "त्रैलोक्योदरवर्त्तिवस्तुविषयज्ञानप्रभावोदयो
दुष्प्रापोऽप्यकलंकदेवसरणिः प्राप्तोऽत्र पुण्योदयात् ।
स्वभ्यस्तश्च विवेचितश्च शतशः सोऽनन्तवीर्योक्तितो
भूयान्मे नयनीतिदत्तमनसस्तद्वोधसिद्धिप्रदः ॥"

3. "गूढमर्थमकलंकवाङ्मयागाधभूमिनिहितं तदर्थिनाम् ।
व्यञ्जयत्यमलमनन्तवीर्यवाग् दीपवर्त्तिरनिशं पदे पदे ॥"

Though such a great writer, Anantavīrya professed utmost humility in saying at the beginning of his commentary on Siddhiviniśchaya :—"It is a great wonder that even Anantavīrya (in another sense 'one who has infinite power') is unable to explain fully the meaning of the work of Akalaṅka"[1].

In this commentary on Siddhiviniśchaya, Anantavīrya has mentioned Dharmottar, Prajñākar and Archata. The date of Archata the author of the commentary on Hetu-vindu is according to Rāhula Sankrityāyana 825 A. D. Ananta-vīrya must have therefore flourished not earlier than the 9th century A. D.

In Prameyaratnamālā, Anantavīrya has referred to Dharmakīrti (page 10) Vyāsa (page 20), Patañjali (page 20) Avadhūta (page 20) and Manu (page 49). He has mentioned the works Āpta-parīkṣā (page 23), Devāgamālaṅkāra also known as Āpta-mīmāṃsā (page 24) by Samantabhadra and Naya-chakra. He has quoted from the Vedas (page 20) and Sāṅkhya-kārika (page 52) of Īśvara-kriṣṇa.

Sāyana-Mādhava in his Sarva-darśana-saṃgraha while explaining Saptabhaṅginaya of Ārhata Darśana has quoted Ananta-vīrya[2].

---

1. "देवस्यानन्तवीर्योऽपि पदं व्यक्तुं तु सर्वतः ।
न जानीतेऽकलंकस्य चित्रमेतद् परं भुवि ॥"

2. "तत्सर्वमनन्तवीर्यः प्रत्यपीपदत्—
तद्विधानविवक्षायां स्यादस्तीति गतिर्भवेत् ।
स्यान्नास्तीति प्रयोगः स्यात्तन्निषेधे विवक्षिते ॥
क्रमेणोभयवाञ्छायां प्रयोगः समुदायभाक् ।
युगपत्तद्विवक्षायां स्यादवाच्यमशक्तितः ॥
आद्यावाच्यविवक्षायां पञ्चमो भंग इष्यते ।
अन्त्यावाच्यविवक्षायां षष्ठभंगसमुद्भवः ॥
समुच्चयेन युक्तश्च सप्तमो भंग उच्यते ॥ इति ।"

Ananta-vīrya has mentioned Prabhāchandra in the beginning of his work : "When there is a moon like the work of Prabhāchandra, how can I resembling a fire-fly expect to be counted ?"[1]

It is mentioned in the beginning of Prameya-ratna-mālā that this commentary 'Pañchikā'[2] on Parīkṣāmukhaṃ was composed for study of Śānti-ṣeṇa at the request of Hīrapa the favourite son of Vaijeya[3]. At the colophon of this work it is mentioned that Vaijeya was born in the family of Vadarīpāla. His wife was Nāṇāmba who was also known as Revatī, Prabhāvatī and Prathitāmbikā. Hīrapa was their son. At his request, Anantavīrya has cleared the meaning of the work of Māṇikya-nandi[4].

Sarvadarśana-saṃgraha Edited by V. S. Abhayankar Pages 83-84.

1. "प्रभेन्दुवचनोदारचन्द्रिकाप्रसरे सति ।
मादृशाः क नु गण्यन्ते ज्योतिरिङ्गणसन्निभा ॥"
Prameya-ratnamālā.

2. Pañchikā is a commentary in which each word of the original work is explained. c.f.
"कारिका स्वल्पवृत्तिस्तु, सूत्रं सूचनकं स्मृतम् ।
टीका निरन्तरं व्याख्या, पंचिका पदभंजिका ॥"

3. "वैजेयप्रियपुत्रस्य हीरपस्योपरोधतः ।
शान्तिषेणार्थमारब्धा परीक्षामुखपंचिका ॥" Prameyaratnamālā.

4. "श्रीमान् बैजेयनामाभूदग्रणीर्गुणशालिनाम् ।
वदरीपालवंशालिव्योमद्युमणिरूर्जितः ॥
तदीयपत्नी भुवि विश्रुतासीन्नाणाम्बनान्मा गुणशीलसीमा ।
यां रेवतीति प्रथिताम्बिकेति प्रभावतीति प्रवदन्ति सन्तः ॥
तस्यामभूद्विश्वजनीनवृत्तिर्दानाम्बुवाहो भुवि हीरपाख्यः ।
स्वगोत्रविस्तारनभोंशुमाली सम्यक्त्वरत्नाभरणार्चिताङ्गः ॥
तस्योपरोधवशतो विशदोरुकीर्त्तेर्माणिक्यनन्दिकृतशास्त्रमगाधबोधम् ।
स्पष्टीकृतं कतिपयैर्वचनैरुदारैर्बालप्रबोधकरमेतदनन्तवीर्यैः ॥"
Colophon to Prameyaratnamālā

Prameyakamalamārtaṇḍa being a voluminous work and full of discussions regarding views of logicians other than Jain logicians, could not easily be tackled by those who wanted to learn the subject-matter only of Parīkṣāmukhaṃ. Prameya-ratna-mālā satisfied their want being a shorter and simpler work though it briefly alluded to the views of other logicians wherever necessary. Many expositions of this commentary Prameyaratnamālā were written. Three of these are preserved in Jain Siddhānta Bhavan, Arrah.

Commentaries on Prameya ratna-mālā.

(a) Artha-prakāśikā.

The first is Arthaprakāśikā. In the verses at the beginning it is mentioned that it is written by Panditāchārya (no specific name being given)[1]. Some attribute it (without however any definite proof) to Chārukīrti. There were several Chārukīrtis and nothing definite can be said as who really was the author of this treatise. The Maṅgalācharaṇa, the colophon and a portion from the middle of this work have been printed from the Mss. in Jain Siddhānta Bhāskara. Bhāga 4. Kiraṇa 1. Praśasti-saṅgraha page 66.

(b) Prameya-ratnamālā-laṅkāra.

The second is Prameya-ratna-mālā-laṅkāra. After saluting Akalaṅka[2], and Māṇikyanandi[3] the author praises Prabhāchandra the author of Prameya-

---

1. "श्रीमन्नेमिजिनेन्द्रस्य वन्दित्वा पादपंकजम् ।
प्रमेयरत्नमालार्थः संक्षेपेण विविच्यते ॥
प्रमेयरत्नमालायाः व्याख्यास् सन्ति सहस्रशः ।
तथापि पण्डिताचार्यकृतिगृ ह्यैव कोविदैः ॥" Arthaprakāśikā.

2. "जित्वा श्लाध्यतमोऽभवत् सपदि तं वंदेऽकलकं मुनिम् ।"
Prameyaratnamālālaṅkāra.

3. "हर्षं वर्षतु सन्ततं हृदि गुरुर्माणिक्यनन्दी मम ।" Ibid.

kamalamārtaṇḍa[1]. The author then mentions his name as Chāru-kīrti and the name of the work as Prameyaratnamālālaṅkāra[2]. From the colophon of this work we learn that this Chārukīrti resided in Śravana Belgola (where the world-renowed image of Gommateśvara exists) and belonged to Deśi Gaṇa[3]. Gommateśvara or Vāhuvali is saluted in two verses at the end[4].

Pandit Bhujavali Śāstrī is of opinion that it is very probable that this Chārukīrti was the author of the same name who composed commentaries on Pārśvābhyudaya, Chandraprabha kāvya, Ādipurāṇa, Yaśodharacharita, Neminirvāṇa etc. The Pattādhīśas of Śravana Belgola are all known by the common name of Chārukīrti. So it is difficult to settle who this particular person was[5].

The Mangalācharaṇa, the colophon and some portions from the middle of this manuscript have been printed in Jain Siddhānta Bhāskar. Bhāga 4. Kiraṇa 1. Praśasti saṅgraha pages 68-71.

---

1. "जयतु प्रभेन्दुसूरिः प्रमेयकमलप्रकाण्डमार्त्तण्डेन ।" Ibid.
2. "श्रीचारुकीर्त्तिधुर्यस्सन्तनुते पण्डितार्यमुनिवर्यः ।
   व्याख्यां प्रमेयरत्नालंकाराख्यां मुनीन्द्रसूत्राणाम् ।।" Ibid.
3. "श्रीमद्देशिगणाग्रगण्यस्य श्रीमद् वेल्गुलपुरनिवासरसिकस्य चारुकीर्त्ति-पण्डिताचार्यस्य कृतौ परीक्षामुखसूत्रव्याख्यायां प्रमेयरत्नमालालंकारसमाख्यायाम् ..." Ibid.
4. "किं च श्रीगुमटेश्वरस्य कृपया विंध्याद्रिचूडामणेः ।" Ibid.
   Also :
   "श्रीमद्वेलगुलमध्यभासुरमहाविन्ध्याद्रिचिन्तामणिः
   श्रीमद् बाहुबली करोतु कुशलं भव्यात्मनां सन्ततम् ।" Ibid.
5. Notes by Pandit K. Bhujavali Śāstrī on Praśasti saṅgraha Page 71 (Jain Siddhānta Bhāskara. Bhāga 4. Kiraṇa 1).

(c) Nyāyamaṇi dīpikā.

The third work is Nyāyamaṇidīpikā. Two Mss. of this work are preserved in Jain Siddhānta Bhavan, Arrah. The name of the author is not found in the Mss. Pandit Subayya Śāstrī says that in some palm leaf Mss. of this work, the name of the writer is mentioned as Ajitasenāchārya. Pandit K. Bhujavali Śāstrī says that this is supported by "Catalogue of Sanskrit and Prākrita Manuscripts in the Central Provinces and Berar by R. B. Hiralal B. A. Appendix B"[1].

The author has made obeisance to Akalaṅka, Anantavīrya, Māṇikyanandi and Prabhāchandra in the Maṅgalācharaṇa of his work[2]. As regards commentaries to Parīkṣāmukhaṃ, he mentions that Prabhāchandra wrote an exhaustive commentary entitled Prameyakamalamārtaṇḍa. Though this work was suitable to scholars, there was a necessity for a shorter and easier commentary. Hīrapa Vaiśya the son of Vaijeya of the family of Badripāla requested Ananta-vīrya to teach Śantiṣeṇa. Ananta-vīrya composed Prameya-ratna-mālā under these circumstances[3].

---

1. Notes by Pandit K. Bhujavali Śāstrī on Praśasti saṅgraha Page 2-3 (Jain Siddhānta Bhāskar Bhāga II. Kiraṇa 1).

2. श्रीवर्द्धमानमकलंकमनन्तवीर्यमाणिक्यनंदियतिभाषितशास्त्रवृत्तिम् ।
"भक्त्या प्रभेन्दुरचितालघुवृत्तिदृष्ट्या नत्वा यथाविधि वृणोमि लघुप्रपञ्चम् ॥" Nyāya-maṇi-dīpikā.

3. "तदनु तत्प्रकरणस्य विशिष्टतमोऽतिस्पष्टं....प्रभाचन्द्रभट्टारकः प्रमेयकमलमार्त्तण्डनामवृहद्वृत्तिं चरीकरोति स्म। तद् वृत्तिग्रन्थस्य....सकलविद्वच्चित्तप्रकाशकत्वेऽपि....बालान्तःकरण....प्रकाशनसामर्थ्याभावमाकलय्य तत्प्रकाशनाय....प्रमेयरत्नमालेत्यन्वर्थनामोद्वहतीं....लघ्वीं वृत्तिं....अनन्तवीर्याचार्यवर्यो....वैजेयप्रियसूनुना हीरपाख्यवैश्योत्तमेन वदरीपालवंशद्युमणिना शान्तिषेणाध्यापनाभिलाषिणा प्रेरितः सन् प्रारीप्सुः...." Ibid.

III. Prameya-kaṇṭhikā.

A commentary named Prameya-kaṇṭhikā on Parīkṣāmukhaṃ was written by Śāntivarṇi. It has not been possible to ascertain details about this Śānti-varṇi or the probable time when his work was written. There are five Sections (**स्तवक**) in this work. Following the Sūtras of Parīkṣāmukhaṃ the author has refuted the views of other logicians (Bauddha etc.) and established the Jain view. A Mss. of this work is preserved in Jain Siddhānta Bhavan, Arrah and the portions at the beginning and the colophon have been published in Jain Siddhānta Bhāskara Bhāga 4, Kiraṇas 1 and 2. Praśasti-Saṅgraha, pages 72 and 73[1].

Parīkṣāmukhaṃ and Pramāṇa-naya-tattvā-lokālaṅkāra.

Vādiveva Sūri (12th century A. D.) composed Pramāṇa-naya-tattvālokālaṅkāra closely following Parīkṣāmukhaṃ. Many aphorisms are exactly the same, only synonyms being used[2]. In some aphorisms, an attempt is seen to show some novelty by giving examples of a different kind but the examples

---

1. The Maṅgalācharaṇa runs thus :

"श्रीवर्धमानमानम्य विष्णुं विश्वसृजं हरं ।
परीक्षामुखसूत्रस्य ग्रन्थस्यार्थं विवृण्महे ॥"

The Colophon is :

"श्रीशान्तिवर्णिविरचितायां प्रमेयकण्ठिकायां पञ्चमः स्तवकः समाप्तः ।
प्रमेयकण्ठिका जीयात् प्रसिद्धानेकसद्‌गुणा ।
लसन् मार्त्तण्ड-साम्राज्ययौवराज्यस्य कण्ठिका ॥
स निष्कलङ्कं जनयन्तु तर्कं वा बाधितकों मम तर्करत्ने ।
केनानिशं ब्रह्मकृतः कलंकश्चन्द्रस्य किं भूषणकारणं न ॥"

2. Compare "हिताहितप्राप्तिपरिहारसमर्थं हि प्रमाणं ततो ज्ञानमेव तत् ॥"
Parīkṣāmukhaṃ. I. 2.

and "अभिमतानभिमतवस्तुस्वीकारतिरस्कारक्षमं हि प्रमाणमतो ज्ञानमेवेदम् ।" Pramāṇanayatattvālokālaṅkāra I. 3.

in Parīkṣāmukhuṃ are more simple and easily understood[1]. In many places some extra words have been introduced in aphorisms[2]. A detailed comparison between Parīkṣāmukhaṃ and Pramāṇa-nayatattvālokālaṅkāra will be found in the article in Hindi entitled 'Pramāṇa-nayatattvālaṅkāra ki samīkṣa' by Pandit Baṅśidhar Ji in Jain Siddhānta Bhāskar, Bhaga 2. Kiraṇas 1 and 2. Pages 18 and 70.

---

1. Compare : "घटमहमात्मना वेद्मि।" Parīkṣāmukhaṃ I. 8.
"करिकलभकमहमात्मना जानामि।"
Pramāṇanayatattvālokālaṅkāra I. 16.
or "प्रदीपवत्।" Parīkṣāmukhaṃ. I. 12.
"मिहिरालोकवत्।"
Pramāṇanayatattvālokālaṅkāra I. 17.
or "यथा नद्यास्तीरे मोदकराशयः सन्ति धावध्वं मानवकाः।"
Parīkṣāmukhaṃ VI. 52.
"यथा मेकलकन्यकायाः कूले तालहिन्तालयोर्मूले सुलभाः पिण्डखर्जुराः सन्ति त्वरितं गच्छत गच्छत शावकाः।"
Pramāṇanayatattvālokālaṅkāra VI. 84.

2. Compare : "सहचारिणोरपि परस्परपरिहारेणावस्थानात् सहोत्पादाच्च।" Parīkṣāmukhaṃ III. 64.
"सहचारिणोः परस्पररुपत्यागेन तादात्म्यानुपपत्तेः सहोत्पादेन तदुत्पत्तिविपत्तेश्च सहचरहेतोरपि प्रोक्तेषु नानुप्रवेशः।"
Pramāṇanayatattvālokālaṅkāra III. 76.
or "उपलम्भानुपलम्भनिमित्तं व्याप्तिज्ञानमूहः॥ इदमस्मिन् सत्येव भवत्यसति न भवत्येवेति च॥" Parīkṣāmukhaṃ. III.11.12.
"उपलम्भानुपलम्भसंभवं त्रिकालीकलितसाध्यसाधनसम्बन्धाद्यालंवनम् इदमस्मिन् सत्येव भवतीत्याद्याकारं संवेदनमूहापरनामा तर्कः॥" Pramāṇa-naya-tattvālokālaṅkāra III. 7.

Hemachandra also wrote his Pramāṇa mīmāṃsā in aphorisms though Sūtra works at such a late period when he flourished were unnecessary. (Vide Pramāṇa mīmāṃsā by S. C. Ghoshal Jain Gazette Vol. XI p. 108).

Subject matter of Parīkṣāmukhaṃ.

Parīkṣāmukhaṃ is divided into six sections (Samuddeśa). In the first section Pramāṇa is defined and explained. In the second section two kinds of Pramāṇa viz. Pratyakṣa and Parokṣa are mentioned and Pratyakṣa with its varieties are described. The third section deals with Parokṣa Pramāṇa and its subdivisions Smriti, Pratyabhijñāna, Tarka, Anumāṇa and Āgama. The greater portion of this section is devoted to Anumāna (inference) the most important subject in all logical works. The two varieties of Anumāṇa viz. Svārtha and Parārtha are described in detail. The fourth section treats with the subject of Pramāṇa with its two varieties Sāmānya and Viśeṣa with their subdivisions. In the fifth section, the result of Pramāṇa is described. The sixth and the last section deals with fallacies.

There are 13 aphorisms in the first, 12 in the second, 101 in the third, 9 in the fourth, 3 in the fifth and 74 in the sixth section of this work.

In the present edition, a new line has been struck out in writing the English commentary. Without entering into the usual refutations and counter-refutations of views of Jain, Hindu and Buddhist logicians as is found in Sanskrit commentaries which will create a volumious work and cloud the main theme, I have taken special pains to make a comparative study of the subject matter and have quoted the views of all important older and later writers on this subject. It is hoped that the reader by going through this commentary will not only gain a thorough idea of Jain Nyāya as succintly put down by the celebrated Digamvara writer Māṇikyanandi who was never surpassed by any other author in making a clear and brief exposition of the subject but he will also have a grasp of the work of other Digamvara as well as Śvetāmvara authors many of whom like Vādideva composed works which attempted to rival that of Māṇikyanandi. My attempt has been to explain in a simple and clear way the views of Jain Nyāya taking great pains to cull authorities from all available important Jain works. I have not left out the views of Hindu and Buddhist philosophers which are referred to in the work itself though I have dealt with the same only so far as is necessary for the understanding of the subject.

The present work was undertaken with the generous help of the trustees of J. L. Jaini Memorial Fund to whom my heartfelt thanks are due. Portions of the work were printed in the Jain Gazette through the courtesy of Pandit Ajit Prasad M.A. LL.B., the Editor of the said journal without whose efforts this work would never have been undertaken.

I am deeply indebted to Brahmachari Sital Prasādji and Pandit Sumerchand Nyāyatīrtha M. A. LL.B. for their valuable suggestions. For loan of rare books and manuscripts my sincerest gratitude is due to the authorities of the Jain Siddhānt Bhavan, Arrah, late Puran Chand Nahar M. A., B. L. Vakil, High Court, Calcutta, Seth Ananda Raj Surana of Delhi and Pandit K. Bhujabali Śāstri, Arrah.

COOCHBEHAR, S. C. GHOSHAL.

August, 1940.

A GUIDE TO TRANSLITERATION

VOWELS

अ—A	उ—U	ऌ—LI	ओ—O
आ—Ā	ऊ—Ū	ॡ—LLI	औ—OU
इ—I	ऋ—ṚI	ए—E	ं—Ṃ
ई—Ī	ॠ—ṚĪ	ऐ—AI	:—Ḥ

CONSONANTS

क—Ka	ट—Ṭa	प—Pa	ष—Ṣa
ख—Kha	ठ—Ṭha	फ—Pha	स—Sa
ग—Ga	ड—Ḍa	ब—Ba	ह—Ha
घ—Gha	ढ—Ḍha	भ—Bha	
ङ—Ṅa	ण—Ṇa	म—Ma	
च—Cha	त—Ta	य—Ya	
छ—Chha	थ—Tha	र—Ra	
ज—Ja	द—Da	ल—La	
झ—Jha	ध—Dha	व—Va	
ञ—Ña	न—Na	श—Śa	

ॐ

परीक्षामुखम्

PARĪKṢĀMUKHAM

प्रमाणादर्थसंसिद्धिस्तदाभासाद्विपर्ययः ।
इति वक्ष्ये तयोर्लक्ष्म सिद्धमल्पं लघीयसः ॥

Pramāṇādarthasaṃsiddhistadābhāsādviparyayaḥ.
Iti vakṣye tayorlakṣma siddhamalpaṃ laghīyasaḥ.

Padapāṭha. प्रमाणात् Pramāṇāt, from Pramāṇa (valid knowledge), अर्थसंसिद्धिः Arthasaṃsiddhiḥ, knowables are rightly ascertained, तदाभासात् Tadābhāsāt, from Pramāṇābhāsa (false knowledge), विपर्ययः Viparyayaḥ, the opposite (happens), इति Iti, for that reason, लघीयसः Laghīyasaḥ, for those who desire a short exposition, तयोः Tayoḥ, of those (i. e. Pramāṇa and Pramāṇābhāsa), सिद्धम् Siddhaṃ, as laid down by authorities, अल्पम् Alpaṃ, short, लक्ष्म Lakṣma, definition, वक्ष्ये Vakṣye, (I shall) speak (describe).

1. From Pramāṇa (valid knowledge) knowables are rightly ascertained and from Pramāṇābhāsa (false knowledge), the opposite happens. For this reason, I shall describe the definitions of these as laid down by authorities in a concise manner for the benefit of those who desire a short exposition (of this subject).

Commentary

Māṇikyanandi the author of Parīkṣāmukhaṃ begins his work by mentioning the subject matter of the treatise and says that he will define and deal with Pramāṇa (valid knowledge) and Pramāṇābhāsa (false knowledge).

Prabhāchandra in his commentary named Prameyakamala-mārtaṇḍa on Parīkṣāmukhaṃ writes that the wise only appreciate a work which has coherence in its subject-matter, which has some object in view and this object is possible of attainment. Incoherent words like those of a mad man find no hearing. Useless attempts like counting the hairs of an ass or teeth of a crow or finding the weight of an egg of a sheep (which are impossibilities) are not made by wise men.[1] They are not also attracted to a task which is unpalatable such as finding out another husband to one's own mother or to follow an advice to perform a task incapable of being fulfilled like the finding out of a jewel on the head of a snake known as Takṣaka which is said to cure all kinds of fever.[2]

Prabhāchandra quotes these verses to support his view :

"At the beginning of every Śāstra, the object with its connection should be mentioned, for a hearer pays attention to only a definite subject and things connected with the same. Who would pay attention to a treatise or do any kind of work till its necessity is patent ? That Śāstra for which no necessity is explained is not desired by the wise. So at the outset, the necessity is to be explained. When the results of studying a Śāstra are known, the wise begin to read it with the object of attaining these results. Until connection with the subject matter is established, the writing is regarded as speech of a man uttering incoherent words in delirium. So commentators should explain the necessity of a work with its connected subject-matter. Otherwise it will be useless.[3]

---

1 "काकस्य कति वा दन्ता मेषस्याण्डं कियत्पलम् ।
गर्दभे कति रोमाणीत्येवं मूर्खविचारणा ॥"

2 "सम्बन्धाभिधेयशक्यानुष्ठानेष्टप्रयोजनवन्ति हि शास्त्राणि प्रेक्षावद्भिराद्रियन्ते, नेतराणि । सम्बन्धाभिधेयरहितस्योन्मत्तादिवाक्यवत्, तद्वतोऽप्यप्रयोजनवतः काकदन्तपरीक्षावद्, अनभिमतप्रयोजनवतो वा मातृविवाहोपदेशवद्, अशक्यानुष्ठानस्य वा सर्वज्वरहरतक्षकचूडारत्नालंकारोपदेशवद्, तैरनादरणीयत्वात् ॥"

3 "सिद्धार्थं सिद्धसम्बन्धं श्रोता श्रोतुं प्रवर्त्तते ।
शास्त्रादौ तेन वक्तव्यः सम्बन्धः सप्रयोजनः ॥

The necessity for studying logic and attaining right knowledge will be evident from the following. The path of liberation according to Jain doctrines, consists of right faith, right knowledge and right conduct.[1] These three are called the three jewels in Jain works. These are attained in a particular stage of development by the householder. Their perfection is attained in the Arhat stage. Right faith is the belief in the seven Tattvas (essential principles) of Jainism.[2] The Tattvas are Jīva, Ajīva, Āsrava, Bandha, Saṃvara, Nirjarā and Mokṣa.[3]

सर्वस्यैव हि शास्त्रस्य कर्मणो वापि कस्यचित् ।
यावत् प्रयोजनं नोक्तं तावत्तत् केन गृह्यताम् ।।
अनिर्दिष्टफलं सर्वं न प्रेक्षापूर्वकारिभिः ।
शास्त्रमाद्रियते तेन वाच्यमग्रे प्रयोजनम् ।।
शास्त्रस्य तु फले ज्ञाते तत्प्राप्त्याशावशीकृताः ।
प्रेक्षावन्तः प्रवर्त्तन्ते तेन वाच्यं प्रयोजनम् ।।
यावत् प्रयोजनेनास्य सम्बन्धो नाभिधीयते ।
असम्बद्धप्रलापित्वाद्भवेत्तावदसङ्गतिः ।।
तस्माद् व्याख्याङ्गमिच्छद्भिः सहेतुः सप्रयोजनः ।
शास्त्रावतारसम्बन्धो वाच्यो नान्योऽस्ति निष्फलः ।।"

1 "सम्यग्दर्शनज्ञानचारित्राणि मोक्षमार्गः ।"
Tattvārthādhigama Sūtra I. 1.

"कृत्स्नकर्मक्षयो मोक्षो भव्यस्य परिणामिनः ।
ज्ञानदर्शनचारित्र-त्रयोपायः प्रकीर्त्तितः ।।"
Chandraprabha-charitaṃ XVIII. 123.

"ज्ञानदर्शनचारित्रैरुपायैः परिणामिनः ।
भव्यस्यायमनेकाङ्गविकल्पैरेव जायते ।।"
Dharmaśarmābhyudayaṃ XXI. 161.

2 "तत्वार्थश्रद्धानं सम्यग्दर्शनम् ।"
Tattvārthādhigama Sūtra I. 2.

3 "जीवाजीवास्रवबंधसंवरनिर्जरामोक्षास्तत्वम् ।"
Tattvārthādhigama Sūtra I. 4.

A sincere belief in the Tattvas which is called right faith or Samyaktva arises either of itself or through instruction.[1] That is to say, it may arise from intuition independently of any precept or it may come to exist from external sources e. g. from precept of others or by reading the scriptures. There is no necessity for any work on Logic for those who get right faith through intuition, but as regards others, Pramāṇa and Naya are the means of instruction.[2] Thus the connection of Pramāṇa with the highest goal viz. the attainment of liberation is established.[3]

The pursuit of study of Pramāṇas accordingly cannot be unpalatable. It is the object of every being to acquire what is desirable and leave what is un-desirable. In Nyāya philosophy, an example is commonly cited that people like to have garlands of flowers, sandal paste etc. while they wish to avoid snakes, thorns etc. This like or dislike arises from actual perception. People act accordingly towards these objects to acquire or avoid the same. Vātsyāyana, the writer of the Bhāṣya on the Nyāya Sūtras of Gautama writes "The knower by Pramāṇa only understands the real nature of knowables and wishes to have or leave the same."[4]

These Tattvas have been explained in detail in Dravya-saṃgraha (Edited by S. C. Ghoshal), Vol. I, Sacred Books of the Jainas.

1 "तन्निसर्गादधिगमाद् वा ।"

Tattvārthādhigama Sūtra I. 3.

2 "प्रमाणनयैरधिगमः ।"

Tattvārthādhigama sūtra I. 6.

3 Dharmabhūṣana Yati has begun his Nyāya-dīpikā in the above strain :

'प्रमाणनयैरधिगम इति महाशास्त्रतत्वार्थसूत्रम् । तत् खलु परमपुरुषार्थनिःश्रेयसाधनसम्यग्दर्शनादिविषयीभूत-जीवादि-तत्वाधिगमोपायनिरुपणपरम् । प्रमाणनयाभ्यां हि विवेचिता जीवादयः सम्यगधिगम्यंते । तद्व्यतिरेकेण जीवाद्यधिगमे प्रमाणान्तरासंभवात् । तत एव जीवाद्यधिगमोपायभूतौ प्रमाणनयावपि विवेक्तव्यौ ॥"

4 "प्रमाणेन खल्वयं ज्ञाताऽर्थमुपलभ्य तमर्थमभीप्सति जिहासति वा ।"

In spiritual activities also, a man who understands the transitory character of the worldly objects of enjoyment and the eternal nature of the supreme being, leaves the temporal things and turns to God. This knowing of the real nature of things is a path to liberation and this knowledge is Pramāṇa. Māṇikyanandi has expressed the same idea in the third aphorism of Samuddeśa I of Parīkṣāmukhaṃ.[1]

The result of Pramāṇa has been mentioned to be the destruction of wrong knowledge, leaving (undesirable objects), acquiring (desirable objects) or acting indifferently towards objects.[2] Siddhasena Divākara has mentioned in his Nyāyāvatāra : "The immediate effect of Pramāṇa is the removal of ignorance, the mediate effect of the absolute knowledge is bliss and equanimity while that of the ordinary practical knowledge is the facility to select or reject".[3] (Translation by Dr. Satis Chandra Vidyabhusan)

In another way, it may be urged that it is only when we use our faculties after understanding the real nature of a thing, that our efforts succeed. If a man wants water but wrongly supposes oil to be water, his efforts towards the oil would be fruitless in the attainment of his object. By Pramāṇa we understand the real nature of objects and by Pramāṇābhāsa, we get false knowledge. So we must leave Pramāṇābhāsa and through Pramāṇas, understand the real nature of objects. This is the meaning of the first

---

1 "हिताहितप्राप्तिपरिहारसमर्थं हि प्रमाणं ततो ज्ञानमेव तत् ।"

Parīkṣāmukhaṃ I. 3.

2 "अज्ञाननिबृत्तिर्हानोपादानोपेक्षाश्च फलम् ।"

Parīkṣāmukhaṃ V. 1.

3 "प्रमाणस्य फलं साक्षादज्ञानविनिवर्त्तनम् ।
केवलस्य सुखोपेक्षे शेषस्यादानहानधीः ॥"

Nyāyāvatāra Ed. by S. C.
Vidyābhusana p. 26.

line of the first Śloka of Parīkṣāmukhaṃ. The same has been mentioned by Vātsyāyana[1] and by Vidyānanda Svāmi.[2]

The importance of Pramāṇa is thus established both as regards our worldly pursuits and as regards the attainment of liberation by understanding the way to it with the removal of hindrances by Pramāṇas and Nayas.[3]

In Parīkṣāmukhaṃ the author deals mainly with Pramāṇas without discussing the Nayas. Many authors like Hemachandra have held that Nayas are part of Pramāṇas and many authors on Jain Logic have set out only the word "Pramāṇa" in the title though they discussed both Pramāṇas and Nayas in their works. For example, Hemachandra has named his work "Pramāṇa-mīmāṃsā" though he dealt with both Pramāṇas and Nayas in his treatise. Hemchandra writes in his Bhāṣya to the first aphorism of Pramāṇa-mīmāmsā : "In this work we have not only a discussion of Pramāṇas but also of Nayas which form part of Pramāṇas and by which a correct knowledge is obtained by refutation of wrong Nayas".[4] There are also separate works like Saptabhaṅgitaraṅgiṇi in which Nayas have been discussed in detail.

Prabhāchandra mentions that the word "Pramāṇa" is used in the singular number in the Śloka, in the general sense as the author has no intention to set up the various kinds of Pramāṇas in the enumeration.[5]

---

1 "प्रमाणतोऽर्थप्रतिपत्तौ प्रवृत्तिसामर्थ्यादर्थवत् प्रमाणं, प्रमाणमन्तरेण नार्थप्रतिपत्तिः, नार्थप्रतिपत्तिमन्तरेण प्रवृत्तिसामर्थ्यं ।"

2 "प्रमाणादिष्ट-संसिद्धिः ।"

3 Hemachandra affirms this : "तत् स्थितमेतत् प्रमाणनयपरिशोधितप्रमेयमार्गं सोपायं सप्रतिपक्षमोक्षं बिवक्षितुं ।" Pramāṇa Mīmāṃsā I. 1.

4 "न प्रमाणमात्रस्यैव विचारोऽत्राधिकृतः किन्तु तदेकदेशभूतानां दुर्णयनिराकरणद्वारेण परिशोधितमार्गानां नयानामपि ।" Pramāṇa Mīmāṃsā

[Translated by S. C. Ghoshal.

Jain Gazette (1915) Vol. XI. Page 278]

5 'वक्ष्यमाणलक्षणलक्षितप्रमाणभेदमनभिप्रेत्यानन्तरसकलप्रमाणविशेषसाधारणप्रमाणलक्षणपुरःसरः 'प्रमाणाद्' इत्येकवचननिर्देशः कृतः ।"

An objection is raised by the commentator Prabhāchandra "Does the author Māṇikyanandi wish to define Pramāṇa and Pramāṇā-bhāsa according to the previous authors on the subject or according to his own inclination ? If the former, there is no reason for his undertaking this labour, for a thing which has already been reduced to powder, should not be powdered again. If the latter, there is no necessity to take all this trouble, for scholars would not consider with regard any compilation produced according to one's own inclination (as opposed to the works of old writers)." The commentator replies to this objection by saying that (i) by the use of the word "Siddhaṃ", it is meant that the author will follow the definitions as laid down by venerable writers of old and (ii) by the use of the word "Alpaṃ" it is meant that the method of treatment will be different viz. that the author will treat the subject in a concise manner leaving aside the detailed exposition of writers like Akalaṅka. That is to say, though the writer will follow the definitions of the older writers, the method of treatment being new (as it will be brief as distinguished from the detailed statement of older writers) there cannot be any apprehension that the work will be a use-less repetition. Those who do not want a very lengthy and detailed treatment of a subject would be satisfied with a short exposition. The author whose mind is always prone to doing good to others cannot be said to have any intention of cheating the disciples by promulgating definitions opposed to older writers and invented by himself.[1]

---

1 "ननु चेदं वक्ष्यमाणं प्रमाणलक्षणं पूर्वशास्त्राप्रसिद्धं तद्विपरीतं वा, यदि पूर्वशास्त्राप्रसिद्धं, तर्हि तद्व्युत्पादनप्रयासो नारम्भणीयः, स्वरुचिविरचितत्वेन सतामनादरणीयत्वात्। तत्प्रसिद्धं तु नितरामेतन्न व्युत्पादनीयं, पिष्टपेषणप्रसंगाद् इत्याहः 'सिद्धमल्पम्'। प्रथमविशेषणेन व्युत्पादनवत् तल्लक्षणप्रणयने स्वातन्त्र्यं परिहृतम्। तदेवाकलंकमिदं पूर्वशास्त्रपरम्पराप्रमाणप्रसिद्धं लघूपायेन प्रतिपाद्य प्रज्ञापरिपाकार्थं व्युत्पद्यते, न स्वरुचिविरचितं ; नापि प्रमाणानुपपन्नं, परोपकारनियतचेतसो ग्रन्थकृतो विनेयसंवादने प्रयोजनाभावात्। तथाभूतं हि वदन् विसंवादकः स्यात्। 'अल्प' मिति विशेषणेन यदन्यत्राकलंकदेवैर्विस्तरेणोक्तं प्रमाणेतरलक्षणं, तदेवात्र संक्षेपेण विनेयव्युत्पादनार्थं अभिधीयते इति पुनरुक्तत्वनिरासः।"

In older works of Jain writers, logic was mixed up with metaphysics and religion. Subsequent writers composed separate works confining themselves exclusively to the subject of pure Logic. These writers however did not depart from the original definitions of older works though in delineation they adopted different methods and even when they tried to modify the definitions, they laid down that the modified meaning was the intention of the old writers. The veneration to the oldest propounders of Logic will be universally found in the works of all subsequent writers. So Māṇikyanandi also begins his work by saying that he will lay down the definitions of Pramāṇa and Pramāṇābhāsa according to ancient authorities ("Siddhaṃ").

The same fact appears in Hindu philosophies where the authors attempt to base their theories on texts of the Vedas which are universally accepted as undisputable authorities. We find attempts to explain a particular passage from the Vedas in diverse ways to suit the purpose of different expositors.

Māṇikyanandi has based his Parīkṣāmukhaṃ on the work of Akalaṅka Deva. Anantavīrya the writer of Prameyaratnamālā a commentary on Parīkṣāmukhaṃ has offered his obeisance to Māṇikyanandi thus: "Salutation to that Māṇikyanandi who has churned the nectar of Nyāya-vidyā from the ocean of Akalaṅka's words."[1] Prabhāchandra also states that as the work of Aklaṅka would not be easily understood by all, Māṇīkyanandi has composed the Prakaraṇa Parīkṣāmukhaṃ.[2] In Nyāyamaṇidīpikā the same has been mentioned.[3]

---

1 "अकलंकवचोऽम्भोधेरुद्दध्रे येन धीमता।
न्यायविद्यामृतं तस्मै नमो माणिक्यनन्दिने ॥"

Prameyaratnamālā 2.

2 "श्रीमदकलंकार्थोऽव्युत्पन्नप्रज्ञैरबगतुं न शक्यते, इति तद्व्युत्पादनाय करतलामलकवत् तदर्थमुद्धृत्य प्रतिपादयितुकामस्तत्परिज्ञानानुग्रहेच्छाप्रेरितस्तदर्थप्रतिपादनप्रवणं प्रकरणमिदमाचार्यः प्राह।" Prameyakamala-Mārtaṇḍa.

3 "भगवान् भट्टाकलंकदेवो विश्वविद्वन्मण्डलहृदयाल्हादियुक्तिशास्त्रेण जगत्-

The commentators of Parikṣāmukhaṃ were faced with the fact that there is no Maṅgalācharaṇa in this work. In most of Brahmanical works, Maṅgalācharaṇa verses are found and even where there are no special verses, attempts are made by commentators to show that the first words of such works e. g. "Atha" is auspicious and serves the purpose of Maṅgalācharaṇa.[1] The Jain writers also hold that Maṅgalācharaṇa should be used to remove obstacles to a successful completion of the work, as even the great men are subject to many obstructions even in good work.[2] The use of Maṅgalācharaṇa is also supported by Śiṣṭāchāra (practice of the good or the respectable).

Prabhāchandra and Anantavīrya write that salutation can be made by words, by the body and also mentally. So though salutation in words is not found in this work, it can be urged that salutation by bodily movements or a mental salutation has been made. If any one is unwilling to accept this, it can be said that the words in the beginning viz. "Pramāṇa" can have a secondary meaning which would serve the purpose of salutation. "Mā" means "Lakṣmī" and "Āṇa" means "Śabda". He who has "Pra" (Prakriṣta =

सद्धर्मप्रभावमवूबुधत्तमाम् । तदनु वालानुजिवृक्षुः······माणिक्यनन्दिमुनिवृन्दारकस्तत्-प्रकाशित-शास्त्रमहोदधेरुद्धृत्य तदवगाहनाय पोतोपमं परीक्षामुखनामधेयमन्वर्थमुद्वहत् प्रकरणमारचयन्······" Nyāyamaṇi-dīpikā. (This work has not been printed. The quotation is from a MSS. preserved in the Jain Siddhānta Bhaban, Arrah. See also Jaina Siddhānta Bhāskara, Bhāga. II. Kiraṇa I. Praśasti-saṅgraha P. 1.)

1 "ओंकारश्चाथशब्दश्च द्वावेतौ ब्रह्मणः पुरा ।
कन्ठं भित्वा विनिर्यातौ तेन मांगलिकावुभौ ॥"

2 "श्रेयांसि वहुविघ्नानि भवन्ति महतामपि ।
अश्रेयसि प्रवृत्तानां क्वापि यान्ति विनायकाः ॥
तस्मादशेषप्रत्यूहोपशमनाय मंगलमभिधेयम् ।"
Śilāṅkāchārya's Commentary on the Āchārāṅga Sūtras.

excellent) Māṇa is Pramāṇa (i. e. the omniscient Arhat) from whom right knowledge can be obtained (Arthasaṃsiddhiḥ) and from his Ābhāsa (viz. Gods like Hari, Hara etc.) the opposite happens.[1] It must be confessed that this interpretation is too farfetched. There are instances of writers like Dharma-kīrti beginning his work[2] without any Maṅgalācharaṇa, which was completed and there are instances of works like Bāṇa-bhatta's Kādambari which was never completed though it began with a Maṅgalācharaṇa. To readers of the present day, this question of Maṅgalācharaṇa may appear to be of little importance, but in old texts and commentaries, a good deal of ingenuity has been displayed to

---

1 "ननु निःशेषविघ्नोपशमनायेष्टदेवतानमस्कारः शास्त्रकृता कथं न कृत इति न वाच्यम्। तस्य मनःकायाभ्यामपि सम्भवात्। अथवा वाचनिकोऽपि नमस्कारोऽनेनैवादिवाक्येनाभिहितो वेदितव्यः। केषांचिद् वाक्यानामुभयार्थप्रतिपादनपरत्वेनापि दृश्यमानत्वात्।....तत्रादिवाक्यस्य नमस्कारपरताभिधीयते।....अनन्तचतुष्टयस्वरूपान्तरंगलक्ष्मणा समवसरणादिस्वभावा वहिरंगलक्ष्मणा लक्ष्मीर्मा इत्युच्यते। आणः शब्दः। मा च आणश्च माणौ। प्रकृष्टौ माणौ यस्यासौ प्रमाणः। हरिहराद्यसंभविविभूतियुक्तो दृष्टेष्टाविरुद्धवाक् च भगवान् अर्हन्नेव अभिधीयते, इत्यसाधारणगुणोपदर्शनमेव भगवतः संस्तवनमभिधीयते। तस्माद् प्रमाणाद् अवधिभूताद् अर्थसंसिद्धिर्भवति। तदाभासाच्च हरिहरादेरर्थसंसिद्धिर्न भवति।"

Prameyaratnamālā.

2 Dharmakīrti the celebrated Buddhist philosopher is said to have flourished in the 7th Century A.D. He is mentioned by the Jain writer Vidyānandi Svāmi in Aṣta-sāhasri and Patra-parīkṣā. He begins his work without any Maṅgalācharaṇa thus: "सम्यग्ज्ञानपूर्विका सर्वपुरुषार्थसिद्धिः।" Prabhāchandra hints that Dharma-kīrti must have made mental or bodily obeisance though not verbal salutation : "दृश्यते धर्मकीर्त्त्यादीनामप्येवंविधा प्रवृत्तिः, वाङ्नमस्कारमन्तरेणैव 'सम्यग्ज्ञानपूर्विका सर्वपुरुषार्थसिद्धिः' इत्यादि वाक्योपन्यासात्।"

Prameyakamalamārtaṇḍa.

explain away the exceptional cases of works of Dharma-Kīrti and Bāṇa-bhatta. It is mentioned in Muktāvalī that in cases where the work is completed without any hindrance though no Maṅgalācharaṇa is made, the explanation is that a counteraction of bad luck by Maṅgalācharaṇa was made in a previous life and where we see that in spite of a Maṅgalācharaṇa, the work is not completed, we should suppose that the evil karma of the writer offering hindrances to a successful completion was so great that the merit obtained by Maṅgalācharaṇa is not sufficient to counteract the same.[1]

1 "इत्थं च यत्र मंगलं न दृश्यते तत्र जन्मान्तरीयं तत् कल्प्यते। यत्र च सत्यपि मंगले समाप्तिर्न दृश्यते तत्र बलवत्तरो विघ्नो विघ्नप्राचुर्यं च बोध्यम्।"
Muktāvalī.

In Jain tradition Maṅgalācharaṇa is observed in three ways :

(i) by reciting the word Namaḥ, especially bowing to the worshipful, as Samantbhadra has done in the beginning of Ratṇa Karaṇda Śrāvakāchāra, नमः श्रीवर्द्धमानाय etc.

(ii) by singing a song of victory in the name of the worshipful, as has been done by Amritachandra in Puruṣārtha Siddhyupāya, तज्जयति परं ज्योतिः etc.

(iii) by proclaiming the basic principles so as to include both the above ideas, as has been done by Umasvāmi in Tattvārthādhigama Sūtra, सम्यग्दर्शनज्ञानचारित्राणि मोक्षमार्गः।

All these modes show the good and pious thought-activities of the writer. According to Jainism thoughts are the main causes of bondage, liberation, or decrease in the intensity or duration of Karmas already bound. Thoughts bring about a change in the nature of the obstructive Karma. If that Karma is mild, it will be altered ; if very strong, it cannot be altered. That is why some authors succeed in their undertaking, while others do not. Pious motives of an author considerably help in combating vicious Karmas, if they are not of a very strong kind.

प्रथमः समुद्देशः

स्वापूर्वार्थव्यवसायात्मकं ज्ञानं प्रमाणम् ।१।

I. Svāpūrvārthavyavasāyātmakaṃ jñānaṃ Pramāṇaṃ.

I. Pramāṇa is valid knowledge of itself and of things not proved before.

Commentary

The word 'Apūrvārtha' will be explained in sūtra 4 which follows and the word 'Sva-vyavasāya' will be explained in sūtra 6. Briefly speaking, Apūrvārtha is that whose nature was not definitely ascertained before by any Pramāṇa. The valid knowledge of such an object is Pramāṇa. Knowledge illumines itself at the same time as well as its object. That is to say, Pramāṇa knows itself simultaneously with the object not definitely ascertained before.

This view of the Jains is in great contrast with the view as laid down in the Nyāya philosophy of the Hindus. In Tarkasaṅgraha we find "of whatever description anything is, when our idea of that thing is of that same description, it is called a right notion; as in the case of silver, the idea of its being silver. This is called Pramā (commensurate with its object). The supposing a thing to be as the thing is not, is called a wrong notion ; as in the case of a shell, the notion of its being silver. This is called Apramā." (Dr. Ballantyne's translation).[1]

The principle of Pramāṇa in the Nyāya philosophy of the Hindus, is that there are causes which produce right notion (Pramā)

---

1 "तद्वति तत्प्रकारकोऽनुभवो यथार्थः। यथा रजत इदं रजतमिति ज्ञानम्। सैव प्रमेत्युच्यते। तदभाववति तत्प्रकारकोऽनुभवोऽयथार्थः। यथा शुक्ताविदं रजतमिति ज्ञानम्। सैवाप्रमेत्युच्यते।" Tarka-sangraha.

and because these causes produce Pramā they are called Pramāṇas. The causes are of four kinds and the right notion produced by them are also of four kinds. In Tarka-saṅgraha we find "Right notion is of four kinds through the divisions of Pratyakṣa (Perceptions), Anumiti (Inferences) Upamiti (conclusions from similarity) and Śābda (Authoritative Assertions) understood. The efficient (peculiar) cause of those also is of four kinds, through the divisions of Perception, Inference, Recognition of similarity and Authoritative Assertion" (Dr. Ballantyne's translation).[1]

Vātsyāyana in his Bhāṣya on Nyāyasūtras of Gautama says "Pramā is the right knowledge of objects"[2] that is to say "it is a notion of that which exists in its right form"[3] or in other words "it is a knowledge of a thing in the same form as it really is".[4] The instrument of this Pramā is Pramāṇa.

The Jain doctrine is that Pramāṇa is not the cause of right knowledge but right knowledge of itself and of the objects not previously ascertained rightly.

The subject of Pramāṇa is treated in older Jain works like the Tattvārthādhigama Sūtra in connection with knowledge. Umāsvāmi writes "Mati, Śruta, Avadhi, Manaḥparyaya and Kevala (are right) knowledge".[5] These (five kinds of knowledge) are the (two kinds of) Pramāṇas".[6] "The first two (kinds

---

1 "यथार्थानुभवश्चतुर्विधः प्रत्यक्षानुमित्युपमितिशाब्दभेदात् । तत्करणमपि चतुर्विधं प्रत्यक्षानुमानोपमानशब्दभेदात् ।" Tarka-saṅgraha.

2 "यदर्थविज्ञानं सा प्रमा ।" Vātsyāyana Bhāṣya.

3 "यदत्र यदस्ति तत्र तस्यानुभवः ।" Vātsyāna Bhāṣya.

4 "तद्वति तत्प्रकारको ज्ञानम् ।" Vātsyāyana Bhāṣya.

5 "मतिश्रुतावधिमनःपर्ययकेवलानि ज्ञानम् ।" Tattvārthādhigama Sūtra I. 9.

6 "तत् प्रमाणे ।" Tattvārthādhigama Sūtra I. 10.

of knowledge viz. Mati and Śruta) are Paroksa (Pramaṇas)"[1] and "the remaining (three) are Pratyakṣa (Pramāṇas)[2]

With these five kinds of knowledge, Kumati, Ku-Śruta and Vibhangāvadhi are added to make up eight kinds of knowledge. These three are nothing but false knowledges of Mati, Śruta and Avadhi, that is to say, Kumati is Ajñāna (false knowledge) of Mati ; Kuśruta is Ajñāna of Śruta and Vibhaṅgābadhi is Ajñāna of Avadhi. Kundakundāchārya has mentioned all these eight varieties of Jñāna in Pañchāstikāyasamayasāra : "Ābhinibodhika or Mati, Śruta, Avadhi, Manaḥ-paryaya and Kevala—these are the five varieties of Jñāna. Kumati, Ku-śruta and Vibhaṅga—these three also are connected with Jñāna."[3]

Mati Jñāna is knowledge derived through the senses including the knowledge which arises from the activity of the mind. In Jain psychology, four stages of Mati Jñāna which follow Darśana (inexpressible contact of an object with sense consiousness) have been mentioned. These are (i) Avagraha (ii) Īhā (iii) Avāya and (iv) Dhāranā. When an object is brought in contact with a sense-organ, we have a general knowledge of an object. There is an excitation in the sense-organ by the stimulus i.e. the object present in the outside world. Then there is an excitation in the consciousness. Thus, in the first stage, a person is barely conscious of the existence of an object. This is Avagraha.[4] The second stage Īhā consists in the desire to know

1 "आद्ये परोक्षम् ।" Tattvārthādhigama Sūtra I. 11.

2 "प्रत्यक्षमन्यत् ।" Tattvārthādhigama Sūtra I. 12.

3 "आभिणिवोधिसुदोधिमणकेवलाणि णाणाणि पंचभेयाणि ।
कुमदिसुद-विभंगाणि य तिण्णि वि णाणेहिं संजुत्ते ॥"
Pañchāstikāya samayasāra 41.

4 "अक्षार्थयोगे दर्शनानन्तरमर्थग्रहणमवग्रहः ।"
Pramāṇa-mimāṃsā I. 1. 27.

whether it is this or that, That is to say, similarities and differences of the object with and from other objects become the subject of consciousness in this stage.[1] For example, when we see a man, the first stage is that we are simply conscious that it is a human being and in the second stage we want to know the particulars such as that this man is a resident of Karṇāta or Lāta country[2]; or, when we hear a noise, at first we are conscious of merely a sound, then we desire to know whether it is from blowing a conch shell or from blowing a horn.[3]

In the third stage Avāya, there is a definite finding of the particulars which we desired to know in the second stage. The

---

"विषयविषयिसंनिपातसमनंतरमाद्यग्रहणमवग्रहः ।"

Tattvārtharājavārttika.

"विषयविषयिसंनिपातानन्तर--समुद्भूत--सत्तामात्र--गोचरदर्शनाज्जातमाद्य--मवान्तर-सामान्याकार-विशिष्टवस्तुग्रहणमवग्रहः ।"

Pramāṇa-Naya-tattvālokālaṅkāra. II. 7.

"अक्षार्थयोगजाद् वस्तुमात्रग्रहणलक्षणात् ।
जातं यद्वस्तुभेदस्य ग्रहणं तदवग्रहः ॥" Tattvārthaślokavārttika.

1 "अवगृहीतविशेषकाङ्क्षणमीहा ।" Pramāṇa Mīmāṁsā I. I. 28.

"अवगृहीतार्थविशेषकाङ्क्षणमीहा ।"

Pramāṇa-Naya-tattvālokālaṅkāra II. 8.

"अवगृहीतेऽर्थे तद्विशेषाकाङ्क्षणमीहा ।" Tattvārtharājavārttika.

"तद्गृहीतार्थसामान्ये यद्विशेषस्य काङ्क्षणम् ।
निश्चयाभिमुखं सेहा संशीतेर्भिन्नलक्षणा ॥" Tattvārthaślokavārttika.

2 "अवग्रहेण विषयीकृतो योऽर्थोऽवान्तर-मनुष्यत्वादिजातिविशेषलक्षणस्तस्य विशेषः कर्णाट-लाटादिभेदस्तस्याकाङ्क्षणं भवितव्यताप्रत्ययरूपतया ग्रहणाभिमुख्य-मीहेत्यभिधीयते ।" Ratnākarāvatārikā II. 8.

3 "अवग्रहगृहीतस्य शब्दादेरर्थस्य किमयं शब्दः शाङ्खः शार्ङ्गो वेति संशये सति माधुर्यादयः शङ्खधर्मा एवोपलभ्यन्ते न कार्कश्यादयः शार्ङ्गधर्मा इत्यन्वयव्यतिरेक-रूपविशेषपर्यालोचनरूपा मतिश्चेष्टेहा ।" Pramāṇa-mīmāṃsā.

second stage is merely an attempt to know the particulars, while the third stage consists of the ascertainment of these particulars.[1] There may be some doubt in the first and second stages but in the third stage this is absent. For example, in the third stage there is a finding that the sound is of a conch shell and not that of a horn.[2]

The fourth stage Dhāraṇā consists of the lasting impression which results after the object with its particulars is definitely ascertained.[3] It is this impression (Saṃskāra) which enables us to remember the object afterwards.[4]

---

1 "ईहितविशेषनिर्णयोऽवायः ।" Pramāṇa-mīmāṃsā I. 1. 29. and Pramāṇa-Naya-tattvālokālaṅkāra I. 9.
"विशेषनिर्ज्ञानाद्याथात्म्यावगमनमवायः ।" Tattvārtharājavārttika.
"तस्यैव निर्णयोऽवायः ।" Tattvārthaślokavārttika.

2 "इह चावग्रहेहयोरन्तराले अभ्यस्तेऽपि विषये संशयज्ञानमस्त्येव ।"
"ईहाक्रोडीकृते वस्तुनि विशेषस्य शाङ्ख एवायं शब्दो न शार्ङ्ग इत्येवं-रूपस्यावधारणमवायः ।" Pramāṇa-mīmāṃsā.

3 "निर्ज्ञातार्थाविस्मृति र्धारणा ।" Tattvārtharājā-vārttika.
"स एव दृढतमावस्थापन्नो धारणा ।"
Pramāṇa-Nayatattvālokālaṅkāra I. 10.

4 "स्मृतिहेतुः सा धारणा ।" Tattvārthaślokavārttika.
"स्मृतिहेतुर्धारणा ।" Pramāṇa-mīmāṃsā I 1. 30.

All these four stages of Matijñāna have been summarised by Vidyānandi thus :

"अक्षार्थयोगजाद् वस्तुमात्रग्रहणलक्षणात् ।
जातं यद्वस्तुभेदस्य ग्रहणं तदवग्रहः ॥
तद्गृहीतार्थसामान्ये यद्विशेषस्य काङ्क्षणम् ।
निश्चयाभिमुखं सेहा संशयाद् भिन्नलक्षणा ॥
तस्यैव निर्णयोऽवायः स्मृतिहेतुः सा धारणा ।"

Śruta Jñāna is knowledge derived from words spoken or from gestures or facial expressions, from reading books and from all other kinds of signs or symbols.

Avadhi Jñāna is the knowledge directly acquired by the soul without the medium of the activity of the mind or the senses[1]. Knowledge in the hypnotic state is the nearest approach to an illustration. As this knowledge also is acquired through the medium of the brain and the senses according to the Jain view, this can not be accepted as an example of Avadhi Jñāna.

Manaḥparyaya Jñāna is the knowledge of thoughts of others[2]. Thought-reading may be mentioned to convey some feeble idea of this kind of knowledge. According to Jainism, no lay man can have this knowledge. Only a saint in a particular stage of spiritual advancement can acquire or develop this knowledge. Kevala Jñāna is omniscience or knowledge unlimited by space, time or object. According to Jainism, Jain saints who completely practise right faith, right knowledge and right conduct can attain this knowledge. In the Hindu Purāṇas, some saints are said to have such a knowledge and are called Sarvajñas or Trikāladarśis.

These eight kinds of knowledge viz. Mati, Kumati, Śruta, Ku-śrutra, Avadhi, Vibhaṅgāvadhi, Manaḥparyaya and Kevala are classified from another point of view into two classes viz. Pratyakṣa and Parokṣa[3] and these two constitute the Pramāṇas of the Jain Logic[4].

---

1 "परापेक्षां विना ज्ञानं रुपिणां भणितोऽवधिः ।"

Tattvārthasāra by Amritachandra Sūri I. 25.

2 "परकीयमनःस्पार्थज्ञानमक्षानपेक्षया ।
स्यान्मनःपर्ययो ॥" Tattvārthasāra I. 28.

3 "णाणं अट्ठवियप्पं मदिसुदओही अणाणणाणाणि ।
मणपज्जय केवलमवि पच्चक्ख परोक्खभेयं च ॥"

Dravya-saṃgraha 5.

4 "मतिश्रुतावधिमनःपर्ययकेवलानि ज्ञानम् ।"

According to Umasvāmi, Mati and Śruta are Parokṣa knowledge and Avadhi, Manaḥparyaya and Kevala are Pratyakṣa knowledge. A detailed description of Pratyakṣa and Parokṣa will follow in the present treatise and we shall discuss later on the criticism how Mati and Śruta Jñāna described as Parokṣa Pramāṇa in the Tattvārthādhigama Śūtra, can be called Sāṅvyavahārika Pratyakṣa in works on Jain Logic.

We shall now deal with the derivation of the word 'Pramāṇa' according to the writers of Jain Logic.

It has been laid down by Prabhāchandra in Prameyakamalamārtaṇḍa that the word Pramāṇa may be derived in three ways. In the first place, the suffix "Anat" may be held to be used in active voice meaning "That which knows rightly (viz the soul) is Pramāṇa". From the definition of Pramāṇa, we learn that Pramāṇa is right knowledge of itself and of objects not previously ascertained. This derivation means that just as a lamp illumines itself as well as other objects, the soul knows itself as well as other objects. In the second place the suffix may be used in the sense of instrumentality. The meaning would then be "That by which right knowledge is gained is Pramāṇa[1]. In this case just as light appears when obstructions to it are removed, so right knowledge will come on removal of obstructions to it. In the third derivation there is use of the suffix in Bhāva-vāchya (passive intransitive

---

"तत् प्रमाणे ।"

"आद्ये परोक्षम् ।"

"प्रत्यक्षमन्यत् ।" Tattvārthādhigama Sūtra I. 9-12.

1 "अत्र प्रमाणशब्दः कर्तृकरणभावसाधनो ।....तत्र...स्वपरप्रमेयस्वरूपं प्रमिमीते यथावज्जानातीति प्रमाणमात्मा···आत्मन एव हि कर्तृसाधनप्रमाणशब्देनाभिधानं स्वातन्त्र्येन विवक्षितत्वात् स्वपरप्रकाशात्मकस्य प्रदीपादेः प्रकाशाभिधानवत् । साधकतमत्वादिविवक्षायां तु प्रमीयते येन तत् प्रमाणं प्रमितिमात्रं वा प्रतिबंधापाये प्रादुर्भूतविज्ञानपर्यायस्य प्राधान्येनाश्रयणात् प्रदीपादेः प्रभाभारात्मकप्रकाशवत् ।"

Prameyakamalamārtaṇḍa.

voice) where stress is laid on the verb only, the meaning being the same as in active voice.

In Tattvārtharājavārttika it has been mentioned : "What is the meaning of the word Pramāṇa ? The meaning of the word Pramāṇa can be understood according to one's desire by deriving it in Bhāva-vāchya (passive intransitive voice) Kartri-vāchya (active voice) and Karaṇa-vāchya (instrumental voice)"[2].

A grammarian might object that according to Jainendra Vyākaraṇa the suffix Anat is used only in the sense of Karaṇa (instrumentality) and Ādhāra (or Adhikaraṇa, locative sense)[3]. So how can it be suffixed in Kartri or Bhāva-vāchya ? The reply to this is given by a commentator on Prameyaratnamālā that though the aforesaid aphorism exists in Jainendra Vyākaraṇa, we may accept the principle that "There are exceptions in krit suffixes" and this covers cases like the present one where suffixes are used in senses not provided in particular aphorisms[4].

---

2 "प्रमाणशब्दस्य कोऽर्थः ? भावकर्त्तृकरणत्वोपपत्तेः प्रमाणशब्दस्येच्छातोऽर्थाध्यवसायः ।"

"अयं प्रमाणशब्दः, भावे, कर्त्तरि, करणे च वर्त्तते । तत्र भावे, तावत् प्रमेयार्थं प्रति निवृत्तव्यापारस्य तत्वकथनात् प्रमाणमिति । कर्त्तरि, प्रमेयार्थं प्रति प्रमातृत्वशक्ति-परिणतस्याश्रितत्वान् तत् प्रमिणोति प्रमेयमिति प्रमाणं । करणे प्रमातृप्रमेययोः प्रमाणप्रमेययोश्च स्यादन्यत्वात् प्रमिणोत्यनेनेति प्रमाणम् ।"

Tattvārtharājavārttika.

3 "करणाधारे चानट् ।" Jainendra Vyākaraṇa II. 3. 112.

4 "ननु प्रमाणशब्दो···कथं कर्त्तृसाधन इति चेत्, न । 'करणाधारे चानट्' इति करणाधिकरणभावेष्वनटो विहितत्वेऽपि 'कृद्बहुलम्' इति वचनात् अन्यत्र कारकेष्वपि वहुलं कृत्प्रत्ययसद्भावादनटोपि कृत्यादन्यत्रापि भावादपादीयतेऽस्मादित्यपादानं संप्रदीयतेऽस्मादिति संप्रदानमित्यादिवत् ।" Nyāyamaṇi-dīpikā. (A. Mss. in Jain Siddhānta Bhaban, Arrah).

Other writers have derived the word Pramāṇa by holding that the suffix "Anat" is used in the sense of instrumentality as laid down in Jainendra Vyākaraṇa.

Dharmabhūṣaṇa in his Nyāya-dīpikā has laid down that the word Jñāna as well as Pramāṇa are derived with the affix "Anat" in the Karaṇa-vāchya (instrumental voice)[5]. Dharma bhūṣaṇa supports his view by a quotation from Pramāṇa-nirṇaya[6]. Hemachandra in his Pramāṇa-mīmāṃsā writes "That by which the essence of substances is rightly understood by eliminating doubt etc. is Pramāna which is the instrumental cause of Pramā (right knowledge)"[7]. In Pramā lakṣma the same has been laid down in another language[8].

The definition of Pramāṇa as given by other Jain writers may be compared with that of Māṇikyanandi. First, we may mention the definition as laid down in Nyāyāvatāra :

"Pramāṇa (valid knowledge) is the knowledge which illumines itself and other things without any obstruction" (Trans. by Dr. S. C. Vidyābhūṣana)[9].

Dr. Vidyābhūṣana writes in his commentary on this definition : "The Jains maintain that it is only when knowledge illumines itself that it can take cognizance of the external object. So, accord-

---

5 "करणसाधनं खल्वेतत् ज्ञायते अनेन इति ज्ञानमिति ।....एवमेव प्रमाण-पद्मपि प्रमीयतेऽनेनेति करणसाधनं कर्त्तव्यम् ।" Nyāya-dīpikā.

6 "इदमेव हि प्रमाणस्य प्रमाणत्वं यत् प्रमितिक्रियां प्रति साधकतमत्वेन करणत्वम् ।" Pramāṇa-nirṇaya.

7 "प्रकर्षेण संशयादिव्यवच्छेदेन मीयते परिच्छिद्यते वस्तुतत्वं येन तत् प्रमाणं प्रमायां साधकतमं ।" Pramāṇa-mīmāṃsā.

8 "प्रमीयते स्वान्यात्मकोऽर्थोऽनेनेति करणसाधनं प्रमाणं तच्चाव्यवधानेन प्रमितौ साधकतमत्वात् ।" Pramā-lakṣma.

9 "प्रमाणं स्वपराभासि ज्ञानं बाधविवर्जितम् ।" Nyāyāvatāra.

ing to them, knowledge like a lamp illumines itself as well as the object lying outside it.

Those whose sight has been obscured by darkness often see many false images, such as two moons etc.; men bewildered by sophism are found to believe that everything is momentary or the like. With a view to differentiate such kinds of false knowledge from Pramāṇa (valid knowledge) the phrase 'without obstruction' has been used." (Nyāyāvatāra, page 7).

The definition in Pramā-lakṣma of Buddhisāgara is the same as that in Nyāyāvatāra.

In Nyāya-dīpikā we find "Pramāṇa is perfect knowledge[10]." Vidyānanda in his Pramāṇa-parīkṣā also lays down the same definition.

Hemachandra defines Pramāṇa thus : "Pramāṇa is the perfect ascertainment of a knowable"[11] and criticises the definition of Māṇikyanandi in Parīkṣāmukhaṃ. He says "Some say that if we accept that we again know a thing which had been previously ascertained by Pramāṇa, the result would be that a thing which has already been powdered will be powdered again. Also, by accepting this view, Pramāṇa would apply to knowledge of objects already ascertained and in the case of continuous knowledge of an object. So, according to those who object thus, the definition should be that Pramāṇa is ascertainment of objects not previously ascertained. So some one (referring to the definition adopted by Māṇikyanandi) has laid down the definition of Pramāṇa to be 'Pramāṇa is valid knowledge of itself and of things not proved before".[12]

---

10 "सम्यग्ज्ञानं प्रमाणम् ।" Nyāya-dīpikā.

11 "सम्यगर्थनिर्णयः प्रमाणम् ।" Pramāṇa-mīmāṃsā. I. I. 2.

12 "ननु च परिच्छिन्नमर्थं परिच्छिन्दता प्रमाणेन पिष्टं पिष्टं स्यात् । तथाच गृहीतग्राहिणां धारावाहिकज्ञानानामपि प्रामाण्यप्रसङ्गस्ततोऽपूर्वार्थनिर्णय इत्यस्तु लक्षणम्,

Hemachandra criticises the definition of Pramāṇa as mentioned in the Parikṣamukhaṃ on two grounds. First, that this definition excludes the knowledge of a thing already ascertained. According to Hemachandra, it is equally Pramāṇa when a thing is ascertained for the first time, as when a thing which has previously been ascertained, is again known[13]. So Hemachandra says that Pramāṇa is perfect ascertainment of a knowable.

The second objection refers to Dhārābāhik Jñāna. This is a series of states throughout which the same object is presented in consciousness. This for example arises when we see an object continuously for some time. Each state of consciousness in this case lasts only for a moment. Then follows a second state and is lost. Then a third state succeeds and is lost and so on. Now if we define Pramāṇa as knowledge of things not ascertained before, the objection is that in the first state of Dhārābāhik Jñāna, this may apply. But in the second and subsequent stages of the presentation of the object, the object cannot be said to be 'Apūrvārtha' (not previously ascertained) as mentioned in the definition for it was ascertained after it had been cognised in the first momentary state. So Dhārābāhik Jñāna will be excluded from Pramāṇa if we accept the definition of Pramāṇa in Parīkṣāmukhaṃ.

A similar objection was raised and refuted in works in Hindu philosophy. To give an example, we may quote the definition of Pramāṇa in Vedānta-paribhāṣā. The author Dharmarājādhvarīndra writes that if re-collection be included within Pramā (right knowledge), the definition of Pramāṇa will be of one kind and if re-collection be excluded from Pramā, the definition will be of a different kind. According to this writer : "Pramāṇa is the instrumental cause of right knowledge (Pramā). When the defini-

---

यथाहुः 'स्वापूर्वार्थव्यवसायात्मकं ज्ञानं प्रमाणम्' इति तथापूर्वार्थविज्ञानमिति ।" Pramāṇa-mīmāṃsā.

13 "ग्रहीष्यमानग्राहिण इव गृहीतग्राहिणोऽपि नाप्रामाण्यम् ।" Pramāṇa-mīmāṃsā I. 1. 4.

tion of Pramā excludes re-collection, Pramā is defined as consisting in the knowledge of an object, which has not been previously perceived and which is not rejected as false. But when re-collection is included, Pramā consists in the knowledge of an object which is not rejected as false"[1].

Now, in the first place when Pramā is taken to exclude re-collection, the definition being knowledge of an object not previously perceived and not rejected as false, how can this definition apply to Dhārābāhik Jñāna ? For as we have noted before in Dhārābāhik Jñana, in the second and succeeding presentations of an object, it cannot be "not previously perceived" as it was perceived in the first momentary state. This criticism is met by Dharmarājādhvarīndra by saying "In the definition of Pramā from which re-collection is excluded, there is no fault of non-pervasiveness. For since it is admitted that time though destitute of form can be cognised through the sense-organs, even a persistent state of cognition has for its object that which is particularised by association with each separate moment and is not the object of each previous cognition"[2]. That is to say, knowledge of a jar even at the first moment will be different from knowledge of the same jar at the second moment for there will be distinct knowledge in each case e. g. this is a jar seen at the first moment, this is a jar seen at the second moment and so on. "The object known in each moment is particularised or determined by that moment and thus differs from the object presented in each previous or succeeding moment"[3]. Further, the

---

1 Translation by A. Venis. "तत्र प्रमायाः करणं प्रमाणं। तत्र स्मृतिव्यावृत्तं प्रमात्वमनधिगतावाधितार्थविषयज्ञानत्वं, स्मृतिसाधारणन्तु अवाधितार्थ-विषयज्ञानत्वम् ।" Vedānta-paribhāṣā. Chapter I.

2 Translation by A. Venis. "नीरुपस्यापि कालस्य इन्द्रिय-वेद्यत्वाभ्युपगमेन धारावाहिकवुद्धेरपि पूर्वपूर्वज्ञानाविषय-तत्तत्क्षणविशेषविषयकत्वेन न तत्र अव्याप्तिः ।" Vedānta-paribhāṣā.

3 A. Venis. Notes on Vedānta-paribhāṣā.

objection may be met in another way, if we say that really speaking the knowledge in Dhārābāhik Jñāna is one and the same throughout and not different in each of the different moments. Dharmarājādhvarīndra says : "More-over, according to (Vedantic) tenet, there is no variation of knowledge in the case of a persistent cognition ; but as long as there is a presentation of the jar, so long the modification of the internal organ in the form of the jar is one and the same and not various. For the persistence of the modification is admitted until there arises a modification which excludes the former. And thus the knowledge of a jar or like object, consisting in the intelligence which is reflected in the modification of the internal organ persists there during that time and is one and the same. Therefore the fault of non-pervasiveness is not to be feared in our definition"[4].

The criticism of Hemachandra as regards the definition of Pramāṇa as laid dawn by Māṇikyanandi may be met in the manner described above.

We may note that Udayanāchārya in his Kusumāñjali has also said that faults of non-pervasiveness (Avyāpti) and Ativyāpti will arise if we accept the definition of Pramāṇa to be the cause of knowledge of an object which was not perceived before. So Pramāṇa should be defined only as right knowledge[5]. In Jain works like Tattvārathasāra[6] the same has been laid down.

---

4 Translation by A. Venis. "किञ्च सिद्धान्ते धारावाहिकबुद्धिस्थले न ज्ञानभेदः, किन्तु यावद् यावद् घटस्फुरणं तावद् घटाकारान्तःकरणवृत्तिः एकैव, न तु नाना, वृत्तेः स्वविरोधिवृत्त्युत्पत्तिपर्यन्तस्थायित्वाभ्युपगमात्। तथाच तत्प्रतिफलित-चैतन्यरुपं घटादिज्ञानमपि तत्र तावत्कालीनम् एकमेव, इति न अव्याप्ति-शङ्कापि।" Vedānta-paribhāṣā. Chapter I. For a detailed treatment, the reader may refer to Vedantaparibhāṣā edited by S. C. Ghoshal Pages 5-8.

5 "अप्राप्तेरधिकप्राप्तेरलक्षणमपूर्वदृक्।
यथार्थानुभवो मानं अनपेक्षतयेष्यते।" Kusumāñjali.

In the Sāṃkhya philosophy, it is laid down that Pramā (right knowledge) consists of ascertainment of a thing which was not previously ascertained and Pramāṇa (which according to the Sāṃkhya doctrine is of three kinds) is the instrumental cause of Pramā[7]. Prabhākara Bhatta in his exposition of Mīmāṃsā philosophy has defined Pramāṇa to be ascertainment of things not ascertained before.[1] Thus, the definition in Parīkṣāmukhaṃ is in agreement on this point with the Sāṃkhya philosophy.

Though by means of explanation and argument as adopted in Vedānta-paribhāṣā as quoted above, the definition of Pramāṇa can be applied to Dhārābāhika Jñāna even if we hold the ascertainment of things not perceived before (Apūrvārtha) as one of its characteristics, yet commentators of Parīkṣāmukhaṃ have held that Dhārābāhika Jñāna is excluded from Pramāṇa. For example, Anantavīrya in Prameyaratnamālā writes "The adjective Apūrva is used to exclude from Pramāṇa Dhārābāhika Jñāna which cognises things already cognised[2]." This has been expanded in Arthaprakāśikā an unpublished commentary on Prameya-ratnamālā in this manner :—

"Why has the adjective Apūrva been applied to Artha ? We reply, it is to exclude Dhārābāhika Jñāna. Dhārābāhika Jñāna means a series of knowledge like 'this is a pitcher, this is a pitcher, etc'. In this series, the first knowledge is Pramāṇa as this consists

---

6 "सम्यगज्ञानात्मकं तत्र प्रमाणमुपवर्णितम् ।" Tattvārthasāra.

7 "द्वयोरेकतरस्य वाप्यसन्निकृष्टार्थपरिच्छित्तिः प्रमा, तत्-साधकतमं यत् तत् त्रिविधं प्रमाणम् ।" Sāṃkhya-darśana. Chapter I. Sūtra 87. Here the word Asannikrīṣtārtha means the same as Apūrvārtha in Parīkṣāmukhaṃ.

1 In Nyāyadīpikā, this definition of the Mīmāṃsā philosophy is quoted : "'अनधिगततथाभूतार्थनिश्चायकं प्रमाणं' इति भाट्टाः ।"

2 "अस्य चापूर्व-विशेषणं गृहीतग्राहिधारावाहिज्ञानस्य प्रमाणतापरिहारार्थ-मुक्तम् ।" Prameya-ratnamālā.

of ascertainment of the object. The second and succeeding knowledge is not Pramāṇa as in the same the object is not ascertained. As the object is ascertained by the first knowledge, the subsequent knowledge is quite insignificant. So the word Apūrva has been used as an adjective to Artha so that the (definition of Pramāṇa) may not extend to the second and succeeding states of knowledge which would become included (in the definition if merely Pramāṇa be defined) as ascertainment of object. By Apūrva it is understood that which has not become the object of previous knowledge. So in Dhārābāhika Jñāna, in the second and subsequent states of knowledge, the definition does not apply as in the first stage the object has been ascertained and in the second and subsequent stages, the object is not one which is previously unascertained"[1].

Nyāyamaṇidīpikā also follows Artha-prakāśikā by laying down "Dhārābāhika Jñāna is excluded by this adjective, Apūrvārtha[2]." In Nyāyadīpikā it has been mentioned that in Jain logic, Dhārābāhika Jñāna is not recognised as Pramāṇa[3].

---

1 "अर्थस्य अपूर्वविशेषणं किमर्थम् ? इति चेत्, धारावाहिकज्ञानव्यवच्छेदार्थमिति ब्रूमः। घटोऽयं घटोऽयं इत्यादि-ज्ञानपरंपरा धारावाहिकज्ञानम्। तादृशज्ञानपरंपरायां प्राथमिकज्ञानमेव प्रमाणं, तस्यैव विषयपरिच्छित्तिजनकत्वात्। द्वितीयादिज्ञानं तु न प्रमाणं, तस्य विषयपरिच्छित्तिजनकत्वाभावात्। प्रथमज्ञानेनैव परिच्छित्तेः जनितत्वेन द्वितीयादिज्ञानस्य अकिंचित्करत्वात्। तादृशद्वितीयादिज्ञाने अर्थविषयकव्यवसायात्मकत्वज्ञानत्वरूपनिरुक्तलक्षणसत्वेन अतिव्याप्तिनिरासार्थं अर्थे अपूर्वविशेषणम्। अपूर्वत्वं च पूर्वकालीनज्ञानान्तराविषयत्वं। तथाच, धारावाहिकज्ञानेषु द्वितीयादिज्ञाने प्राथमिक-ज्ञानगृहीतार्थविषयकत्वस्यैव सत्वेन पूर्वकालीनज्ञानान्तरागृहीतार्थविषयकव्यवसायात्मकत्वरूपलक्षणस्य अभावात् नातिव्याप्तिः।" Artha-prakāśikā (from a Mss. in Jain Siddhānta Bhavan, Arrah.)

2 "अनेन अपूर्वार्थविशेषणेन धारावाहिविज्ञानमेव निरस्यते।" Nyāyamaṇidīpikā (from a Mss. in Jain Siddhānta Bhavan, Arrah)

3 "अथापि धारावाहिकवुद्धिष्वतिव्याप्तिस्तासां सम्यगज्ञानत्वात्। न च तासामार्हतमते प्रामाण्याभ्युपगम इति। उच्यते एकस्मिन्नेव घटे घटविषयाज्ञानविघटनार्थं आद्ये ज्ञाने प्रवृत्ते तेन घटप्रमितौ सिद्धायां पुनर्घटोऽयं घटोऽयमित्येवमुत्पन्नान्युत्तरोत्तर

We have thus seen that in all earlier works on Nyāya philosophy Pramāṇa has been taken to consist of knowledge of an object not ascertained before. The Mīmāṃsā philosophy of the Hindus have accepted that Gautama the propounder of the old school of the Nyāya philosophy of the Hindus must have taken Pramāṇa in this sense and we have shown that the Mīmāṃsakas led by Kumārila Bhatta have defined Pramā as ascertainment of an object not ascertained before. The older writers on Jain logic like Māṅikya–nandī lay down a definition of Pramāṇa which is not at all different in this particular point (though there are differences on other points as already mentioned). Later writers specially those of the new school of Nyāya philosophy of the Hindus led by Gaṅgeśa the author of Tattva-Chintāmaṇi who flourished in the 14th Century have discarded this peculiarity in the definition of Pramāṇa and satisfied themselves by saying that Pramā is knowledge free from fallacy[1]. Their view has been summarised in the extract from Tarka-saṅgraha quoted above. Later Jain writers like Hemachandra who flourished in the twelfth century as shown

---

ज्ञानानि खलु धारावाहिकज्ञानानि। न ह्येषां प्रमितिं प्रति साधकतमत्वं प्रथमज्ञानेनैव प्रमितेः सिद्धत्वात्। कथं तत्र लक्षणमतिव्याप्नोति तेषां गृहीतग्राहित्वात्।" Nyāya-dīpikā. i.e. "This definition that Pramāṇa is right knowledge may overlap the case of Dhārābāhika Jñāna. These knowledges (viz Dhārābāhika knowledges) are not Pramāṇas according to Jain doctrine. It may be mentioned that when a pitcher is seen, first of all there is Pramāṇa of a pitcher when the Ajñāna regarding a pitcher is removed. In the first knowledge, there is right conception of a pitcher. The subsequent knowledges 'this is a pitcher' are Dhārābāhika Jñāna. As by the first knowledge, we have Pramiti (right conception), the subsequent knowledges not being instrumental in producing Pramiti, are not Pramāṇas. So the definition does not overlap as there are cases where a thing already perceived are again perceived."

1 "भ्रमभिन्नन्तु ज्ञानमत्रोच्यते प्रमा।" Vide Viśva.koṣa 1st Edition Vol. X. P. 481.

above similarly discarded this peculiarity in the definition of Pramāṇa and criticised the older writers.

The writers who appeared still later reverted to the definition of the earliest writers and we have shown an example from Vedānta-paribhāṣā how this was done. The writer of the Vedānta-paribhāṣā was later than Gaṅgeśa as he wrote a commentary on the works of Gaṅgeśa. The main object of attack of writers like Hemachandra was the inapplicability of the definition of Pramāṇa in Dhārābāhika Jñāna. Though some of the Jain commentators lay down that only the first state of knowledge in Dhārābāhika Jñāna is Pramāṇa, if we follow the arguments in Vedānta-paribhāṣā, the object cognised in the second and subsequent stages can also be said to be Apūrvārtha and hence the knowledge in these stages also would be Pramāṇa. The main point of attack being thus met, we do not see any fault in the definition as adopted by Māṇikya-nandī. The subtle discussions in the new school of Nyāya philosophy on this point will necessitate a seperate work and so we refrain from embodying the same in this commentary.

In Prameya-ratnamālā each of the words in the definition of Pramāṇa as laid down by Māṇikya-nandī has been explained as refuting definitions of other philosophies. According to this commentary, the word Jñāna (knowledge) shows that the Jain doctrine does not follow the view of Naiyāyikas that Pramāṇa consists of connection of the senses with the objects[1]. The word Vyavasāya is used refuting the view of the Buddhists viz. Pramāṇa consists of Nirvikalpa Pratyakṣa of four kinds i.e. Sva-saṃvedana-pratyakṣa (understanding of the self), Indriya-pratyakṣa, (cognition through senses), Manopratyakṣa (understanding by mind) and Yogipratyakṣa (cognition of the Yogis)[2]. The Buddhists do

---

1 "तस्य च ज्ञानमिति विशेषणं अज्ञानरूपस्य सन्निकर्षादे-र्नैयायिकादि-परिकल्पितस्य प्रमाणत्वव्यवच्छेदार्थमुक्तम् ।" Prameyaratnamālā.

2 "तथा ज्ञानस्यापि स्वसंवेदनेन्द्रियमनोयोगिप्रत्यक्षस्य निर्विकल्पकस्य प्रत्यक्षत्वेन प्रामाण्यं सौगतैः परिकल्पितं तन्निरासार्थं व्यवसायात्मकग्रहणम् ।" Ibid.

not accept Vyavasāya or Niśchaya to be essential in Pramāṇa. The word Artha is used to refute the views of those who deny the existence of external objects like Vijñānādvaitavādins, Māyāvādins and Mādhyamikas[1]. The view of Vijñānādvaitavādins is that every object consists of knowledge and there is nothing to be cognised. Knowledge according to this view is of two kinds Ālaya-vijñāna and Pravrittivijñāna. Ālaya-vijñāna is the self and Pravritti-vijñāna is jar, cloth etc.[2] A verse is quoted in Arthaprakāśikā meaning "That is Ālaya-vijñāna which consists of the self and the knowledge of bluishness etc., is Pravrittivijñāna"[3]. The persons holding this view say that everything is knowledge and there is nothing to be cognised. The Māyāvādins say that everything is Brahma, that what we see as a jar, a cloth etc., are all unreal, and only Brahma is real. Mādhyamikas are Śūnyavādins who say that the essence is void. It does neither exist, nor is non-existent, nor existent as well as non-existent, nor distinct from existence and non-existence[4]. The word 'Sva' is used to refute the views of the

---

For details of Bauddha Nyāya view on this point, the reader may refer to the work Nyāyavindu of Dharma-kīrti.

1 "तथा वहिरर्थापह्नोतॄणां विज्ञानाद्वैतवादिनां पुरुषाद्वैतवादिनां पश्यतोहराणां शून्यैकान्तवादिनां च विपर्यासव्युदासार्थमर्थ- ग्रहणम् ।" Prameyaratnamālā.

2 "तत्र तावद्विज्ञानाद्वैतवादि···सर्वं वस्तु ज्ञानात्मकमेव, तदितरज्ञेयाकारस्तु नास्त्येव। तच्च ज्ञानं द्विविधं, आलयविज्ञानं प्रवृत्तिविज्ञानं च तत्र आलयविज्ञानं आत्मपदवाच्यं, प्रवृत्तिविज्ञानं तु घटपटादिपदवाच्यम् ।" Arthaprakāśikā.

3 "तत् स्यादालयविज्ञानं यत्तु स्यादहमास्पदं ।
तत् स्यात् प्रवृत्तिविज्ञानं यत्तु नीलादिगोचरं ।"

Verse quoted in Arthaprakāśikā.

4 'माध्यमिकास्तु....शून्यमेव तत्वं। तथाहि सर्वं जगत्। न सत्, नास्तित्वप्रतीतिविरोधात्। नाप्यसत्, अस्तित्वप्रतीतिविरोधात्। नापि सदसत्, सत्वासत्वयोरत्यन्तविरूद्धयोरेकत्र समावेशासंभवात्। नापि सदसद्विलक्षणं सत्वादि-प्रतीतिविरोधादेव। तस्मान्निरूक्तचतुःप्रकाररहितं शून्यमेव तत्वं। तदुक्तं

Nyāya, Sāṃkhya, Mīmāṃsā and Yoga philosophies in which Pramāṇa does not include the knowledge itself as well as the objects known at the same time[1].

We have thus seen that most of the definitions of Pramāṇa lay down that it is the right knowledge of objects. Some hold like Māṇikyanandi that the object must be one which was not ascertained before; while others are of view that this is not at all essential. The main difference in Jain doctrine is that knowledge as Pramāṇa like the sun or a lamp illumines itself as well as the objects simultaneously.

हिताहितप्राप्तिपरिहारसमर्थं हि प्रमाणं, ततो ज्ञानमेव तत् ॥ २ ॥

2. Hitāhitaprāptiparihārasamartham hi prmāṇaṃ tato jñānameva tat.

2. Because Pramāṇa enables acquiring beneficial things and leaving non-beneficial objects, this is nothing but knowledge.

Commentary

Pramāṇa leads to the acquirement of pleasure and its causes and abstention from sorrow and its causes. When a man is thirsty, he searches for an object to quench the thirst and begins to seek water. That Pramāṇa which points out this water is sought by a thirsty man, for by a right knowledge that this is water acquired by Pramāṇa there is no want of receipt of the object desired viz., water[2].

न सन्नासन्न सदसन्न चाप्यनुभयात्मकं ।
चतुष्कोटिविनिर्मुक्तं तत्वं माध्यमिका विदुः ॥

इति तथाच शून्यमेव तत्वमिति वदन्ति ।" Arthaprakāśikā. (Mss.)

1 "तथा परोक्षज्ञानवादिनां मीमांसकानामस्वसंवेदनज्ञानवादिनां सांख्यानां ज्ञानान्तरप्रत्यक्षज्ञानवादिनां यौगानां च मतमपाकर्तुं स्वपदोपादानम् ।"

Prameyaratnamālā.

2 This is shortly expressed by Prabhāchandra as follows :

"हितं सुखं तत् साधनं च, तद्विपरीतं अहितं, तयोः प्राप्तिपरिहारौ । प्राप्तिः खलूपादेयभूतार्थक्रियाप्रसाधकार्थप्रदर्शकत्वम् । अर्थक्रियार्थी हि पुरुषः तन्निष्पादनसमर्थं

The acquirement of desired objects depends on the activities (Pravritti) and not on Pramāṇa. One first desires to have an object and then performs activities. It cannot be said that without the activity to acquire the object, Pramāṇa points out objects because this view is contrary to our every day experience. It is known to every body that even such prominent objects like the sun and the moon are not seen by men when they do not direct their activities to the same[1]. Where the sun and the moon are not causes of activities (Pravritti), there is no showing (Pradarśakattva) and hence there is no Pratyakṣa. The function of Pramāṇa is not to give objects (Prāpaka) but to show them (Pradarśaka).

By this aphorism the view that Pramāṇa can be anything which is not knowledge like connection of the senses with external objects (which is technically called Sannikarṣa) is refuted[2]. Chandraprabha Sūri in his Nyāyāvatāra-vivriti has mentioned that as the Jains accept that knowledge illumines itself as well as the object, they refute the views of Yogāchāra Buddhists who hold that knowledge only illumines itself and the views of Mīmāṃsakas, Naiyāyikas etc., who maintain that knowledge illumines the external object alone, as it cannot illumine itself[3].

प्राप्तुकामस्तत्प्रदर्शकमेव प्रमाणमन्वेषत इत्यस्य प्रदर्शकत्वमेव प्रापकत्वम् । न हि तेन प्रदर्शितेऽर्थे प्राप्त्यभावः" Prameyakamala-mārtaṇda.

1 "प्रवृत्तिमूला तूपादेयार्थप्राप्तिर्न प्रमाणाधीना तस्याः पुरुषेच्छाधीन प्रवृत्तिप्रभवत्वात् । न च प्रवृत्त्यभावे प्रमाणस्यार्थप्रदर्शकत्वलक्षणव्यापाराभावो वाच्यः प्रतीतिविरोधात् । न खलु चन्द्रार्कादिविषयं प्रत्यक्षमप्रवर्त्तकत्वात् न तत् प्रदर्शकमिति लोके प्रतीतिः ।" Prameyakamala-mārtaṇda.

2 "यस्माद्धिताहितप्राप्तिपरिहारसमर्थं प्रमाणं, ततस्तत् प्रमाणत्वेनाभ्युपगतं वस्तु ज्ञानमेव भवितुमर्हति । नाज्ञानरूपं सन्निकर्षादि ।" Prameyaratnamālā.

3 "ये स्वाभास्येव ज्ञानं मन्यन्ते ते ज्ञानवादिनो बौद्धविशेषाः, ये च पराभास्येव मीमांसकनैयायिकादयः, ते निरस्तास्ते हि बहिरर्थाभावात् ज्ञानं स्वांशपर्यवसितसत्ताकम् इत्याचक्षीरन् । तदयुक्तम् । ज्ञेयार्थाभावे ज्ञानाभावप्रसङ्गात् ।....पराभास्यपि

This is laid down in "An Epitome of Jainism" as follows :

"The question, therefore, to begin with is, what is Pramāṇa from our point of view ? Pramāṇa, we define, is the valid knowledge which reveals itself as well as its knowable. It is worthy of note that by this we, first, put aside the Buddhist view that there being nothing external, knowledge only reveals itself and secondly, we contradict as well the Naiyāyika and the Mīmāṃsaka schools of thought who teach that knowledge does not reveal itself but reveals external relations. We hold however, that just as colour reveals itself as well as the object to which it belongs, so knowledge revealing itself reveals the knowable as well."[1]

तन्निश्चयात्मकं समारोपविरुद्धत्वादनुमानवत् ॥ ३ ॥

3. Tanniśchayātmakaṃ samāropaviruddhatvādanumānavat.

3. That (viz. Pramāṇa) being opposed to Samāropa (viz. fallacies) consists of definiteness like Anumāna (inference).

Commentary

Pramāṇa must be free from Samāropa (fallacies) which is of three kinds Saṃśaya, Anadhyavasāya and Viparyaya[2]. Saṃśaya arises when there is a doubt about an object i.e. when our mind sways between this or that, without being able to assert the true nature of a thing[3]. For example, when a person sees some-

---

स्वप्रकाशाभावात् अभिदधीरन् तदप्यसम्बद्धम् । स्वप्रकाशाभावे परप्रकाशायोगात् । न हि प्रदीपः स्वरुपमनुद्योतयन् घटाद्युद्योतने व्याप्रियते ।" Nyāyāvatāra-vivriti

1 An Epitome of Jainism by Nahar & Ghosh. P. 70.

2 "अतस्मिंस्तदध्यवसायः समारोपः ।" Pramāṇa-nayatattvālokālaṅkāra. I. 7

"स विपर्ययसंशयानध्यवसायभेदात् त्रेधा ।" Pramāṇa-nayatattvālokālaṅkāra. I. 8.

3 "अनुभयत्रोभयकोटिसंस्पर्शी प्रत्ययः संशयः।"

Pramāṇa-mimāṃsā I. I. 5.

"साधकवाधकप्रमाणाभावादनवस्थिताऽनेककोटिसंस्पर्शि ज्ञानं संशयः ।"

Pramāṇa-naya-tattvālokālaṅkāra. I. 11.

thing at a distance in the darkness, a doubt arises in his mind whether it is a man or a post[1]. The knowledge in this case touches two ideas without being able to fix it to a particular right knowledge of the object seen. It must be understood that when a thing is capable of two conceptions, there is no Doubt, though there are two ideas in the same object. For example in the Saptabhaṅgi Naya in Jain philosophy a pitcher is in one sense, said to exist while in another, it is said not to exist[2]. When the details of the head, hands etc. of a man or the branches, hollow etc. of a tree are not perceived being at a distance and in the darkness, we have knowledge of only something high. In this case a doubt arises whether it is a tree or a man[3].

When we have a knowledge that this is something without any clear idea what it is, we have Anadhyavasāya which is also known as Vibhrama (Indefiniteness). If a man touches something when he walks but does not understand what it is, his knowledge is Anadhyavasāya. He is conscious that he has touched something but is unable to say what its real nature is[4].

---

1 "यथाऽयं स्थाणुर्वा पुरुषो वा ।" Pramāṇanayatattvālokālaṅkāra. I. 12.

"यथान्धकारे दूरादूर्द्धाकारवस्तूपलम्भात् साधकवाधकप्रमाणाभावे सति स्थाणुर्वा पुरुषो वेति प्रत्ययः ।" Pramāṇa-mimāṃsā. Bhāṣya to Aphorism I. 1. 5.

2 To emphasize this, Hemachandra has used the word "Anubhayatra" in the definition of Saṃśaya quoted above e. g. "अनुभयत्र-ग्रहणमुभयरुपे वस्तुन्युभयकोटिसंस्पर्शोऽपि संशयत्वनिराकरणार्थं, यथाऽस्ति च नास्ति च घटः नित्यश्चानित्यश्चात्मेत्यादि ।" (Pramāṇa-mimāṃsā.)

3 "विरुद्धानेककोटिस्पर्शि ज्ञानं संशयः । यथाऽयं स्थाणुर्वा पुरुषो वेति । स्थाणुपुरुषसाधारणोर्द्धतादिदर्शनाद् तद्विशेषस्प वक्रकोटर-शिरः-पाण्यादेः साधकप्रमाणस्याभावादनेककोट्यवलंवित्वं ज्ञानस्य ।" Nyāya-dipikā.

4 "किमित्यालोचनमात्रमनध्यवसायः । यथा गच्छतस्तृणस्पर्शज्ञानम् ।" Pramāṇa-naya-tattvālokālaṅkāra. I. 13. 14.

The knowledge of an object as quite the contrary to its real self is known as Viparyaya or Vimoha. When we think nacre to be silver or a rope to be a snake, we have a knowledge vitiated by Viparyaya or Vimoha (Perversity[1]). Such is also the case when a person attacked by a particular disease tastes a sweet thing as bitter, or sees two moons by a defect in vision or thinks trees to be moving while travelling in a boat or a railway carriage or sees a circle of fire when a burning brand is spun round[2].

Pramāṇa is free from these three kinds of fallacies. These

"किमित्यालोचनमात्रमनध्यवसायः । यथा पथि गच्छतस्तृणस्पर्शादिज्ञानम्"

Nyāya-dīpikā. Dharmabhūṣana lays down that Anadhyavasāya does not touch different ideas, so it is not Saṃśaya. It is also not Viparyaya as it does not comprehend the reality of the opposite idea :

"इदं हि नानाकोट्यवलंवनाभावाद् न संशयः ।
विपरीतैककोटि-निश्चयाभावान्न विपर्ययः ।" Nyāya-dīpikā.

"विशेषानुल्लेख्यमनध्यवसायः ।" Pramāṇa-mīmāṃsā I. 1. 7.

"दूरान्धकारादिवशादसाधारणधर्मावमर्शरहितः प्रत्ययोऽनिश्चयात्मकत्वादनध्यवसायः यथा किमेतदिति ।" Bhāṣya on Ibid.

1 "विपरीतैककोटिनिष्टंकनं विपर्ययः । यथा शुक्तिकायामिदं रजतमिति ।" Pramāṇanayatattvālokālaṅkāra. 1. 9. 10.

"अतस्मिंस्तदेवेति विपर्ययः ।" Pramāṇa-mimāṃsā I. 1. 7.

"विपरीतकोटिनिश्चयो विपर्ययः । यथा शुक्तिकायामिदं रजतमिति ज्ञानम् । अत्रापि सादृश्यादिनिमित्तवशात् शुक्तिविपरीते रजते निश्चयः ।" Nyāya-dīpikā.

2 "यथा धातुवैषम्यान्मधुरादि-द्रव्येषु तिक्तादिप्रत्ययः, तिमिरादिदोषादेकस्मिन्नपि चन्द्रे द्विचन्द्रादिप्रत्ययः, नौयानादगच्छत्स्वपि वृक्षेषु गच्छत्-प्रत्ययः आशुभ्रमणादलातादावचक्रेऽपि चक्रप्रत्ययः ।" Bhāṣya to Aphorism 1, 1. 7 in Pramāṇa-mīmāṃsā.

are termed Pramāṇābhāsas by Māṇikyanandi and are mentioned in the sixth chapter of Parikṣāmukhaṃ[1].

According to the Jain doctrine, liberation is attained by a soul possessed of certain characteristics, viz. right faith, right knowledge and right conduct. Right faith or Samyaktva is a sincere belief in the seven Tattvas (essential principles) of Jainism viz. Jīva, Ajīva, Āsrava, Bandha, Saṃvara, Nirjarā and Mokṣa. It is only after a person has right faith that he can attain right knowledge. Right knowledge or Samyak Jñāna is the detailed cognition of the ego and non-ego and is free from the fallacies Saṃśaya, Anadhyavasāya and Viparyaya as described above[2]. A person may have a knowledge of the aforesaid seven principles of Jainism but that knowledge may be vague or indefinite or it may be full of doubts or it may be entirely wrong. When indecision, doubts or belief in opposite principles disappear from removal of fallacies, a person attains perfect knowledge. The understanding of Pramāṇas is therefore not useless even to a person who has given up worldly pursuits and is bent upon obtaining liberation.

Anantavīrya says that the Buddhists might say that they agree to the view that Pramāṇa is knowledge as mentioned in the second aphorism but they do not agree that all Pramāṇas consist of definite knowledge. According to them it is only in case of one variety of Pramāṇa viz. inference that correctness can be asserted. In other cases for example in Nirvikalpaka Pratyakṣa as understood by the Buddhists, definiteness is not essentially found. In opposition to this view this aphorism has been laid down in which

---

1 "अस्वसंविदितगृहीतार्थदर्शनसंशयादयः प्रमाणाभासाः ।" Parikṣāmukhaṃ VI. 2.

2 "संसयविमोहविब्भमविवज्जियं अप्पपरसरुवस्स ।
गहणं सम्मं णाणं सायारमणेयभेयं च ॥"

Dravya-saṃgraha. Verse. 42.

it has been mentioned that not only in Anumāna but in all kinds of Pramāṇa, there is definite knowledge[1].

अनिश्चितोऽपूर्वार्थः ॥ ४ ॥

4. Aniśchitohpūrvārthaḥ.

4. Apūrvārtha is that which has not been ascertained.

Commentary

In the definition of Pramāṇa as laid down in the first aphorism, the word Apūrvārtha has been used. This word is explained in this aphorism. Apūrvārtha is that which has not previously been ascertained by any Pramāṇa by making it free from fallacies like Doubt, Indefiniteness or Perversity[2].

We have previously mentioned that there are four stages of knowledge. First, we have a general knowledge of a thing brought into contact with a sense organ (Avagraha). Then we have a desire to know the particulars (Īhā). A doubt may be started by saying that as Avagraha precedes Īha, the knowledge in the second stage viz. Īhā cannot be said to be a knowledge of a thing not ascertained before as in the first stage (Avagraha) it has already been ascertained. The reply to this is that as details are not ascertained by Avagraha but only by Īhā it cannot be said that ascertainment of the object takes place during the first stage viz. Avagraha[3]. The ascertainment consists of a perfect and correct idea of the thing.

---

1 "अत्राह सौगतः, भवतु नाम सन्निकर्षादिव्यवच्छेदेन ज्ञानस्यैव प्रामाण्यं, न तदस्माभिर्निषिध्यते। तत्तु व्यवसायात्मकमेवेत्यत्र न युक्तिमुत्पश्यामः। अनुमानस्येव व्यवसायात्मनः प्रामाण्याभ्युपगमात्। प्रत्यक्षस्य तु निर्विकल्पकत्वेऽप्यविसंवादकत्वेन प्रामाण्योपपत्तेरिति तत्राह।" Prameyaratnamālā.

2 "यः प्रमाणान्तरेण संशयादिव्यवच्छेदेनानध्यवसितः सोऽपूर्वार्थः।" Prameyaratnamālā.

3 "तेनेहादिज्ञानविषयस्यावग्रहादिगृहीतत्वेऽपि न पूर्वार्थत्वम्। अवग्रहादिनेहादिविषयभूतावान्तरविशेषनिश्चयाभावात्।" Prameyaratnamālā.

दृष्टोऽपि समारोपात्तादृक् ॥ ५ ॥

5. Driṣṭohpi samāropāttādrik.

5. Even an ascertained thing becomes so (i. e., unascertained) through Samāropa (fallacies).

Commentary

It is urged in this aphorism that by Apūrvārtha, we not only mean a thing not ascertained before but also a thing previously ascertained but which has subsequently become involved in fallacies[1]. In the latter class, we do away with the fallacies and ascertain the thing again correctly. This subsequent ascertainment is also said to be of a thing not ascertained before as in the interval there were fallacies destroying the true idea of the object.

Dharmabhūṣaṇa has quoted this aphorism in Nyāya-dipikā saying that after we see a pitcher, we may see other things and then again see the pitcher and the question may arise whether the subsequent knowledge of the pitcher is Pramāṇa as it had been already ascertained before. The answer to this question is that in this case the pitcher is to be taken as unascertained because there may be fallacies in the interval[2].

This however can be explained in another way following the argument in the case of Dhārāvāhika Jñāna. Though a section of Jain writers exclude Dhārāvāhika Jñāna from Pramāṇa, we have shown how it can be fitted to the definition of Pramāṇa. Similarly when we have knowledge of a pitcher followed by knowledge of other things and then again we have knowledge of the pitcher it

---

1. "अथोक्तप्रकार एवापूर्वार्थः किमन्योऽप्यस्तीत्याह···दृष्टोऽपि गृहीतोऽपि न केवलमनिश्चित एवेत्यपिशब्दार्थः। तादृगपूर्वार्थो भवति। समारोपादिति हेतुः।" Prameyaratnamālā.

2. ननु घटे दृष्ट पुनरन्यव्यासंगे पश्चाद् घट एव दृष्टे पश्चात्तमं ज्ञानमप्रमाणं प्राप्नोति···इति चेत्, न। दृष्टस्यापि मध्ये समारोपे सत्यदृष्टत्वात्। तदुक्तं 'दृष्टोऽपि समारोपात्तादृक्' इति।" Nyāya-dipikā.

may be said that different knowledges of the pitcher on the two occasions are different ascertainments characterised by different time, place, etc. So the second ascertainment can be Pramāṇa as well as the first.

The view is therefore clear that not only an object never ascertained before can be Pramāṇa but the same object after previous ascertainment can again be Pramāṇa for fallacies may vitiate the first ascertainment making it necessary for another ascertainment of the true characteristics of the object. In our everyday life we may see an object previously perceived but be unable to find out its real nature owing to its being covered by dirt etc., when we see it for the second time. But if this dirt be removed we get a real knowledge of it. So a Pramāṇa also may be vitiated by fallacies and again become Pramāṇa when the fallacies are removed[1].

स्वोन्मुखतया प्रतिभासनं स्वस्य व्यवसायः ॥ ६ ॥

6. Svonmukhatayā pratibhāsanaṃ svasya vyavasāyaḥ.

6. The ascertainment of self is the illumination of it towards itself.

Commentary

This aphorism explains the words "Sva . . . vyavasāya" used in the definition of Pramāṇa in the first aphorism.

When the knowledge becomes its own object, it illumines itself and we say that in Pramāṇa there is ascertainment of itself (as well as of the object)[2].

This is further explained in the next aphorism.

---

1. "एतदुक्तं भवति, गृहीतमपि ध्यामलिताकारतया यन्निर्णेतुं न शक्यते तदपि वस्त्वपूर्वमिति व्यपदिश्यते प्रवृत्तसमारोपाव्यवच्छेदात् ।" Prameyaratnamālā.

2. The word स्वोन्मुखतया is explained as स्वविषयकत्वम् i.e. becoming its own object of ascertainment or in other words, स्वतः प्रकाशनं ज्ञानं i.e. the knowledge illumines itself. (Arthaprakāśikā)

अर्थस्येव तदुन्मुखतया ॥ ७ ॥

7. Arthasyeva tadunmukhatayā.

7. It becomes its own object, like other objects.

Commentary

This aphorism gives an example explaining the preceding aphorism. As the ascertainment of external objects results from directing attention towards them, so the knowledge itself is ascertained by it. In every knowledge there is a subject and an object and in valid knowledge the object as well as the knowledge itself is ascertained. A concrete example is given in the next aphorism to elucidate this.

घटमहमात्मना वेद्मि ॥ ८ ॥

8. Ghatamahamātmanā vedmi.

8. I know the pitcher through myself.

Commentary

Here "I" is the subject (Pramātā) and "the pitcher" is the object (Prameya), "knowing" is the action (Pramiti) and "through myself" is the instrumental cause of this knowledge (Pramāṇa). Thus in such a knowledge we have an understanding of a subject, an object, an instrumental cause and a verb signifying action. This is mentioned in the next aphorism.

Aphorisms 6, 7, 8 are embodied in a different language in a single Sūtra in Pramāṇanayatattvālokālaṅkāra. Instead of a pitcher, the example given there is that of a baby elephant[1].

कर्मवत्कर्तृकरणक्रियाप्रतीतेः ॥ ९ ॥

9. Karmavatkartrikaraṇakriyāpratīteḥ.

---

1. "स्वस्य व्यवसायः स्वाभिमुख्येन प्रकाशनं वाक्यस्येव तदाभिमुख्येन करिकलभकमहमात्मना जानामि ।" Pramāṇanayatattvālokālaṅkāra, I. 17.

9. Because (in our knowledge) we have an understanding of the subject, an instrumental cause and the verb, in the same manner as the object.

Commentary

Anantavīrya says that this aphorism denies the views of those who maintain that knowledge ascertains only the object but not itself, others who hold that knowledge ascertains either itself or an object, others again who lay down that in knowledge there is understanding of only the subject and the object and of others who say that in knowledge there is understanding of subject, object and a verb[1]. By this aphorism it is laid down that according to the Jain view, in knowledge there is understanding of four things, a subject, an object, a verb and an instrumental cause. The thing which is known is the object. The subject is the self. Pramāṇa is the instrumental cause and Pramiti is the verb.

In Arthaprakāśikā, it is mentioned that this is in contra-distinction with the view of Naiyāyikas who hold that in Pratyakṣa Pramāṇa only the object (Prameya) is understood e. g. that this is a pitcher and that the knowledge does not know itself or the subject (Pramātā) or the result (Pramiti). It is urged that this is also in opposition to the view of Mimāṃsakas following Prabhākara who say that objects like pitchers and the self are ascertained by Pratyakṣa Pramāṇa and who deny that Pramiti or the instrumental cause is ascertained by such Pramāṇa. Further it is mentioned that this refutes the view of the followers of Jaimini who admit the understanding of Pramāṇa, Prameya and Pramiti in Pratyakṣa Pramāṇa but deny the instrumental cause[2].

---

1. "ननु ज्ञानमर्थमेवाध्यवस्यति न स्वात्मानम् । आत्मानं फलं वेति केचित् । कर्त्तृकर्मणोरेव प्रतीतिरित्यपरे । कर्त्तृकर्मक्रियाणामेव प्रतीतिरित्यन्ये । तेषां मतमखिलमपि प्रतीतिबाधितमिति दर्शयन्नाह ।" Prameyaratnamālā.

2. "अत्राहुर्नैयायिकादयः अज्ञानं प्रमेयमेव प्रत्यक्षीकरोति । अयं घट इत्याकारेण ज्ञानेन प्रमेयरूपघटादेरेव प्रत्यक्षीकरणात् । अतः तादृशज्ञानं न स्वस्वरूपं, नाप्यात्मानं प्रमातारं, नापि प्रमितिरूपं फलं वा प्रत्यक्षीकरोति ।

शब्दानुच्चारणेऽपि स्वस्यानुभवनमर्थवत् ॥ १० ॥

10. Śabdānuchchāraṇehpi svasyānubhavanamarthavat.

10. Just as in the case of objects, there is understanding of itself (the knowledge) without utterance of the word (signifying it).

Commentary

It is our everyday knowledge that though the word "pitcher" is not uttered, we can have experience of a pitcher. So we can have experience of the knowledge itself though no word signifying knowledge is uttered. This is urged to meet the view of those who say that there can be no experience without the help of words. It cannot be urged that as there is no use of the word 'knowledge' in an experience of an object, the knowledge cannot become its own object ; for we see that even when the word 'pitcher' is not uttered we can have experience of a pitcher.

को वा तत्प्रतिभासिनमर्थमध्यक्षमिच्छंस्तदेव तथा नेच्छेत् ॥११॥

11. Ko vā tatpratibhāsinamarthamadhyakṣamichchhaṃstadeva tathā nechchhet.

11. Who does not accept it (i. e. knowledge) to be of that manner (i. e. being the subject-matter of experience) when one admits that in Pratyakṣa the object is illumined by knowledge ?

प्रदीपवत् ॥ १२ ॥

12. Pradīpavat.

12. Like a lamp.

भाट्टास्तु प्रमाणप्रमेययोरेव प्रत्यक्षतः प्रतिपत्तिः। प्रत्यक्षेण प्रमेयस्य घटादेः प्रमातुश्च आत्मनः प्रत्यक्षीकरणात्। न तु प्रमितिकरणज्ञानयोरपि प्रत्यक्षतः प्रतिपत्तिः सम्भवतीति वदन्ति।

प्रमाणप्रमेयप्रमितीनामेव प्रत्यक्षतः प्रतिपत्तिः, न तु प्रमितिकरणज्ञानस्येति जैमिनीयाः।

तेषां सेर्वेषामपि मतमनुभवपराहतमिति दर्शयन्नाह।" Arthaprakāśikā.

Commentary

Just as a lamp illumines itself as well as objects like a jar etc., so knowledge illumines itself as well as objects known. There cannot be any one who would accept objects as knowable by knowledge but deny that knowledge itself can be known.

In Pramāṇanayatattvālokālaṅkāra, aphorisms 11 and 12 of Parīkṣāmukham are written in a slightly different language[1]. The example there given is that of the sun instead of a lamp.

The fact that knowledge illumines itself is accepted by later Jain writers like Hemachandra though in the definition of Pramāṇa accepted by them they exclude this. Hemachandra mentions that older writers have laid down that as objects are ascertained by knowledge, so the knowledge itself becomes its own object. Hemachandra quotes two definitions of older writers : one is of Siddhasena in Nyāyāvatāra in which it is laid down that Pramāṇa illumines itself as well as other objects and the other is of Māṇikyanandi in Parīkṣāmukhaṃ as we have already discussed[2]. Hemachandra admits following the example as given by Māṇikyanandi 'I know a pitcher', that the knowledge illumines itself in such a case like the subject and object[3]. He also mentions that as an object reveals itself, so the knowledge reveals itself and consequently a knowledge can know itself[4]. It is also stated by him that like a lamp, knowledge reveals an object capable of revealing itself as knowledge has the power of illumination[5]. It cannot be urged that

1. "कः खलु ज्ञानस्यालंबनं वाह्यं प्रतिभातमभिमन्यमानस्तदपि तत्प्रकारं नाभिमन्येत मिहिरालोकवत् ।" Pramāṇanayatattvālokālaṅkāra, I. 18.

2. "नन्वर्थनिर्णयवत् स्वनिर्णयोऽपि वृद्धैः प्रमाणलक्षणत्वेनोक्तः 'प्रमाणं स्वपराभासि' इति, 'स्वार्थव्यवसायात्मकं प्रमाणम्' इति च" Pramāṇamīmāṃsā. Bhāṣya to 1. 1. 2.

3. "घटमहं जानामीत्यादौ कर्तृकर्मवज् ज्ञप्तेरप्यवभासमानत्वात्" Ibid.

4. "अर्थोन्मुखतयेव स्वोन्मुखतयापि ज्ञानस्य प्रतिभासात् स्वनिर्णयात्मकत्वमप्यस्ति ।" Ibid.

5. "तथाहि ज्ञानं प्रकाशमानमेवार्थं प्रकाशयति प्रदीपवत् ।" Ibid.

as illumination is the very essence of knowledge, it cannot be the illuminator for its illuminating characteristic is established by the destruction of wrong knowledge[1]. But admitting all these Hemachandra propounds the following aphorism "The ascertainment of itself though it happens, is not the definition (of Pramāṇa) as this happens also in fallacies (which are not Pramāṇas)"[2].

Hemachandra himself in his own Bhāṣya to this aphorism writes that the views of others who lay down that knowledge illumines itself is approved by me. But in laying down a definition that quality only which distinguishes the object defined should be mentioned and not all the qualities which exist in a thing. In other words, a definition is not a description. Hemachandra adds that there is no knowledge whether right or wrong which does not illumine itself. So even in doubt etc., the knowledge illumines itself but this kind of knowledge being false is excluded from Pramāṇas. For this reason, Hemachandra says that he has excluded self-illumination as a characteristic of Pramāṇa in his definition[3].

But he supports the older writers by saying that they have not committed any fault by using this characteristic in the definition of Pramāṇa as they have done so for examination of the characteristics of Pramāṇa[4].

---

1. "संवेदनस्य प्रकाशत्वात् प्रकाशकत्वमसिद्धमिति चेत्, न, अज्ञाननिरासादिद्वारेण प्रकाशकत्वोपपत्तेः ।" Ibid.

2. "स्वनिर्णयः सन्नप्यलक्षणमप्रमाणेऽपि भावात् ॥"

Pramāṇamimāṃsā. 1. 1. 3.

3. "सन्नपि परोक्तमनुमोदते अयमर्थों, नहि अस्तीत्येव सर्वं लक्षणं वाच्यं किन्तु यो धर्मो विपक्षाद् व्यावर्त्तते, स्वनिर्णयस्त्वप्रमाणेऽपि संशयादौ वर्त्तते, नहि काचित् ज्ञानमात्रा सास्ति या न स्वसंविदिता नाम ततो न स्वनिर्णयो लक्षणमुक्तोऽस्माभिः ।" Bhāṣya to Aphorism I. 1. 3. in Pramāṇa-mīmāṃsā.

4. "वृद्धैस्तु परीक्षार्थमुपक्षिप्त इत्यदोषः ।" Ibid.

तत्प्रामाण्यं स्वतः परतश्च ॥१३॥

13. Tatprāmāṇyaṃ svataḥ parataścha.

13. The validity of Pramāṇa rises from itself or through another (Pramāṇa).

Commentary

In this aphorism, the point how a Pramāṇa establishes its validity, is discussed. In the Nyāya philosophy as propounded by Gautama, it has been laid down that the validity of Pramāṇa arises through other help. Vātsyāyana the writer of the Bhāṣya of Nyāya-sūtras of Gautama says that through inference, the validity of a Pramāṇa is established. We know that Pramāṇa is not the opposite of a correct understanding by the help of inference. So we must say in such a case that the validity of Pramāṇa is established through another viz. inference.

An example will make this clear. A thirsty man seeks water. That which causes a knowledge of water in a mirage is not Pramāṇa, for in a mirage the thirst of that man cannot be mitigated. Such a knowledge is a fallacy. Conformity with the object presented is known as the validity of Pramāṇa, and non-conformity with the object presented is the opposite of Pramāṇa[1].

A criticism may be made of the view that if by inference, the validity of a Pramāṇa is established, we may ask : if an inference which is itself a Pramāṇa confirms another Pramāṇa to establish its validity, how will this inference be validated ? If we say, that another inference will validate this, the result would be an endless chain of inferences. So we must accept that in some cases Pramāṇa validates itself and in other cases, its validity is established by inference. Jain writers accordingly hold that validity of Pramāṇa

---

1. "किमिदं प्रमाणस्य प्रामाण्यं नाम ? प्रतिभातविषयाव्यभिचारित्वम् ।"
Nyāyadīpikā.

"ज्ञानस्य प्रमेयाव्यभिचारित्वं प्रामाण्यम् । तदितरत्त्वप्रामाण्यम् ।"
Pramāṇanayatattvālokālaṅkāra, I. 19. 20.

arises either from itself or through another Pramāṇa (like inference).

It may be asked, in what case does the validity of a Pramāṇa arises of itself and in what case through another Pramāṇa ? The answer is that in the case of objects with which we are already familiar, the Pramāṇa rises of itself. For example, when we look at our palm and have a knowledge of the same, no inference is necessary to establish its validity. Similarly when we see a pond previously seen many times in our own village, the validity does not require the help of inference but arises of itself. This is shown by the fact that immediately afterwards we go to it to wash ourselves or drink water. But when we see a reservoir of water not seen before at any time, we may have a doubt at first whether this is really water or a mirage. Then we use our inference and say that as we are having a smell of lotuses, feeling cool wind etc., it must be water and no mirage and so our former knowledge of water is Pramāṇa and not a fallacy[1].

Hemachandra also mentions that we become certain of the validity of a Pramāṇa either by itself or through the help of others[2]. When we look at our palm of hand which is familiar to us, we have no wish to examine whether this knowledge is valid or not, for we have not the slightest doubt regarding it. Similarly

---

1. "तत्र तावदभ्यस्तविषये जलमिदमिति ज्ञाने जाते ज्ञानस्वरूपज्ञप्तिसमय एव तद्गतं प्रामाण्यमपि ज्ञायत एव। अन्यथोत्तरक्षण एव निःश्ंकप्रवृत्तेर-योगात्। अस्ति हि जलज्ञानोत्तरक्षण एव निःश्ंका प्रवृत्तिः। अनभ्यस्ते तु विषये जलज्ञाने जाते जलज्ञानं मम जातमिति ज्ञानस्वरूपनिर्णयेऽपि प्रामाण्य-निर्णयोऽन्यत एव। अन्यथोत्तरकाले संदेहानुपपत्तेः। अस्ति हि संदेहो जल-ज्ञानं मम जातं, तत् किं जलमुत मरीचिकेति ? ततः कमलपरिमलशिशिरमंदमरुत्-प्रचारप्रभृतिभिरवधारयति। प्रमाणं प्राक्तनं जलज्ञानं, कमलपरिमलाद्यन्यथानुपपत्तेः।" Nyāyadipikā.

2. "प्रामाण्यनिश्चयः स्वतः परतो वा।" Pramāṇa-mimāṃsā, I. I. 8.

when we are afflicted by thirst and want to drink water, or when we want to bathe or to assuage the heat of our body and see a tank already familiar to us, we at once proceed to it without stopping to examine, whether the knowledge is valid or not. But in other cases regarding objects with which we are not already familiar, we take the help of inference etc., to establish the validity of the knowledge[1].

Vidyānanda has affirmed this by saying "Pramāṇa establishes itself regarding objects with which we are already familiar and takes the help of other in other cases".[2]

In Pramāṇanayatattvālokālaṅkāra, it is mentioned that Prāmāṇya and Aprāmāṇya (validity and its opposite) arise through others, but regarding their knowledge, they arise by themselves or through others.[3] In Prameyaratnamālā also we find that Prāmāṇya arises by itself.[4]

In Arthaprakāśikā it is mentioned that in this aphorism the words "utpattau" ("when it arises") and "svakārye" ("in its working") may be taken as understood. The meaning would then be that when Prāmāṇya arises it takes help of others but regard-

---

1. "प्रामाण्यनिश्चयः क्वचित् स्वतो यथाऽभ्यासदशापन्ने स्वकरतलादिज्ञाने स्नानपानावगाहनोदन्योपशमादावर्थक्रियानिर्भासे वा प्रत्यक्षज्ञाने, नहि तत्र परीक्षाकांक्षाऽस्ति प्रेक्षावताम्, तथाहि जलज्ञानं ततो दाहपिपासार्त्तस्य तत्र प्रवृत्तिस्ततस्तत्प्राप्तिः ततः स्नानपानादीनि ततो दाहोदन्योपशम इत्येतावतैव भवति कृती प्रमाता न पुनर्दाहोदन्योपशमज्ञानमपि परीक्षते इत्यस्य स्वतः प्रामाण्यम् ।....क्वचित् परतः प्रामाण्य निश्चयो यथाऽनभ्यासदशापन्ने प्रत्यक्षे ।" Bhāṣya to Pramāṇa-mimāṃsā I. 1. 8.

2. "प्रामाण्यं तु स्वतः सिद्धमभ्यासात् परतोऽन्यथा ॥"

Pramāṇa-parikṣā.

3. "तदुभयमुत्पत्तौ परत एव ज्ञप्तौ तु स्वतः परतश्च ।"

Pramāṇa-nayatattvālokālaṅkāra I. 11.

4. "अथवा प्रामाण्यमुत्पत्तौ परत एव ।" Prameyaratnamālā.

ing its work viz. determination of objects, it takes its own help in the case of familiar objects and help of others in other cases.[1]

Here ends the first chapter of Parīkṣāmukhaṃ. We have seen that in the first aphorism of this chapter, the definition of Pramāṇa has been given. In the aphorisms which follow this definition is explained. For example in the second aphorism it is laid down that Pramāṇa cannot be anything else than knowledge as indicated in the definition. The words "sva-vyavasāya" in the definition is explained in aphorisms 6 and 7 and a concrete example is given in aphorism 8. The word "Apūrvārtha" is explained in aphorism 4. Thus defining Pramāṇa and explaining the general characteristics of Pramāṇa in the first chapter the author will proceed in the next chapter to mention the different varieties of Pramāṇa viz. Pratyakṣa and Parokṣa. Pratyakṣa Pramāṇa will be discussed in detail in the second chapter and Parokṣa Pramāṇa will be examined in the third chapter.

End of Chapter I.

---

1. "अथवा उत्पत्तौ स्वकार्यं च इति पदद्वयमपि अस्मिन् सूत्रे अध्याहर्त्तव्यं। तथाच अयमर्थः। प्रामाण्यमुत्पत्तौ परत एव।....विषयपरिच्छित्यादिलक्षणस्वकार्यें प्रामाण्यमभ्यासदशायां स्वतो गृह्यते। अनभ्यासदशायां परतो गृह्यत इति।"

Arthaprakāśikā.

द्वितीयः समुद्देशः

SAMUDDEŚA II

तद्‌द्वेधा ॥ १ ॥

1. Taddvedhā.

1. This (Pramāṇa) is of two kinds.

Commentary

Jain Logic accepts only two kinds of Pramāṇas, Pratyakṣa and Parokṣa. This distinguishes the Jain view from the views of Hindu and Buddhist philosophers. According to the Chārvāka school of philosophy there is only one Pramāṇa named Pratyakṣa. Buddhist philosophy admits two varieties of Pramāṇa viz. Pratyakṣa and Anumāna. In Vaiśeṣika philosophy also Pratyakṣa and Anumāna are the only Pramāṇas which are recognised, for according to this system of philosophy Śabda etc. (which are recognised by some as Pramāṇas) are included within Anumāna. In Sāṃkhya and Yoga philosophies, three kinds of Pramāṇas viz. Pratyakṣa, Anumāna and Āgama (Śabda) are accepted. In Nyāya philosophy four kinds of Pramāṇas, Pratyakṣa, Anumāna, Upamāna and Śabda are recognised. The Mīmāṃsā school of philosophy as propounded by Prabhākara and his followers recognise five Pramāṇas, Pratyakṣa, Anumāna, Upamāna, Śabda and Arthāpatti. The Bhatta school of Mīmāṃsā philosophy recognises one more Pramāṇa viz. Abhāva in addition to the five Pramāṇas accepted by Prabhākara. The Vedānta view as discussed in the Vedānta-paribhāṣā is that there are six kinds of Pramāṇas viz. Pratyakṣa, Anumāna, Upamāna, Śabda, Arthāpatti and Anupalabdhi.

Hemachandra in his Pramāṇamīmāṃsā laying down that "Pramāna is of two varieties[1] mentions in his Bhāṣya that this refutes the views of Chārvāka, Vaiśeṣika, Sāṃkhya, Nyāya,

---

1. "प्रमाणं द्विधा ।" Pramāṇa-mimāṃsā, I. I. 9.

Prābhākara and Bhāṭṭa (the two schools of Mīmāṃsā) philosophy.[1]

In Pramāṇanayatattvālokālaṅkāra we have "Pramāṇa is of two kinds—Pratyakṣa and Parokṣa"[2]. Dharmabhūṣaṇa also lays down the same[3].

प्रत्यक्षेतरभेदात् ॥ २ ॥

2. Pratyakṣetarabhedāt.

2. As it is of two varieties, Pratyakṣa and another (viz. Parokṣa).

Commentary

This is connected with the previous aphorism which lays down that Pramāṇa is of two kinds and this aphorism mentions the two kinds of Pramāṇas. In Pramāṇanayatattvālokālaṅkāra as we have already quoted these two aphorisms have been put down in a single aphorism. Hemachandra follows Māṇikyanandī and after mentioning that Pramāṇa is of two kinds[4] lays down in the next aphorism that the Pramāṇas are Pratyakṣa and Parokṣa[5]. In Nyāyāvatāra we find "Pramāṇa is divided as Pratyakṣa and Parokṣa as knowables are ascertained in two ways"[6]. Haribhadra Sūri lays down "According to the (Jain) view, Pratyakṣa and

---

1. "तेन प्रत्यक्षमेवैकं प्रमाणमिति चार्वाकाः, प्रत्यक्षानुमानागमाः प्रमाणानीति वैशेषिकाः, तान्येवेति सांख्याः, सहोपमानेन चत्वारीति नैयायिकाः, सहार्थापत्त्या पञ्चेति प्राभाकराः, सहाभावेन षडिति भाट्टा इति न्यूनाधिक-प्रमाणवादिनः प्रतिक्षिप्ताः ।" Bhāṣya to Ibid.

2. "तद्द्विभेदं प्रत्यक्षं च परोक्षं च ।" Pramāṇanayatattvālokālaṅkāra, II. I.

3. "प्रमाणं द्विविधं प्रत्यक्षं परोक्षं च ।" Nyāyadīpikā. Prakāśa II.

4. "प्रमाणं द्विधा ।" Pramāṇa-mīmāṃsā. I. I. 9

5. "प्रत्यक्षं च परोक्षं च ।" Ibid I. I. 10

6. "प्रत्यक्षं च परोक्षं च द्विधा मेयविनिश्चयाद् ॥" Nyāyāvatāra I.

Parokṣa are two kinds of Pramāṇas"[1]. In Tattvārtha Sūtra, Pramāṇas have been laid down in three aphorisms : "This knowledge consisting of Mati, Śruta, Avadhi, Manaḥparyaya and Kevala[2] consists of two Pramāṇas[3]. The first two are Parokṣa Pramāṇas[4]. The remaining ones are Pratyakṣa"[5].

विशदं प्रत्यक्षम् ॥ ३ ॥

3. Viśadaṃ Pratyakṣaṃ.

3. (The knowledge) which is clear is Pratyakṣa.

Commentary

The word "Knowledge" (Jñānaṃ) is to be understood in this aphorism[6]. Clearness is the characteristic of Pratyakṣa Pramāṇa. This clearness is expressed by the words Viśada, Spaṣta, Nirmala etc. in works on Jain Logic[7]. The idea may be thus explained by an example. We may have knowledge of fire directly or when we are told by a reliable person whom we believe "Here is fire" or when we see smoke and infer that there is fire. The second and third kind of knowledge is not direct and not therefore styled as clear. That there is difference between this direct and indirect knowledge is understood by every one. This direct knowledge is not dependant on Śabda or Anumāna. It

---

1. "प्रत्यक्षं च परोक्षं च द्वे प्रमाणे तथा मते ।" Ṣaḍdarśanasamuchchaya. Śloka 55.

2. "मतिश्रुतावधिमनःपर्ययकेवलानि ज्ञानम् ।" Tattvārtha Sūtra. I. 9.

3. "तत् प्रमाणे ।" Ibid I. 10.

4. "आद्ये परोक्षं ।" Ibid I. 11

5. "प्रत्यक्षमन्यत् ।" Ibid I. 12.

6. "ज्ञानमिति वर्त्तते ।" Prameyaratnamālā.

7. "स एव नैर्मल्यं वैशद्यं स्पष्टत्वमित्यादिभिः शब्दैरभिधीयते ।" Nyāya-dīpikā.

arises when there is destruction or mitigation of the obstruction to Jñāna[1].

Akalaṅka Deva in Nyāyaviniśchaya has mentioned that the definition of Pratyakṣa has been mentioned to be clear knowledge[2]. Syādvādavidyāpati has explained in the commentary that clearness means perspicuous illumination. This is felt by every one when one proceeds to examine the character of the knowledge[3].

In Pramāṇanayatattvālokālaṅkāra, the word Spaṣta has been used in place of Viśada. The meaning is the same. In Nyāyadīpikā[4] and in Pramāṇa-mīmāṃsā[5] the word Viśada has been followed.

The older Jain logicians have accepted the view which is contrary to that adopted in other philosophies that knowledge derived through the senses is Parokṣa and not Pratyakṣa. Their view is based on the authority of Umāsvāmi (as already quoted), Akalaṅka etc., who maintain that knowledge derived through meditation independant of the senses is Pratyakṣa (direct knowledge). Later writers on Jain logic however have laid down that sense-perception is Pratyakṣa and other kinds of knowledge are Parokṣa. For example Siddhasena Divākara writes "Such knowledge that

---

1. "किमिदं विशदप्रतिभासत्वं नाम ? उच्यते :—ज्ञानावरणस्य क्षयाद्‌-विशिष्टक्षयोपशामाद्वा शब्दानुमानाद्‌यसंभवि यन्नैर्मल्यमनुभवसिद्धं । दृश्यते खल्वग्नि-रस्तीत्याप्तवचनाद्‌ धूमादिर्लिंगाच्चोत्पन्नाज्‌ ज्ञानादयमग्निरित्युत्पन्नस्यैंद्रियिकस्य ज्ञानस्य विशेषः ।" Nyāya-dīpikā.

2. "प्रत्यक्षलक्षणं प्राहुः स्पष्टं साकारमंजसा ।" Nyāyaviniśchayālaṅkāra.

3. "निर्मलप्रतिभासत्वमेव स्पष्टत्वं । स्वानुभवप्रसिद्धं चैतत्‌ सर्वस्यापि परीक्षकस्येति नातीव निर्बाध्यते ।" Comm. by Syādvāda-vidyāpati.

4. "तत्र विशदप्रतिभासं नाम प्रत्यक्षम्‌ ।" Nyāyadīpikā.

5. "विशदः प्रत्यक्षम्‌ ।" Pramāṇa-mīmāṃsā. I. I. 13.

takes cognizance of objects, not beyond the range of the senses, is Pratyakṣa (direct knowledge or perception) ; the other is known as Parokṣa (indirect knowledge) in reference to the manner of taking the cognizance"[1]. (Translation by Dr. S. C. Vidyābhūṣaṇa).

Dr. S. C. Vidyābhūṣaṇa in his notes on the above verse of Siddhasena Divākara has mentioned the difference between the views of the older and later writers on Jain Logic thus :

"The words Pratyakṣa (direct knowledge) and Parokṣa (indirect knowledge) have been used here in their ordinary acceptations, namely, the first for sense-perceptions, and the second for inference and verbal testimony. In the ancient Jaina scriptures, however, Pratyakṣa (direct knowledge) signified perfect knowledge acquired by the soul direct through meditation and not through the channels of the senses, while Parokṣa (indirect knowledge) signified knowledge derived through the medium of the senses or signs comprising perception, inference and the verbal testimony"[2].

Now we may turn to the derivation of the word Pratyakṣa as given by different Jain writers. In Syādvādaratnākara we find that the derivative meaning of Pratyakṣa is that which rests on Akṣa (i. e., a sense). There it is also mentioned that the derivation is by Tatpuruṣa Samāsa. It cannot be Avyayībhāva, as in that case the word should always be in the neuter gender but we use Pratyakṣa in all the three genders[3]. Haribhadra Sūri derives

---

1. "अपरोक्षतयार्थस्य ग्राहकं ज्ञानमीदृशम् ।
प्रत्यक्षमितरत् ज्ञेयं परोक्षं ग्रहणेक्षया ॥" Nyāyāvatāra. 4

2. Nyāyāvatāra Edited by Dr. S. C. Vidyābhūṣaṇa P. 9.

3. "अक्षमिंद्रियं प्रति गतं कार्यत्वेनाश्रितं प्रत्यक्षम् । 'कुगतिप्रादयः' इति ततपुरुषः । ततश्च 'द्विगुप्राप्तापन्नालं पूर्वगतिसमासेषु' परवल्लिंगताप्रतिषेधादभिधेयवल्लिंगतायां विलिंगः प्रत्यक्षशब्दः सिद्धः । एवं च प्रत्यक्षं ज्ञानं, प्रत्यक्षो बोधः, प्रत्यक्षा

the word thus: "Akṣa means Jīva as it enjoys or pervades all Dravya, Kṣetra, Kāla and Bhāva. Akṣa also means Indriya (senses) as it enjoys objects. When Akṣa meets Akṣa we have Pratyakṣa that is to say knowledge arises through the senses"[1]. Hemachandra also lays down the derivation adopted by Haribhadra[2]. These derivations have been criticised in Syādvādaratnākara as already mentioned.

Now a question may be asked, if by the derivation we get that knowledge arising from sense-perception is Pratyakṣa, how can the view of writers who call such knowledge Parokṣa and only direct knowledge derived through meditation Pratyakṣa, be tenable. The answer has been given in Syādvādaratnākara that whatever the derivative meaning of a word may be, in use we do not stick to it. For example the derivative meaning of the word "Gauḥ" (a cow) is that which goes. This meaning can apply to any moving thing but use of the word Gauḥ is not at all made in its derivative sense. So in the case of Pratyakṣa Pramāṇa also, its derivative meaning cannot stop its being applied to knowledge like Avadhi etc., derived without the help of any sense[3].

बुद्धिरित्यादयो व्यपदेशाः प्रवर्त्तन्ते । अक्षमक्षं प्रति वर्त्तत इति प्रत्यक्षमिति त्वव्ययीभावे 'अव्ययीभावश्च' इत्यनेन सदा नपुंसकत्वं स्यात् ।" Syādvādaratnākara, II. 1.

1. "अश्नुतेऽक्ष्णोति वा व्याप्नोति सकलद्रव्यक्षेत्र-कालभावानित्यक्षो जीवोऽश्नुते विषयमित्यक्षमिन्द्रियं च । अक्षमक्षं प्रतिगतं प्रत्यक्षमिंद्रियाण्याश्रित्य व्यवहारसाधकं यज्ज्ञानमुत्पद्यते तत् प्रत्यक्षमित्यर्थः ।" Ṣaḍdarśanasamuchchaya. Comm. on Verse 55.

2. "अश्नुते अक्ष्णोति वा व्याप्नोति सकलद्रव्यक्षेत्रकालभावानित्यक्षो जीवः । अश्नुते विषयमित्यक्षमिंद्रियं च प्रतिः प्रतिगतार्थः अक्षं प्रतिगतं तदाश्रितं अक्षाणि चेंद्रियाणि तानि प्रतिगतमिंद्रियाण्याश्रित्योज्जिहीते यज्ज्ञानं तत् प्रत्यक्षम् ।" Pramāṇa mīmāṃsā. Bhāṣya on I. I. 10.

3. "नन्वेवं प्रत्यक्षशब्दस्य व्युत्पत्तौ कथमिंद्रियानाश्रितस्य मानसस्यावध्यादेश्च प्रत्यक्षव्यपदेशः स्यादिति चेत् ? उच्यते । प्रवृत्तिनिमित्तस्य तत्रापि सद्भावात् ।

We have already mentioned that according to the Jain doctrine, knowledge is of five kinds : (1) Mati (knowledge derived through the senses including the knowledge which arises from the activity of the mind), (2) Śruta (knowledge derived through symbols or signs e. g. words, gestures etc.), (3) Avadhi (psychic knowledge which the soul acquires without the help of any sense), (4) Manaḥparyaya (knowledge of thoughts of others) and (5) Kevala (omniscience). There are false knowledges of Mati, Śruta and Avadhi which make up a total of eight kinds of knowledge recognised in Jainism. We have seen that in Tattvārtha Sūtra, Mati and Śruta Jñāna have been described as Parokṣa Pramāṇas and Avadhi, Manaḥparyaya and Kevala as Pratyakṣa Pramāṇas. The distinction between Pratyakṣa and Parokṣa according to Tattvārtha Sūtra is that in the former the soul gets a clear knowledge of an object without depending upon any other knowledge while in the latter, the cognition is not clear by itself but has to depend upon some other kind of knowledge. We have already given an example of this dependance when, to have a knowledge of fire by seeing smoke, we have to depend on the knowledge of smoke and then infer the existence of fire.

But later writers like Jain logicians have laid down that Mati and Śruta Jñāna are Sāṅvyavahārika Pratyakṣas and Avadhi, Manaḥparyaya and Kevala are Pāramārthika or Mukhya Pratyakṣa. Brahmadeva in his commentary on Dravya-saṃgraha tries to reconcile this contradiction in the following manner. First he raises the question : "The disciple asks 'In Tattvārtha Sūtra, Mati and Śruta have been described as Parokṣa in the aphorism Ādye

---

अक्षाश्रितत्वं हि प्रत्यक्षशब्दस्य व्युत्पत्तिनिमित्तं, गतिक्रियेव गोशब्दस्य, प्रवृत्ति-निमित्तं त्वेकार्थसमवायिनाऽक्षाश्रितत्वेनोपलक्षितमर्थसाक्षात्कारत्वं गतिक्रिययोपलक्षितं गोत्वमिव गोशब्दस्य। अन्यद्धि शब्दस्य व्युत्पत्तिनिमित्तं, अन्यच्च प्रवृत्तिनिमित्तम्। इतरथा गच्छन्नेव गौर्गौरिति व्यपदिश्येत नापरो व्युत्पत्तिनिमित्ताभावात्। जात्यन्तर-विशिष्टं हि तुरगादिकं गति-क्रियापरिणतं व्युत्पत्तिनिमित्तसद्भावात् गोशब्दाभिधेयं स्यात्।" Syādvādaratnākara, II. 1.

Parokṣaṃ (I. 11). How can these be Pratyakṣa (according to the view of Jain writers on Logic ?[1] Brahmadeva then answers this question by saying that the aphorism of Umāsvāmi is to be regarded as a general rule (utsarga) while the sayings of Jain logicians are to be taken as special rules or exceptions (Apavāda). In special or exceptional cases, the general rule is not followed. So though in Tattvārtha Sūtra it has been mentioned that Mati and Śruta Jñānas are Parokṣa knowledge, there are particular cases which may be taken as exceptions where these may be called Pratyakṣa[2]. For example, Śruta Jñāna can be wholly Parokṣa as when it arises from words only or when it consists of knowledge of outside objects e. g. heaven, liberation etc. But when the soul has internal knowledge that it has happiness or misery or it consists of infinite knowledge, this Śruta Jñāna is partially Parokṣa. But Śruta Jñāna is Pratyakṣa in case of ordinary householders (though Parokṣa in case of Kevalins who have omniscience) when it cognizes the soul[3]. Brahmadeva further says that we all know

1 "अत्राह शिष्यः :—'आद्ये परोक्षम्' इति तत्त्वार्थसूत्रे मतिश्रुतद्वयं परोक्षं भणितं तिष्ठति, कथं प्रत्यक्षं भवति ?" Commentary on Dravyasaṃgraha, Verse 5.

2 "परिहारमाह। तदुत्सर्गव्याख्यानम्, इदं पुनरपवादव्याख्यानम्। यदि तदुत्सर्गव्याख्यानं न भवति, तर्हि मतिज्ञानं कथं तत्त्वार्थे परोक्षं भणितं तिष्ठति ? तर्कशास्त्रे सांव्यवहारिकं प्रत्यक्षं कथं जातम् ? यथा अपवादव्याख्यानेन मतिज्ञानं परोक्षमपि प्रत्यक्षज्ञानं तथा स्वात्माभिमुखं भावश्रुतज्ञानमपि परोक्षं सत् प्रत्यक्षं भण्यते।" Brahmadeva : Dravyasaṃgraha—Vritti Verse 5.

3 "शब्दात्मकं श्रुतज्ञानं परोक्षमेव तावत्। स्वर्गापवर्गादिबहिर्विषयपरिच्छित्तिपरिज्ञानं विकल्परूपं तदपि परोक्षं। यत्पुनरभ्यन्तरे सुखदुःखविकल्परूपोऽहमनन्तज्ञानादिरूपोऽहमिति वा तदीषत्परोक्षम्। यच्च निश्चय-भावश्रुतज्ञानं तच्च शुद्धात्माभिमुखसुखसंवित्तिस्वरूपं स्वसंवित्त्याकारेण सविकल्पमपीन्द्रियमनोजनितरागादिविकल्पजालरहितत्वेन निर्विकल्पम्, अभेदनयेन तदेवात्मशब्दवाच्यं, वीतरागचारित्राविनाभूतं केवलज्ञानापेक्षया परोक्षमपि संसारिणां क्षायिकज्ञानाभावात् क्षायोपशमिकमपि प्रत्यक्षमभिधीयते।" Ibid.

that the knowledge of our happiness and misery is Pratyakṣa, but if we say that according to Tattvārtha Sūtra, Mati and Śruta Jñāna are always Parokṣa, the knowledge of our happiness or misery should also become Parokṣa which is absurd[1].

In this connection we may mention the view of Dharmabhūṣaṇa who says: "Some say that Pratyakṣa should only be that which arises through the senses, eye etc., as Akṣa means the senses (and according to the derivative meaning Pratyakṣa means that arising from the senses). This view is not correct. The knowledges Avadhi, Manaḥparyaya and Kevala arise through the soul and are independent of the senses. There is no doubt that these are Pratyakṣa. The characteristic of Pratyakṣa is clearness and not being caused by the senses. For this reason among the five kinds of knowledge Mati, Śruta, Avadhi, Manaḥparyaya and Kevala, it has been mentioned (in the Tattvārtha Sūtra) that the former two are Parokṣa and the others are Pratyakṣa"[2]. Whatever may be the derivative meaning, the meaning fixed by use makes Avadhi, Manaḥparyaya and Kevala to be Pratyakṣa.[3] Or the derivation can be changed in the following manner. Akṣa means the soul as it pervades or knows and that which arises in the soul

---

1 "यदि पुनरेकान्तेन परोक्षं भवति तर्हि सुखदुःखादिसंवेदनमपि परोक्षं प्राप्नोति, न च तथा।" Ibid.

2 "कश्चिदाह 'अक्ष' नाम चक्षुरादिकमिंद्रियं तत् प्रतीत्य यदुत्पद्यते तदेव प्रत्यक्षमुचितं नान्यत्' इति तदप्यसत्। आत्ममात्रसापेक्षाणामवधिमनःपर्ययकेवलानामिंद्रियनिरपेक्षाणामपि प्रत्यक्षत्वाविरोधात्। स्पष्टत्वमेव हि प्रत्यक्षत्वप्रयोजकं नेंद्रियजन्यत्वं। अत एव हि मतिश्रुतावधिमनःपर्ययकेवलानां ज्ञानत्वेन प्रतिपन्नानां मध्ये 'आद्ये परोक्षं', 'प्रत्यक्षमन्यत्' इत्याद्ययोर्मतिश्रुतयोः परोक्षत्वकथनमन्येषां त्ववधिमनःपर्ययकेवलानां प्रत्यक्षत्ववाचो युक्तिः।" Nyāyadīpikā. Prakāśa II.

3 "कथं पुनरेतेषां प्रत्यक्षशब्दवाच्यत्वमिति चेत्? रूढित इति ब्रूमः।" Ibid.

independent of the senses is Pratyakṣa[1]. So if we quarrel that we must follow the derivative meaning, a solution is given by adopting a derivation which fits with the definition.

प्रतीत्यन्तराव्यवधानेन विशेषवत्तया वा प्रतिभासनं वैशद्यम् ॥४॥

4. Pratityantarāvyavadhānena viśeṣavattayā vā pratibhāsanaṃ vaiśadyaṃ.

4. Clearness means illumination without any other intermediate knowledge or illumination in details.

Commentary

In Aphorism 3, it was mentioned that the knowledge which is clear is Pratyakṣa. In the present aphorism, clearness is explained.

Clearness of knowledge means illumination of an object when there is no intermediate knowledge. For example, in inference we have an intermediate knowledge. When we see smoke and infer that there is fire, there is the intermediate knowledge of smoke before we have the knowledge of fire. Where there is no such intervention of another knowledge, we hold that the knowledge is clear. Another definition is also given. Clearness means knowledge of an object with all its details.

Hemachandra has laid down : "Clearness means illumination which does not depend on any other Pramāṇa (Anumāna, Śabda etc.) or understanding that it is of such and such a nature"[2]. In Anumāna and Śabda, the knowledge depends on other Pramāṇas but that is not the case in Pratyakṣa Pramāṇa. There is another

1 "अथवा अक्ष्णोति व्याप्नोति जानातीत्यक्ष आत्मा तन्मात्रापेक्षोत्पत्तिकं प्रत्यक्षमिति ।" Ibid.

2 "प्रमाणान्तरानपेक्षेदन्तया प्रतिभासो वा वैशद्यम् ।" Pramāṇa-mimāṃsā I. 1. 14.

definition of clearness viz. that it grasps all the details and hence forms a correct knowledge by being a Pratyakṣa Pramāṇa[1].

In Syādvādaratnākara this aphorism is criticised. It is mentioned there : "Some say 'Clearness means illumination without any intermediate knowledge'. They say that in Parokṣa Pramāṇas like Anumāna, the knowledge of fire arises after the intermediate knowledge of smoke, so that knowledge is not clear but in Pratyakṣa there is no such intermediate knowledge, so it is clear. Those who hold this view have not got an idea of Jain philosophy even in their dreams. For, how will they establish the knowledge Īhā etc. when connected with doubt ?"[2] So in Syādvādaratnākara, support is given to the definition of clearness as laid down in Pramāṇa-naya-tattvālokālaṅkāra which is as follows :

"Clearness means the illumination of details in excess of that produced by Anumāna etc."[3]. A verse is quoted in Syādvāda-ratnākara meaning the same thing[4].

---

1 "प्रस्तुतात् प्रमाणादन्यत् प्रमाणं शब्दलिंगादिज्ञानं तत् प्रमाणान्तरं, तन्निरपेक्षता वैशद्यम्। न हि शब्दानुमानादिवत् प्रत्यक्षं स्वोत्पत्तौ शब्दलिंगादिज्ञानं प्रमाणान्तरमपेक्षते इत्येकं वैशद्यलक्षणम्। लक्षणान्तरमपि इदन्तया प्रतिभासो वेति। इदन्तया विशेषनिष्ठतया यः प्रतिभासः सम्यगर्थनिर्णयस्य सोऽपि वैशद्यम्। वा शब्दः लक्षणान्तरत्वसूचनार्थः।" Bhāṣya on Pramāṇa-mīmāṃsā I. 1. 14.

2 "केचित्तु तार्किकम्मन्याः प्रतीत्यन्तराव्यवधानेन प्रतिभासनमपि ज्ञानस्य वैशद्यं वदन्ति। अनुमानादिपरोक्षप्रमाणभेदेषु हि धूमादिगोचरप्रतीतिव्यवधानेन धूमध्वजादिवस्तुनः प्रतीतिरित्यवैशद्यं तेषाम्, प्रत्यक्षे तु नैवं प्रतीत्यन्तरव्यवधानमस्तीति वैशद्यं तस्य। न ते जैनदर्शनोपनिषदं स्वप्नेऽपि प्रापुः। एवं प्रकारं वैशद्यं वदन्तस्ते कथमीहादिज्ञानस्य संदेहाद्यपेक्षिणः प्रत्यक्षतां व्यवस्थापयिष्यन्ति ?" Syādvādaratnākara.

3 "अनुमानाद्याधिक्येन विशेषप्रकाशनं स्पष्टत्वम्।"

Pramāṇanayatattvālokālaṅkāra. II. 3

4 "अनुमानाद्यतिरेकेण विशेषप्रतिभासनं।
तद्वैशद्यं मतं बुद्धेरवैशद्यमतः परम्॥"

Verse quoted in Syādvādaratnākara.

We have already mentioned while discussing the definition of Pramāṇa, the four kinds of Mati Jñāna viz. Avagraha, Īhā, Avāya and Dhāraṇā. The first stage is the bare knowledge of an object. In the second stage there is an attempt to know the particulars of the object whereby similarities with or differences from other objects are known. In the third stage there is a definite finding of these particulars and in the fourth stage there is a lasting impression which arises after the object is known with all its particulars.

Now these four stages are accepted in Sāṅvyavahārika Pratyakṣa which will be discussed in the next aphorism. The criticism of Syādvādaratnākara is that as in the case of Sāṅvyavahārika Pratyakṣa we recognise one knowledge after another (viz. Avagraha, Īhā, Avāya and Dhāraṇā) there are intermediate knowledges and so the definition of clearness that it is bereft of intermediate knowledge cannot be correct. For clearness being the characteristic of Pratyakṣa Pramāṇa we see that it cannot apply to Sāṅvyavahārika Pratyakṣa where four stages of knowledge arise one after another.

This criticism however has been met in the commentaries of Parīksāmukhaṃ and other works on Jain Logic. In Prameyaratnamālā, it is mentioned that "by intervention of another knowledge" it should be understood that the intermediate knowledge is of a quite different object and not of the same object. For example, in Anumāna we have knowledge of one object, smoke and a quite different object, fire, later on. But in Sāṅvyavahārika Pratyakṣa we have knowledge of the same object in four stages. For example, first we are merely conscious of a man ; then we desire to know his particulars. In the third stage we ascertain the particulars that he belongs to such and such a country etc., and in the fourth stage we get a lasting impression[1]. In Prameyakamalamārtaṇḍa, the

1 "यद्यप्यवायस्यावग्रहेहाप्रतीतिभ्यां व्यवधानं, तथापि न परोक्षत्वं विषयविषयिणोर्भेदे सति व्यवधानं तत्र परोक्षत्वम्। तर्हि अनुमानाध्यक्षविषयस्यैकात्मग्राह्यस्याग्नेरभिन्नस्योपलम्भादध्यक्षस्य परोक्षतेति तदप्ययुक्तम्। भिन्नविषयत्वाभावात्।

definition of Māṇikyanandī has been supported. That view has again been criticised in Syādvādaratnākara[1]. It will serve no purpose to go into details of this controversy. We have explained the main point fully and we have seen that no fault appears in the definition of clearness as given by Māṇikyanandī. Though in Pramāṇa-naya-tattvālokālaṅkāra an attempt is made to give a different definition, later writers like Hemachandra have followed Māṇikyanāndī.

इन्द्रियानिन्द्रियनिमित्तं देशतः सांव्यवहारिकम् ॥ ५ ॥

5. Indriyānindriyanimittaṃ deśataḥ sāṇvyavahārikaṃ.

5. (The knowledge)which is partially clear and arises from Indriya (the senses) and Anindriya (the mind) is Sāṅvyavahārika Pratyakṣa.

विसदृशसामग्रीजन्यभिन्नविषया प्रतीतिः प्रतीत्यन्तरमुच्यते नान्यदिति न दोषः ।" Prameyaratnamālā.

1 "नन्वेवमीहादिज्ञानस्यावग्रहाद्यपेक्षत्वादव्यवधानेन प्रतिभासनलक्षण-वैशद्याभावात् प्रत्यक्षता न स्यात्तदसारम् । अपरापरेन्द्रियव्यापारादेवावग्रहादीनामुत्पत्तेस्तत्र तदपेक्षत्वासिद्धेः । एकमेव चेदं विज्ञानमवग्रहाद्यतिशयवदपरापरचक्षुरादि-व्यापारादुत्पन्नं सत् स्वतन्त्रतया स्वविषये प्रवर्त्तत इति प्रमाणान्तराव्यवधानमत्रापि प्रसिद्धमेव । अनुमानादिप्रतीतिस्तु लिंगादिप्रतीत्यैव जनिता सति स्वविषये प्रवर्त्तते इत्यव्यवधानेन प्रतिभासनाभावान्न प्रत्यक्षता" Prameya-kamala-mārtaṇḍa

The above has been criticised in Syādvādaratnākara thus : "अथ ब्रयुरपरापरेन्द्रियव्यापारादेवेहादीनामुत्पत्तेः सन्देहाद्यनपेक्षत्वात् प्रतीत्यन्तरा-व्यवधानेन प्रत्यक्षतेति, तदपि प्रतीतिपराङ्मुखत्वम् । ईहादयो हि संदेहादिभ्यः समुपजायमानाः प्रतीयन्त एवेति कथं तदनपेक्षत्वम् ? प्रतीयमानस्यापि कार्यकारणभाव-स्यात्रापह्नवे सर्वत्र तदपह्नवः किं न स्यात् ? अथैकमिदं संवेदनमवग्रहाद्यतिशयोपेत-मित्यत्रापि प्रतीत्यन्तराव्यवधानमस्तीति, ननु तथापि तदनेकत्वपक्षे प्रतीत्यन्तरव्यव-धानमलब्धसमाधानं, स्याद्वादिना ह्यवग्रहादीनामेकत्वमिवानेकत्वमपि वक्तव्यम् ।"

Commentary

Pratyakṣa Pramāṇa is subdivided into two classes Sāṅvyavahārika and Mukhya or Pārarmārthika. In this aphorism the definition of Sāṅvyavahārika Pratyakṣa is given[1]

In Pramāṇaparīkṣā, Vidyānanda Svāmī has divided Pratyakṣa into three classes Indriya-pratyakṣa, Anindriya-pratyakṣa and Atīndriya-pratyakṣa.[2] The first two however can be included under Sāṅvyavahārika Pratyakṣa. So the twofold division of Pratyakṣa will be sufficient. In Pramāṇa-nayatattvālokālaṅkāra, Pratyakṣa has been divided into Sāṅvyavahārika and Pāramārthika and Sāṅvyavahārika again has been subdivided into Indriya-nivandhana and Anindriya-nivandhana[3]. In Pramāṇa-mimāṃsā Pratyakṣa has been divided into Mukhya and Sāṅvyavahārika[4] and in Nyāyadīpikā the divisions are Sāṅvyavahārika and Pāramārthika[5]. Mukhya or Pāramārthika are one and the same thing.

---

1 "तच्च प्रत्यक्षं द्वेधा मुख्यसंव्यवहारभेदाद् इति मनसि कृत्य प्रथमं सांव्यवहारिकप्रत्यक्षस्योत्पादिकां सामग्रीं तद्भेदं च प्राह।" Prameyaratnamālā.

2 "तत् त्रिविधं, इन्द्रियानिन्द्रियातीन्द्रियप्रत्यक्षविकल्पनात्।"

Pramāṇaparīkṣā.

3 "तद्द्विप्रकारं सांव्यवहारिकं पारमार्थिकं च।"

"तत्राद्यं द्विविधमिन्द्रियनिवन्धनमनिन्द्रियनिवन्धनं च।"

Pramāṇanayatattvālokālaṅkāra. II. 4. 5

4 "तत् सर्वथावरणविलये चेतनस्य स्वरूपाविर्भावो मुख्यं केवलम्।"

Pramāṇa-mimāṃsā I. 1. 15

"तत् तारतम्येऽवधिमनःपर्ययौ च।" Ibid 1. 1. 18

"इन्द्रियमनोनिमित्तावग्रहेहावायधारणात्मा सांव्यवहारिकम्।"

Ibid, 1. 1. 21

5 "तत् प्रत्यक्षं द्विविधं सांव्यवहारिकं पारमार्थिकं च।"

Nyāya-dīpikā.

The knowledge which is partially clear is Sāṅvyavahārika Pratyakṣa and the knowledge which is fully clear is Mukhya or Pāramārthika Pratyakṣa[1].

Saṅvyavahāra is the perfect satisfaction of a desire to cognize[2]. That which arises from Saṅvyavahāra is called Sāṅvyavahārika[3] The knowledge in Sāṅvyavahārika Pratyakṣa being partially clear, it is also called Amukhya Pratyakṣa as opposed to Mukhya Pratyakṣa where the knowledge is fully clear[4].

Sāṅvyavahārika Pratyakṣa is caused by Indriya and Anindriya. According to Jainism, the Indriyas (senses) are five viz. touch, taste, smell, sight and hearing[5]. Mind is called Anindriya or No-indriya. But by this distinction it should not be supposed that mind is not Indriya. Akalaṅka Deva in Tattvārtharāja-vārttika has laid down "We call a female who is unable to conceive, 'a woman without a belly'. This does not mean that really this female has no belly at all but the meaning is that she is unable to conceive. So when we call mind to be Anindriya it means that it does not produce impressions of objects like organs of sense eye etc. on contact. This does not however mean that mind is not a sense".[6]

---

1 "यज्ज्ञानं देशतो विशदमीषन्निर्मलं तत् सांव्यवहारिकप्रत्यक्षम् ।"
"यजज्ञानं साकल्येन स्पष्टं तत् पारमार्थिकप्रत्यक्षं मुख्यप्रत्यक्षमिति यावत् ।"
Nyāya-dīpikā.

2 "समीचीनः प्रवृत्तिनिवृत्तिरूपो व्यवहारः संव्यवहारः ।"
Pramāṇa-Mīmāṃsā Vritti on I. I. 21.

3 "समीचीनः प्रवृत्तिनिवृत्तिरूपो व्यवहारः संव्यवहारः, तत्र भवं सांव्यवहारिकम् ।" Prameya-ratna-mālā.

4 "इदं च अमुख्यप्रत्यक्षमुपचारसिद्धत्वात् ।" Nyāya-dīpikā.

5 'स्पर्शरसगन्धरूपशब्दग्रहणलक्षणानि स्पर्शनरसनघ्राणचक्षुःश्रोत्राणीन्द्रियाणि द्रव्यभावभेदानि ।" Pramāṇa-mīmāṃsā I. 1. 22.

6 "अनिंद्रियं मनोऽनुदरावत् ।" Tattvārtharājavārttika on Sūtra I. 14. It is thus explained in the Commentary on this :

In Nyāya philosophy of the Hindus, mind has been accepted as Indriya. But a distinction has been made from other senses. It has been mentioned that the true senses touch, taste etc. are fixed in their particular objects. For example, the sense of smell can produce a knowledge of smell but not of taste, sight etc. The mind however can apply itself to every object in all its qualities. In mind there is no special quality like those existing in senses e. g. smell etc.[1] This has been affirmed by Uddyotkara[2] and in substance this view is the same as that of Hemachandra already quoted in the footnote.

Gautama has taken consideration of the five Jñānendriyas, eye, ear etc., but in Smritis and other philosophies of the Hindus, five Karmendriyas (Vāk, Pāda, Pāṇi, Pāyu and Upastha) have also been mentioned as senses. Thus the total number of senses according to this view is ten. Manu has mentioned that mind is

---

"मनोऽतंकरणमनिन्द्रियमित्युच्यते । कथं इंद्रियप्रतिषेधेन मन उच्यते ?.... यथानुदरा कन्या इति नास्या उदरं न विद्यते, किन्तु गर्भभारोद्वहनसमर्थोदराभावादनुदरा । तथानिंद्रियमिति नास्येंद्रियत्वाभावः । किन्तु चक्षुरादिवत् प्रतिनियतदेशविषयावस्थानाभावादनिन्द्रियं मन इत्युच्यते ।"

This is affirmed in Pramāṇa-mīmāṃsā : "सर्वार्थग्रहणं मनः ।" I. 1. 25. The Bhāṣya on it lays down "सर्वे न तु स्पर्शनादीनां स्पर्शादिवत् प्रतिनियता एवार्था गृह्यन्ते तेनेति सर्वार्थग्रहणं मनोऽनिन्द्रियमिति नो इन्द्रियमिति चोच्यते ।"

1 "भौतिकानीन्द्रियाणि नियतविषयाणि, सगुणानाञ्चैषामिन्द्रियभाव इति । मनस्तु अभौतिकं सर्वविषयञ्च, नास्य सगुणस्येन्द्रियभाव इति । सति चेन्द्रियार्थसन्निकर्षे सन्निधिमसन्निधिश्चास्य युगपज्ज्ञानाऽनुत्पत्तिकारणं वक्ष्याम इति । मनश्चेन्द्रियभावान्न वाच्यं लक्षणान्तरमिति । तन्त्रान्तरसमाचाराच्चैतत् प्रत्येतव्यमिति ।" Vātsyāyana Bhāsya to Nyāya-sūtra I. 1. 4.

2 "मनः सर्वविषयं स्मृतिकारणसंयोगाधारत्वात् आत्मवत् सुखग्राहकसंयोगाधिकरणत्वात् समस्तेन्द्रियाधिष्ठातृत्वात् ।" Nyāya-vārttika.

the eleventh sense[1] In Sāṅkhya Sūtra[2] and Sāṅkhyakārikā[3] of Īśvarakriṣṇa we find that mind is both Jñānendriya and Karmendriya.

In Vedānta paribhāṣā however it is laid down that mind is not a sense[4]. To support this view the following is quoted from Kaṭha Upaniṣad III. 10 : "Objects are beyond the organs of senses, mind is beyond the sense-organs."[5] In Vedānta Sūtra however (II. 4. 17) we find mind accepted as a sense. Śaṅkar-āchārya in his Bhāṣya to the above Sūtra has taken mind as a sense supporting his view by quoting Smriti. In Bhāmatī, Vāchaspati Miśra quoted different views regarding the acceptance of mind as a sense but his own conclusion is that mind is a sense. In Śrimad-bhagavadgītā mind has been accepted as a sense[6].

---

1 "एकादशेन्द्रियाण्याहुर्यानि पूर्वे मनीषिणः ।
तानि सम्यक् प्रवक्ष्यामि यथावदनुपूर्वशः ॥
श्रोत्रं त्वक् चक्षुषी जिह्वा नासिका चैव पञ्चमी ।
पायूपस्थं हस्तपादं वाक् चैव दशमी स्मृता ॥
बुद्धीन्द्रियाणि पञ्चैषां श्रोत्रादीन्यनुपूर्वशः ।
कर्मेन्द्रियाणि पञ्चैषां पाय्वादीनां प्रचक्षते ॥
एकादशं मनो ज्ञेयं स्वगुणेनोभयात्मकम् ।"

Manusaṃhitā II. 89-92

2 "उभयात्मकं मनः ।" Sāṅkhya Sūtra II. 26.

3 "उभयात्मकमत्र मनः ।" Sāṅkhya-kārikā 27.

4 "न तावत् अन्तःकरणम् इन्द्रियम् इत्यत्र मानमस्ति ।"

Vedānta-paribhāṣā.

5 "'इन्द्रियेभ्यः परा ह्यर्थाः अर्थेभ्यश्च परं मनः ।'
इत्यादि श्रुत्या मनसोऽनिन्द्रियत्वावगमाच्च ।" Vedānta-paribhāṣā.

6 "वेदानां सामवेदोऽस्मि देवानामस्मि वासवः ।
इन्द्रियाणां मनश्चास्मि भूतानामस्मि चेतना ॥" Gitā X. 22.

Thus the view of the Jain Logic is in accordance with the view which preponderates in the Hindu philosophy regarding mind being a sense. But though Jain Logic accepts mind as a sense it calls it a small or intangible sense (No-indriya or Īṣat-indriya) because it is not materially cognisable like the other senses. Its function according to Jain view is discernible only by highly developed souls who have Manaḥparyayajñāna as described in the commentary on Aphorism I. Samuddeśa I of this work.

नार्थालोकौ कारणं परिच्छेद्यत्वात्तमोवत् ॥ ६ ॥

6. Nārthālokau kāraṇaṃ parichchedyatvāttamovat.

6. The object and light is not the instrument (of Pratyakṣa knowledge) as the same are capable of being ascertained as in the case of darkness.

"ममैवांशो जीवलोके जीवभूतः सनातनः ।
मनःषष्ठानीन्द्रियाणि प्रकृतिस्थानि कर्षति ॥" Ibid XIV. 7.

In Vedānta-paribhāṣā the latter verse has been tried to be explained away thus : "If you object that the quotation from the Bhagavadgīta is conclusive 'the organs of sense with the mind to make up six' ('मनःषष्ठानीन्द्रियाणि'), we reply, no ; for no contradiction results in filling up the number six with mind, though mind be not reckoned as an organ of sense. There is no positive injunction restricting the completion of the number relating to the organs of sense to such an organ only. Instance the text : 'the five including the sacrificer eat the Iḍā oblation' ; here we notice that the completion of the number five, relating to the Ritvik priests, is effected by means of the sacrificer (himself the fifth) who is not a Ritvik. And in the quotation 'He taught the five, the Vedas and Mahābhārata, we observe that the completion of the number five relating to the Vedas, is effected by the Mahābhārata which is not a Veda." (Trans. by A. Venis)

But this argument is use-less as in the first verse (X. 22), it is unmistakably mentioned "I am Manas (the Mind) among the senses," where the best among the senses is meant.

Commentary

In the preceding aphorism, it has been mentioned that mind and the senses cause Pratyakṣa knowledge. One may urge that light or a particular object is also necessary to give rise to Pratyakṣa knowledge. So these should also be mentioned as cause of Pratyakṣa knowledge. To refute this, it is mentioned in the present aphorism that an object or light does not cause Pratyakṣa knowledge. The example of darkness is cited to establish this for it is well-known that we have a knowledge of darkness though it obstructs perception and is not the cause[1]

This is further elucidated in the following two aphorisms.

तदन्वयव्यतिरेकानुविधानाभावाच्च केशोंडुकज्ञानवन्नक्तंचरज्ञानवच्च ॥ ७

7. Tadanvayavyatirekānuvidhānābhāvāchcha keśoṅduka-jñānavannaktañcharajñānavachcha.

7. That (is established) from universal affirmative and universal negative propositions like the knowledge of mosquito on a hair and like the knowledge of animals which see during the night.

Commentary

Some may urge, that it may be established by inference that an object or light is the cause of Pratyakṣa knowledge[2]. To refute this it is mentioned that even by inference this cannot be established. For a deduction by inference follows from a knowledge of a concomitance expressed in an universal affirmative proposition (Anvayavyāptijñāna) e. g. where there is smoke, there is fire or from a knowledge of a concomitance expressed in a universal negative proposition e. g. where is no smoke, there is no fire.

---

1. "प्रसिद्धं हि तमसो विज्ञानप्रतिबन्धकत्वेनातत्कारणस्यापि परिच्छेद्यत्वम् ।" Prameyakamala-mārtaṇḍa.

2. "अथानुमानात् तत्कार्यतावसायः । तथा हि, 'अर्थालोककार्यं विज्ञानं तदन्वयव्यतिरेकानुविधानात् । यद् यस्यान्वयव्यतिरेकावनुविधत्ते, तत् तस्य कार्यम् ।

To establish an inference, it will be necessary to hold where there is light, there is knowledge but we see that even where there is no light there can be knowledge as in the case of cats or owls in a dark night when there is no light. Further lice cannot see even when there is light. So, it cannot be propounded that where there is an object there is knowledge, for some persons in a particular state may have a knowledge of a mosquito on a hair though really there is no such mosquito[1]. A person suffering from jaundice may perceive yellowness while really there is no yellowness. So the relationship of cause and effect which is recognised by concomitance expressed in an universal affirmative or negative proposition cannot be found in light or object with knowledge.

Hemachandra in his Pramāṇa-mīmāṃsā also affirms this by saying "An object or light is not the cause of knowledge as knowledge can arise without the universal negative proposition (viz. where there is no object or light, there is no knowledge)."[2] Hemachandra cites examples of knowledge of water in a mirage though there is really no water or knowledge of objects in darkness by certain animals and the knowledge of Yogis about things in the past and the future and urges that this proves that object or light is not the cause of knowledge[3].

यथा अग्नेर्धूमः । अन्वयव्यतिरेकावनुविधत्ते चार्थालोकयोर्ज्ञानम्', इति । न चात्रासिद्धो हेतुस्तत्सद्भावे सत्येवास्य भावादभावे चाभावाद् ।" Prameyakamalamārtaṇḍa.

1. "अन्वयव्यतिरेकगम्यो हि कार्यकारणभावः। तत्रालोकस्तावन्न ज्ञानकारणं तदभावेऽपि घूकादीनां तदनुत्पत्तेः। तद्वदर्थोऽपि न ज्ञानकारणं तदभावेऽपि केशमशकादिज्ञानोत्पत्तेः। तथा च कुतोऽर्थजत्वं ज्ञानस्य ? तदुक्तं परीक्षामुखे 'नार्थालोकौ कारणं' इति। प्रामाण्यस्य चार्थाव्यभिचार एव निबंधनं, न त्वर्थजन्यत्वं, स्वसंवेदनस्य विषयाजन्यत्वेऽपि प्रामाण्याभ्युपगमात्। नहि किंचित् स्वस्मादेव जायते।" Nyāya-dipikā.

2. "नार्थालोकौ ज्ञानस्य निमित्तमव्यतिरेकात्।" Pramāṇa-mīmāṃsā I. 1. 26

3. "मरुमरीचिकादौ जलाभावेऽपि जलज्ञानस्य वृषदंशादीनां चालोका-

अतज्जन्यमपि तत्प्रकाशकं प्रदीपवत् ॥ ८ ॥

8. Atajjanyamapi tat-prakāśakaṃ pradīpavat.

8. Though it (i. e. knowledge) is not caused by it (i. e. the object), it (i. e. knowledge) illumines it (i. e. the object) like a lamp.

Commentary

The knowledge of an object though not caused by the object illumines the object. By the expression 'without being caused by it', it is also implied "though of not the same shape". An object is illuminated by a lamp which is neither caused by an object, nor is of the same shape as the object[1].

स्वावरणक्षयोपशमलक्षणयोग्यतया हि प्रतिनियतमर्थं व्यवस्थापयति ॥ ९ ॥

9. Svāvaraṇakṣayopaśamalakṣaṇayogyatayā hi pratiniyatamarthaṃ vyavasthāpayati.

9. Surely (Pratyakṣa knowledge) always illumines objects according to its power characterised by the mitigation of its hindrances.

Commentary

According to Jain philosophy, Upayoga is the sole characteristic of Jīva. Upayoga is a sort of inclination which arises from consciousness. This inclination is either towards Darśana or towards Jñāna. Darśana is of four kinds Chakṣu, Achakṣu, Avadhi

---

भावेऽपि सान्द्रतमतमःपटलविलिप्तदेशगतवस्तुप्रतिपत्तेश्च दर्शनात् योगिना चातीतानागतार्थग्रहणे किमर्थस्य निमित्तत्वं, निमित्तत्वे चार्थक्रियाकारित्वेन सत्त्वादतीतानागतत्वक्षतिः ।" Bhāsya to Aphorism I. I. 26 in Pramāṇa-mīmāṃsā.

1. "अर्थाजन्यमप्यर्थप्रकाशकमित्यर्थः । अतज्जन्यत्वमुपलक्षणम् । तेनातदाकारमपीत्यर्थः । उभयत्रापि प्रदीपो दृष्टान्तः । यथा प्रदीपस्यातज्जन्यस्याऽतदाकारधारिणोऽपि तत्प्रकाशकत्वं, तथा ज्ञानस्यापि ।" Prameyaratnamālā.

and Kevala[1] and Jñāna as already expounded in commentaries of previous aphorisms in this work is of eight kinds viz. Mati, Śruta, Avadhi, Manaḥparyaya and Kevala and false knowledges of Mati, Śruta and Avadhi.

In Darśana, details are not perceived but in Jñāna details are perceived. "Before we know things in a detailed way, there is the stage where we simply see, hear, or otherwise become conscious of it in a general way without going into its ins and outs. This is the first state of knowledge: it may be called indefinite cognition (Darśana). If this stage is not experienced, there can be no knowledge of the thing"[2]. In Jñāna, there is cognition of details.

Jain philosophy lays down that there are certain classes of Karma which obscure the four kinds of Darśana as well as the eight kinds of Jñāna. "Darśana is of four kinds: Chakṣu, Achakṣu, Avadhi and Kevala; so there are also four kinds of Karma which obscure each of these varieties. When there is a cessation or mitigation (Kṣayopaśama) of one or more of these varieties of Karma, the corresponding class or classes of Darśana is or are evolved. Thus by the removal of these Karmas, which obscure the Darśana which is received through the eye, a Jīva can see through the eyes. This is Chakṣu Darśana (Darśana through the eye). Again, by the removal of that Karma which obscures the Darśana through any sense other than the eye, or mind, a Jīva can cognize through the four organs of sense—ear, nose, tongue or skin and through the mind.

---

1. "उवओगो खलु दुविहो णाणेण य दंसणेण संजुत्तो ।
जीवस्स सव्वकालं अणण्णभूदं वियाणीहि ॥
दंसणमवि चक्खुजुदं अचक्खुजुदमवि य ओहिणा सहियं ।
अणिधणमणंतविसयं केवलियं चावि पण्णत्तं ॥"

Pañchāstikāyasamayasāra 40, 42.

"उवओगो दुवियप्पो दंसण णाणं च दंसणं चदुधा ।
चक्खु अचक्खू ओही दंसणमध केवलं णेयं ॥" Dravya-saṃgraha 4.

2. Jainism by Herbert Warren, Page 29.

This is called Achakṣu Darśana (Darśana not through the eye). Similarly, when Karmas obscuring Avadhi Darśana are removed, a Jīva can have Avadhi Darśana (conation before particular kind of psychic knowledge, limited by space and time and obtained directly by the soul e.g. clairvoyance). Lastly by the removal of the Karmas which obscure Kevala Darśana, a Jīva can have Kevala (or perfect) Darśana (in which everything in the three worlds existent in the present, past and future is at once cognized).

Besides the four varieties of Karmas obscuring Darśana already mentioned, there are also five others mentioned by Umāsvāmi e. g. Nidrā (sleep), Nidrānidrā (deep sleep), Prachalā (Trance), Prachalāprachalā (drowsiness) and Styānagriddhi (Somnambulistic state)[1]. These together with the Karmas obscuring Chakṣu, Achakṣu, Avadhi and Kevala Darśana already mentioned, make up nine Darśanāvaraṇīya Karmas[2].

Just as there are Darśanāvaraṇīya Karmas which obscure Darśana, so there are Jñānāvaraṇīya Karmas which obscure Jñāna. Umāsvāmi has mentioned that there are five sorts of Jñānāvaraṇīya Karmas which obscure Mati, Śruta, Avadhi, Manaḥparyaya and Kevala knowledge[3].

One may argue that in a knowledge of a pitcher, the pitcher and nothing else is the object of knowledge. Here the substance is the cause of its being the object of knowledge. But by denying as in the previous aphorism that the object is not the cause of knowledge, you must satisfy us by laying down the cause which particularises that such and such a thing would produce such and such a knowledge.

---

1. 'चक्षुरचक्षुरवधिकेवलानां निद्रानिद्रानिद्राप्रचलाप्रचलाप्रचलास्त्यानगृद्धयश्च ।' Tattvārthādhigama Sūtra VIII. 7.

2. Dravyasaṃgraha Edited by S. C. Ghoshal Page 10.

3. "मतिश्रुतावधिमनःपर्ययकेवलानाम् ।" Tattvārthādhigama Sūtra VIII. 6.

Raising this objection in Nyāyadipikā, Dharmabhūṣaṇa meets it by saying that Yogyatā is the cause regarding the object of knowledge and this Yogyatā is nothing but the mitigation or cessation of Karma obstructing knowledge. Dharmabhūṣaṇa quotes the present aphorism of Parīkṣāmukhaṃ to support his view[1].

That is to say when a Karma obstructing a particular kind of Jñāna is mitigated or entirely removed, knowledge arises and illumines objects like a lamp. This knowledge is not therefore caused by the object and is not of the same shape as the object.

In Vedānta-paribhāṣā it has been laid down that just as water goes out from a pond and entering fields of different shape, assumes different shape, so mind getting out through the sense-organs eye etc. goes to objects like pitchers and is changed like those objects[2]. This view is not accepted by Jain logicians as laid down in this aphorism. According to Jain view, the object is neither the cause nor the transformer of the mind to its shape.

कारणस्य च परिच्छेद्यत्वे करणादिना व्यभिचारः ॥ १० ॥

10. Kāraṇasya cha parichchedyatve karaṇādinā vyabhichāraḥ.

10. There will be non-application in the case of senses etc. if you accept the cause as the thing perceived.

Commentary

This aphorism is laid down to refute the view that a cause of a knowledge can be the object of knowledge. We know that the

---

1. "यदुक्तं घटज्ञानस्य घट एव विषयो, न पर इति। अर्थजत्वं हि विषयं प्रति नियमकारणं, तज्जन्यत्वात्। यद्विषयमेव चैतदिति। तत्तु भवता नाभ्युपगम्यते इति चेत्, यौग्यतैव विषयं प्रति नियमकारणमिति ब्रूमः। का नाम योग्यतेति, उच्यते—स्वावरणक्षयोपशमः। तदुक्तं 'स्वावरणक्षयोपशमलक्षणयोग्यतया हि प्रतिनियतमर्थं व्यवस्थापयति' इति।" Nyāyadipikā.

2. "तत्र यथा तड़ागोदकं छिद्रान्निर्गत्य कुल्यात्मना केदारान् प्रविश्य तद्वदेव चतुष्कोणाद्याकारं भवति तथा तैजसमन्तःकरणमपि चक्षुरादिद्वारा निर्गत्य घटादिविषय-देशं गत्वा घटादिविषयाकारेण परिणमते ॥" Vedānta-paribhāṣā Chapter I.

senses or mind are instrumental in producing knowledge. In this sense, these can be said to be the cause of knowledge. But these cannot be the objects of knowledge for when we get knowledge of objects through these, we have not the knowledge of the senses or mind. So we cannot accept that a cause of knowledge is the object of knowledge.

सामग्रीविशेषविश्लेषिताखिलावरणमतीन्द्रियमशेषतो मुख्यम् ॥११॥

11. Sāmagrīviśeṣaviśleṣitākhilāvaraṇamatīndriyamaśeṣato mukhyam.

11. Mukhya or supreme (Pratyakṣa) is clear in every respect, has no dependance on any sense and arises after destruction of all obstructions by perfection of Sāmagrī (Dravya, Kṣetra, Kāla and Bhāva).

Commentary

That knowledge which is absolutely clear is called Pāramārthika or Mukhya Pratyakṣa. This is of two kinds, Sakala and Vikala. Vikala Pratyakṣa is subdivided into Avadhi and Manaḥparyaya (which we have previously described)[1].

Vikala Jñāna is knowledge of certain things while Sakala Jnāna is knowledge of all things or omniscience[2]. Sakala Jnāna is also known as Kevala Jñāna. Ordinary individuals do not have this knowledge. According to Jain view it is only the Arhats who can have this knowledge[3]. When Mohanīya or alluring Karmas are destroyed and the Karmas obstructing Jñāna and Darśana are

---

1. "सर्वतो विशदं पारमार्थिकं प्रत्यक्षं। यज्ज्ञानं साकल्येन स्पष्टं तत् पारमार्थिकप्रत्यक्षं मुख्यप्रत्यक्षमिति यावत्। तद्द्विविधं सकलं विकलं च।...तदपि द्विविधं अवधिज्ञानं मनःपर्ययज्ञानं चेति।" Nyāyadīpikā.

2. "तत्र कतिपयविषयं विकलं...सर्वद्रव्यपर्यायविषयं सकलं ॥"

Nyāyadīpikā.

3. "तद्वानर्हन्निर्दोषत्वात्।"

Pramāṇanayatattvālokālaṅkāra. II. 14.

removed and the Antarāyas (obstructive Karmas) are also destroyed, Kevala knowledge arises[1].

Siddhasena defines Mukhya Pratyakṣa as follows: "That which is characterised as free from all obstructions and shines as the absolute is called supreme or transcendental perception; it uninterruptedly illumines the nature of all objects."[2]

In Mukhya Pratyakṣa, knowledge is acquired by the soul direct without the intervention of senses or signs[3].

In Pramāṇanayatattvālokālaṅkāra, the two varieties of Pārmārthika Pratyakṣa viz. Vikala and Sakala have been mentioned. The two subdivisions (Avadhi and Manaḥparyaya Jñāna) of Vikala have also been laid down[4]. Hemachandra defines Kevala

---

1. "मोहक्षयाज्ज्ञानदर्शनावरणान्तरायक्षयाच्च केवलम् ।"

Tattvārthādhigama Sūtra X. 1.

During different stages of development, these Karmas disappear. At the end of the tenth Guṇasthāna, Mohanīya Karmas are destroyed and at the end of the twelfth Guṇasthāna, Antarāya Karmas disappear.

2. Nyāyāvatāra. Tr. by S. C. Vidyābhūṣaṇa Pages 25-26. The original verse is as follows :—

"सकलावरणमुक्तात्मकेवलं यत् प्रकाशते ।
प्रत्यक्षं सकलार्थात्मसततप्रतिभासनम् ॥" Nyāyāvatāra 27.

3. "पारमार्थिकं पुनरुत्पत्तावात्ममात्रापेक्षम् ।"

Pramāṇanayatattvālokālaṅkāra II. 18.

4. "तद्विकलं सकलं च ।"

"तत्र विकलमवधिमनःपर्यायज्ञानतया द्वेधा ।" Ibid. II. 19 and II. 20.

The difference between Avadhi and Manaḥparyaya is shown in the next two aphorisms :

Pratyakṣa as the appearance of the true nature of itself when all the obstructions are thoroughly removed[1]. Hemachandra also mentions that besides Kevala, Avadhi and Manaḥparyaya are also Mukhya Pratyakṣa and Avadhi is of two kinds Bhava-pratyaya and Guṇa-pratyaya. Bhava-pratyaya concerns celestials or inmates of hell and Guṇapratyaya concerns human and sub-human beings[2].

When we establish Kevala Jñāna, we must accept the existence of omniscient beings. So, the celebrated Jain writer Samantabhadra in his work Āpta-mīmāṃsā has laid down :

"सूक्ष्मान्तरितदूरार्थाः प्रत्यक्षाः कस्यचिद् यथा ।
अनुमेयत्वतोऽग्न्यादिरिति सर्वज्ञ-संस्थितिः ॥"

i.e. The existence of an omniscient being is established from the fact that to some beings invisible things like atoms, things or persons remote in time or things far beyond (like the Meru hill) become known as objects of direct perception just like the knowledge of the existence of fire in a hill (which ordinary people know through inference by seeing the smoke) is also the subject of perception.

This knowledge can not be derived through the senses for in that case it could not have cognated all objects, for the senses can only stimulate knowledge of objects which can be perceived by them. So when there is knowledge of things beyond the perception of

---

"अवधिज्ञानावरणविलयविशेषसमुद्भवं भवगुणप्रत्ययं रूपिद्रव्यगोचरमवधिज्ञानम् ।" Ibid II. 21.

"संयमविशुद्धिनिबन्धनाद् विशिष्टावरणविभेदाज्जातं मनोद्रव्यपर्यायालंबनं मनःपर्ययज्ञानम् ।" Ibid II.22.

1. "तत् सर्वथावरणविलये चेतनस्य स्वरूपाविर्भावो मुख्यं केवलम् ।"
Pramāṇa-mīmāṃsā. I. 1. 15

2. "तत्तारतम्येऽवधिमनःपर्ययौ च ।" Ibid I. 1. 18.
"स द्वेधा भवप्रत्ययगुणप्रत्ययश्च ।" Ibid I. 1. 19.

senses it must be held that this arises without the intervention of senses and so it is Atīndriya and acquired by the soul direct.

सावरणत्वे करणजन्य च प्रतिबन्धसम्भवात् ॥ १२ ॥

12. Sāvaraṇatve karaṇajanya cha pratibandhasambhavāt.

12. Obstruction may arise in the case of a knowledge which is caused by senses and which has hindrances.

Commentary

It has been mentioned in the previous aphorism that in Mukhya Pratyakṣa, we have a knowledge absolutely clear in all respects. A question may now be asked "What is the cause which may give rise to such a clearness ?" The answer is "Removal of all obstruction is the cause of clearness." Where there is possibility of obstruction there may be hindrance of knowledge and similarly where there is dependance on the senses knowledge might not arise of things which are beyond the perceptive power of the senses. So in this aphorism the definition of the previous aphorism is supported by saying that we have defined Mukhya Pratyakṣa as not arising through senses and as arising after destruction of hindrances because there is possibility of obstruction of perfect knowledge when hindrances exist or senses are depended on for acquiring knowledge.

The second chapter ends here. In this chapter we have seen that Pratyakṣa Pramāṇa is of two kinds Sāṅvyavahārika and Mukhya. Māṇikyanandi has not given the subdivisions of these two kinds of Pratyakṣa but we have shown from other works on Jain logic that Sāṅvyavahārika Pratyakṣa is of four kinds Avagraha, Īhā, Avāya and Dhāraṇā and Mukhya or Pāramārthika or Atīndriya Pratyakṣa is of two kinds Vikala and Sakala or Kevala. Vikala Pratyakṣa is of two kinds Avadhi and Manaḥparyaya. Avadhi again may be of Bhava-pratyaya or Guṇapratyaya and Manaḥparyaya is of two kinds Riju (the knowledge of simple impressions in the mind of another) and Vipula (the knowledge of all kinds of thoughts and impressions whether simple or complex).

End of Chapter II.

CHART I.

[CHAPTER II]

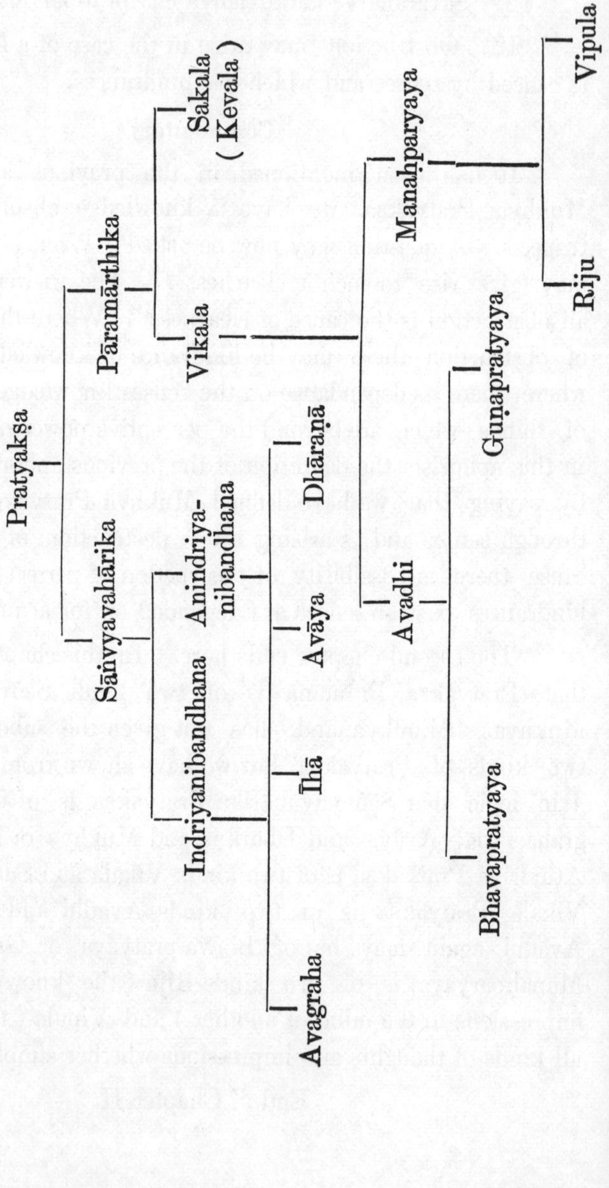
Pratyakṣa
Sāṁvyavahārika
Pāramārthika
Indriyanibandhana
Anindriya-
nibandhana
Vikala
Sakala
(Kevala)
Avagraha
Īhā
Avāya
Dhāraṇā
Avadhi
Manaḥparyaya
Bhavapratyaya
Guṇapratyaya
Riju
Vipula

CHART II.

[Chapter III.]

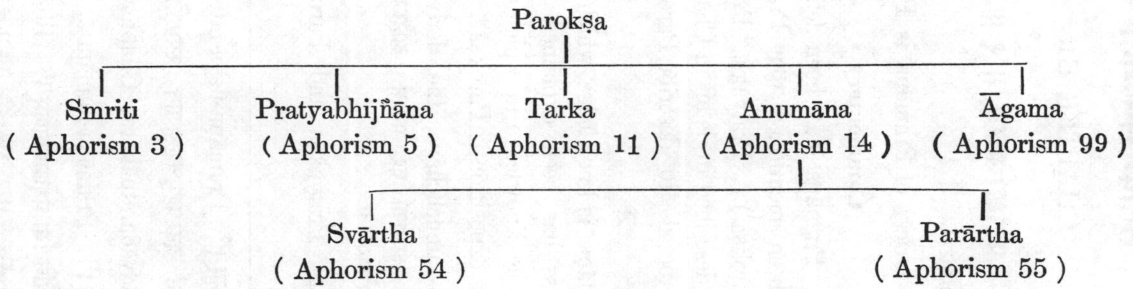

तृतीयः समुद्देशः ।

CHAPTER III.

परोक्षमितरत् ॥ १ ॥

1. Parokṣamitarat.

1. The other variety of Pramāṇa is Parokṣa.

Commentary

In Chapter I Pramāṇa has been defined. In Chapter II, aphorism I it has been mentioned that Pramāṇa is of two kinds (Pratyakṣa and Parokṣa). Pratyakṣa Pramāṇa with its subdivisions has been described in detail in Chapter II. In the third chapter, the author proceeds to describe Parokṣa Pramāṇa with its varieties.

Parokṣa Pramāṇa is knowledge which is not clear.[1]. What is meant by clearness has been explained in Aphorism II. 4 of Parīkṣā-mukhaṃ. The knowledge in which the illumination is not clear according to this exposition is Parokṣa[2].

In Ṣaḍdarśana-samuchchaya, the derivation of Parokṣa has thus been given: "अक्षाणां परं परोक्षं, अक्षेभ्यः परतो वर्त्तत इति वा, परेणेन्द्रियादिना वोक्ष्यते परोक्षम्" ।

In Nyāyāvatāra, Pratyakṣa and Parokṣa have thus been defined:

---

1. "अस्पष्टं परोक्षम् ।" Pramāṇa-naya-tattvālokālaṅkāra III. I.

"स्वपरव्यवसायज्ञानं यदस्पष्टमुक्तलक्षणात् स्पष्टाद्विपरीतमविशदं तत् परोक्ष-मित्यवगन्तव्यम् ।" Syādvādaratnākara, Chapter III. I.

"अविशदः परोक्षम् ।" Pramāṇa-mīmāṃsā, I. 2. I.

"अविशदः सम्यगर्थनिर्णयः परोक्षप्रमाणम् ।" Bhāṣya to Ibid.

"अविशदप्रतिभासं परोक्षम् ।" Nyāya-dīpikā.

2. "यस्य ज्ञानस्य प्रतिभासो विशदो न भवति तत् परोक्षप्रमाणम् ।"

Nyāya-dīpikā.

"Such knowledge that takes cognizance of objects, not beyond the range of the senses, is Pratyakṣa (direct knowledge or perception) ; the other is known as Parokṣa (indirect knowledge) in reference to the manner of taking the cognizance" (Trans. by Dr. S. C. Vidyābhūṣaṇa)[1].

In a note to this Dr. Vidyābhūṣaṇa writes "The words Pratyakṣa (direct knowledge) and Parokṣa (indirect knowledge) have been used here in their ordinary acceptations, namely, the first for sense-perceptions, and the second for inference and verbal testimony. In the ancient Jain Scriptures, however, Pratyakṣa (direct knowledge) signified perfect knowledge acquired by the soul direct through meditation and not through the channels of the senses, while Parokṣa (indirect knowledge) signified knowledge derived through the medium of the senses or signs comprising perception, inference and the verbal testimony." Nyāyāvatāra p. 9.

In defining clearness, Māṇikyanandī has mentioned in Parīkṣā-mukhaṃ II. 4 that in case of clear knowledge there is no existence of any intermediate knowledge. In Parokṣa there is always an intermediate knowledge. For example, Parokṣa Pramāṇa as will be mentioned in the next aphorism is of five kinds : Smriti, Pratyabhijñāna, Tarka, Anumāna and Āgama. Of these Smriti (remembrance) is dependant on a previous experience. Pratyabhijñāna (recognition) depends on Smriti (remembrance) and cognition, Tarka depends on cognition, Smriti and Pratyabhijñāna ; Anumāna depends on recognition of Liṅga (middle term) and Āgama depends on hearing of words. In each variety of Parokṣa

---

1. "अपरोक्षतयार्थस्य ग्राहकं ज्ञानमीदृशम् ।
प्रत्यक्षमितरत् ज्ञेयं परोक्षं ग्रहणेक्षया ॥"

Nyāyāvatāra IV.

This is identical with Verse 86 in Ṣaḍdarśana-samuchchaya of Haribhadra Sūri.

Pramāṇa, therefore, there is a dependance on another cognition while as shown before there is no such dependance in Pratyakṣa Pramāṇa[1].

प्रत्यक्षादिनिमित्तं स्मृतिप्रत्यभिज्ञानतर्कानुमानागमभेदम् ॥ २ ॥

2. Pratyakṣādinimittaṃ smritipratyabhijñānatarkānumānāgamabhedaṃ.

2. (Parokṣa) consists of varieties Smriti, Pratyabhijñāna, Tarka, Anumāna and Āgama and is caused by Pratyakṣa etc.

Commentary

In this aphorism the five kinds of Parokṣa Pramāṇa are enumerated. It is mentioned that all these are caused by Pratyakṣa etc. In Prameya-ratnamālā it is mentioned that by the word "etc."[2] Parokṣa is to be understood as included as a cause. That is to say that some variety of Parokṣa Pramāṇa may be caused by Pratyakṣa Pramāṇa and some may be caused by Pratyakṣa as well as Parokṣa Pramāṇa or only by Parokṣa Pramāṇa. We have mentioned in the commentary on the previous aphorism how each of these varieties of Parokṣa Pramāṇa is dependant on Pratyakṣa and Parokṣa Pramāṇa.

Hemachandra mentions these varieties of Parokṣa mentioning "Ūha" in place of "Tarka" which is merely a synonym[3]. In

---

1. "पंचविधस्याप्यस्य परोक्षस्य प्रत्ययांतरसापेक्षत्वेनैवोत्पत्तिः । तद् यथा, स्मरणस्य प्राक्तनानुभवापेक्षा, प्रत्यभिज्ञानस्य स्मरणानुभवापेक्षा, तर्कस्यानुभवस्मरणप्रत्यभिज्ञानापेक्षा, अनुमानस्य च लिंगदर्शनाद्यपेक्षा, आगमस्य शब्दश्रवणसंकेतग्रहणाद्यपेक्षा । प्रत्यक्षं तु न तथा, स्वातंत्र्येणैवोत्पत्तेः ।" Nyāya-dīpikā.

2. "प्रत्यक्षादिनिमित्तमित्यत्रादिशब्देन परोक्षमपि गृह्यते ।" Prameya-ratna-mālā.

3. "स्मृतिप्रत्यभिज्ञानोहानुमानागमास्तद्विधयः ।"

Pramāṇa-mīmāṃsā, I. 2. 2.

Pramāṇanayatattvālokālaṅkāra, the varieties are the same as mentioned in Parīkṣāmukhaṃ[1].

Maṇibhadra mentioning these five varieties of Pramāṇa adds that Mati-jñāna and Śruta-jñāna also are Parokṣa Pramāṇa[2].

संस्कारोद्बोधनिबन्धना तदित्याकारा स्मृतिः ॥ ३ ॥

3. Saṃskārodbodhanivandhanā tadityākārā smritiḥ.

3. Remembrance is of the form "it is that" produced by the raising up of previous experience.

Commentary

We have mentioned before that when an object with all its particulars is definitely ascertained, we get a lasting impression of the object which is called Dhāraṇā. This impression is the Saṃskāra which enables us to remember the object afterwards. Remembrance consists of the knowledge "this is that" when this impression is aroused by any cognition.

In Pramāṇa-naya-tattvālokālaṅkāra it is mentioned "Remembrance arises from the awakening of the impression regarding an object previously cognised to the effect that this is that"[3]. Hemachandra calls this impression (Saṃskāra) Vāsanā and defining remembrance as caused by the awakening of Vāsanā to the form

---

1. "स्मरणप्रत्यभिज्ञानतर्कानुमानागमभेदतस्तत् पञ्चप्रकारम् ।"

Pramāṇanayatattvālokālaṅkāra, III. 2.

2. "परोक्षं स्मरणप्रत्यभिज्ञानतर्कानुमानागमभेदम् । अमुयैव भङ्ग्या मतिश्रुतज्ञाने अपि परोक्षमेव ।" Commentary on Ṣaḍdarśana-samuchchaya.

Dharmabhūṣaṇa also mentions the same five varieties of Parokṣa thus : "तत् पंचविधं—स्मृतिः प्रत्यभिज्ञानं तर्कोऽनुमानागमश्चेति ।" Nyāyadīpikā.

3. "तत्र संस्कारप्रबोधसंभूतमनुभूतार्थविषयं तदित्याकारं वेदनं स्मरणम् ।"

Pramāṇanayatattvālokālaṅkāra III. 3.

that 'this is that'[1] lays down that though the impression exists always, it does not become the cause of remembrance unless it is awakened from its dormant state by the mitigation or disappearance of the obstructions and cognition of the previously experienced objects[2].

In remembrance, therefore, there must be a previous cognition. For example, when we see a man named Devadatta and subsequently again see him, the impression of him derived at the first cognition is aroused on the second occasion and we have a knowledge "This is that Devadatta". Remembrance cannot arise when there is no previous cognition[3].

The root of remembrance is Dhāraṇā[4]. Avagraha, Īhā and Avāya cannot cause remembrance as there is no Dhāraṇā in these stages of cognition. We have already stated that in the first stage (Avagraha) we have simply a knowledge of an object e. g. a man ; in the second stage (Īhā) we desire to know particulars about the man and in the third stage (Avāya) we find the particulars. It is not until we go to the fourth stage (Dhāraṇā) that we acquire a lasting impression. This Dhāraṇā so modifies the soul that it produces knowledge in that object even after a lapse of time[5].

---

1. "वासनोद्बोधहेतुका तदित्याकारा स्मृतिः ।"

Pramāṇa-mīmāṃsā I. 2. 3.

2. "चिरकालस्थायिन्यपि वासनाऽनुद्बुद्धा न स्मृतिहेतुः, आवरणक्षयोपशमसदृशदर्शनादिसामग्रीलब्धप्रबोधा तु स्मृतिं जनयति ।" Bhāṣya to Ibid.

3. "तत्र का नाम स्मृतिः ? तदित्याकारा प्रागनुभूतवस्तुविषया स्मृतिः । यथा स देवदत्त इति । अत्र हि प्रागनुभूत एव देवदत्तस्तत्तया प्रतीयते, तस्मादेषा प्रतीतिस्तत्तोल्लेखिन्यनुभूतविषया च, अननुभूतविषये तदनुत्पत्तेः ।" Nyāya-dīpikā.

4. "स्मृति-हेतुर्धारणा ।" Pramāṇa-mīmāṃsā I. I. 29.

"तन्मूलं चानुभवो धारणारूप एव ।" Nyāyadīpikā.

5. "अवग्रहाद्यनुभूतेऽपि धारणाया अभावे स्मृतिजननायोगात् । धारणा हि तथात्मानं संस्करोति यथासावात्मा कालान्तरेऽपि तस्मिन् विषये ज्ञानमुत्पादयति ।" Nyāya-dīpikā.

One may object that Smriti can never be Pramāṇa as it cognises an object already once cognised. The reply to this is that this objection is not maintainable. For as the different stages of Avagraha, Īhā, Avāya and Dhāraṇā are Pramāṇas though an object is perceived through these stages owing to peculiarities of each stage as distinct from those in other stages, so remembrance having a peculiarity viz. the knowledge "this is that" is a separate Pramāṇa being not identical with the simple knowledge of an object on the first occasion[1]. Further, remembrance is opposed to forgetfulness, doubt etc. and so is recognised as a separate Pramāṇa[2].

Again, when one sees smoke and infers a fire, he goes to the spot to get fire if he wants it. Here the knowledge of fire is at first Parokṣa Pramāṇa being caused by inference and then when the person goes to the spot and sees the fire with his eyes, there is Pratyakṣa Pramāṇa. If we say that there cannot be any Pramāṇa when there is a first cognition, this Pratyakṣa knowledge of fire which follows an inference of fire does not also become Pramāṇa[3].

स देवदत्तो यथा ॥ ४ ॥

4. Sa devadatto yathā.

4. As for example, "This is Devadatta".

Commentary

This is an example of remembrance defined in the previous aphorism. When one sees a man named Devadatta previously seen

---

1. "नन्वेवं धारणागृहीत एव स्मरणस्योत्पत्तौ गृहीतग्राहित्वादप्रामाण्यं प्रसज्यत इति चेन्न, विषयविशेषसद्भावादीहादिवत्। यथा हि अवग्रहादिगृहीत-विषयानामीहादीनां विषयविशेषसद्भावात् स्वविषयसमारोपव्यवच्छेदकत्वेन प्रामाण्यं तथा स्मरणस्यापि धारणागृहीतविषयप्रवृत्तावपि प्रामाण्यमेव। धारणाया हीदन्ता-वच्छिन्नो विषयः, स्मरणस्य तु तत्तावच्छिन्नः।" Nyāya-dipikā.

2. "विस्मरणसंशयविपर्यासलक्षणः समारोपोऽस्ति तन्निराकरणाच्चास्याः स्मृतेः प्रामाण्यम्।" Prameyakamala-mārtaṇḍa.

3. "यदि चानुभूते प्रवृत्तमित्येतावता स्मरणप्रमाणं स्यात्, तर्हि अनुमिते अग्नौ पश्चात् प्रवृत्तं प्रत्यक्षमपि अप्रमाणं स्यात्।" Nyāya-dipikā.

and remembers that this is Devadatta we have Smriti. In Pramāṇanayatattvālokālaṅkāra, this example is given "As for example, this is that image of the Tīrthaṅkara"[1].

दर्शनस्मरणकारणकं संकलनं प्रत्यभिज्ञानम्, तदेवेदं तत्सदृशं तद्विलक्षणं तत्प्रतियोगीत्यादि ॥ ५ ॥

5. Darśanasmaraṇakāraṇakaṃ saṃkalanaṃ pratyabhijñānaṃ tadevedaṃ tatsadriśaṃ tadvilakṣaṇaṃ tatpratiyogītyādi.

यथा स एवायं देवदत्तः ॥ ६ ॥

6. Yathā sa evāyaṃ devadattaḥ.

गोसदृशो गवयः ॥ ७ ॥

7. Go-sadriśo gavayaḥ.

गोविलक्षणो महिषः ॥ ८ ॥

8. Go-vilakṣaṇo mahiṣaḥ.

इदमस्माद् दूरम् ॥ ९ ॥

9. Idamasmād dūraṃ.

वृक्षोऽयमित्यादि ॥ १० ॥

10. Vrikṣoyamityādi.

5. Pratyabhijñāna is the deduction following from Darśana and Smriti e. g. this is verily that, this is like that, this is different from that, this is opposite to that etc.

6. As for example, this is that Devadatta.

7. A Gavaya is like a cow.

8. A buffalo is different from a cow.

9. This is far from this.

10. This is a tree etc.

---

1. "तत्तीर्थंकरविम्बमिति यथा।"

Pramāṇa-naya-tattvālokālaṅkāra III. 4.

Commentary

In Pratyabhijñāna, we recognise an object by noticing similarities and differences. The differences between Smriti and Pratyabhijñāna may be illustrated thus. We see a certain man. We then remember that we have seen him previously. This is Smriti or Smaraṇa. Then if we deduce that this is that very man named Devadatta, we have Pratyabhijñāna. Again, we may go to a forest and see a strange creature like a Gavaya. Then we remember that we have read or heard about such a creature and deduce from its similarities with a cow and the description read or heard before, that this is a Gavaya. We notice the characteristics of a buffalo and distinguish it from a cow. We judge the distance of an object and say that this is far or near. We decide that this is a tree or other object. All these and others are examples of Pratyabhijñāna.

In Hindu philosophics, a deduction from similarities has been recognised as a separate Pramāṇa named Upamāna[1]. The Jain

---

1. "उपमितिकरणमुपमानम्। तच्च सादृश्यज्ञानात्मकम्। उपमितित्व-जातिमत्युपमितिः। कथमियम् उत्पद्यत इति चेदुच्यते। गवयमजानन् कश्चिन्नागरिकः कंचिद्वनेचरं कीदृशो गवयपदवाच्य इति पृच्छति। ततस्तेनोक्तो गोसदृशो गवयपदवाच्य इत्युत्तरितः स कदाचिद् वनं गतो गोसदृशं पिंडं पश्यन् प्रागुक्तातिदेशवाक्यार्थं स्मृत्वासौ गवयपदवाच्य इति प्रतिपद्यते सोपमितिः।" Tarka-kaumudi

"तत्र सादृश्यप्रमाकरणमुपमानम्। तथाहि नगरेषु दृष्टगोपिण्डस्य पुरुषस्य वनं गतस्य गवयेन्द्रियसन्निकर्षे सति भवति प्रतीतिः अयं पिंडो गोसदृश इति। तदनन्तरञ्च भवति निश्चयः अनेन सदृशी मदीया गौरिति।" Vedānta-paribhāṣā. Chapter IV.

"Comparison or the recognition of likeness, is the cause of an inference from similarity. Such an inference consists in the knowledge of relation between a name and the thing so named. Its instrument is the knowledge of a likeness. The recollection of the purport of a statement of resemblance is the operation of that instrument. For example, a person not knowing what is meant by view is that there is no necessity to recognise a separate Pramāṇa named Upamāna arising from noticing similarities as this can be included within Pratyabhijñāna and not only similarities but dissimilarities (e. g. those distinguishing a buffalo from a cow) and knowledge of distance or nearness is got from Pratyabhijñāna. Dharmabhūṣaṇa summarises this and a detailed exposition of the same has been made by Prabhāchandra[1].

Hemachandra has followed the definition of Pratyabhijñāna as laid down in Parīkṣā-mukhaṃ[2]. The substance of the definition in Pramāṇa-nayatattvālokālaṅkāra is the same though the language is somewhat different[3].

---

the word Gavaya having heard from some inhabitant of the forest that a Gavaya is like a cow, goes to the forest. Remembering the purport of what he has been told, he sees a body like that of a cow. Then this inference from similarity arises (in his mind) that this is what is meant by the word Gavaya." Tarka-saṅgraha, Translated by Jacob. Page 12.

1. "सादृश्यप्रत्यभिज्ञानमुपमानाख्यं पृथक् प्रमाणमिति केचित् कथयन्ति तदसत्। स्मृत्यनुभवपूर्वकसंकलनज्ञानत्वेन प्रत्यभिज्ञानत्वानतिवृत्तेः। अन्यथा गोविलक्षणो महिष इत्यादिविसदृशत्वप्रत्ययस्य इदमस्माद दूरम् इत्यादेश्च प्रत्ययस्य सप्रतियोगिकस्य पृथक्-प्रमाणत्वं स्यात्। ततो वैसादृश्यादि-प्रत्ययवत् सादृश्यप्रत्ययस्यापि प्रत्यभिज्ञानलक्षणाक्रान्तत्वेन प्रत्यभिज्ञानत्वमेवेति प्रामाणिकपद्धतिः।"

Nyāya-dīpikā.

"गोसदृशगवयाभिधानयोर्वाच्यवाचकसंबंधं प्रतिपद्य पुनर्गवयदर्शनात् तत्प्रतिपत्तिः प्रत्यभिज्ञा किं नेष्यते ?" Prameyakamala-mārtaṇḍa.

2 "दर्शनस्मरणसंभवं तदेवेदं तत्सदृशं तद्विलक्षणं तत्प्रतियोगीत्यादिसंकलनं प्रत्यभिज्ञानम्।" Pramāṇa-mīmāṃsā I. 2. 4.

3. "अनुभवस्मृतिहेतुकं तिर्यगूर्ध्वतासामान्यादिगोचरं संकलनात्मकं ज्ञानं प्रत्यभिज्ञानम्।"

"यथा तज्जातीय एवायं गोपिण्डो गोसदृशो गवयः स एवायं जिनदत्त इत्यादि।"

Pramāṇanayatattvālokālaṅkāra. III. 5. 6.

In the tenth aphorism, the word "etc." has been used. In Prameya-ratna-mālā, it is mentioned that by this word the recognition of other objects from distinguishing characteristics is included. For example, a swan is recognised from its power of separating milk from water, a bee is recognised from having six legs, a Saptaparṇa tree is recognised from having seven leaves, a Mechaka jewel is recognised from its having five colours, a young woman is recognised from her high breasts, a rhinoceros is recognised from its single horn, a Śarabha (a fabulous creature) is recognised from its eight legs and a lion is recognised from its manes"[1].

उपलम्भानुपलम्भनिमित्तं व्याप्तिज्ञानमूहः ॥११॥

11. Upalambhānupalambhanimittaṃ vyāptijñānamūhaḥ.

इदमस्मिन् सत्येव भवत्यसति न भवत्येवेति च ॥१२॥

12. Idamasmin satyeva bhavatyasati na bhavatyeveti cha.

यथाग्नावेव धूमस्तदभावे न भवत्येवेति च ॥१३॥

13. Yathāgnāveva dhūmastadabhāve na bhavatyeveti cha.

11. The knowledge of universal concomitance arising from finding and not finding, is Ūha (or Tarka).

17. Such as, this exists when that exists and this does not exist when that does not exist.

13. For example, smoke exists only in fire and when there is no fire, there is no smoke.

---

1. "पयोंबुभेदी हंसः स्यात् षट्पदैः भ्रमरः स्मृतः ।
सप्तपर्णैस्तु तत्त्वज्ञैर्विज्ञेयो विषमच्छदः ॥
पंचवर्णैर्भवेद् रत्नं मेचकाख्यं पृथुस्तनी ।
युवतिश्चैकशृंगोऽपि गण्डकः परिकीर्त्तितः ॥
शरभोऽप्यष्टभिः पादैः सिंहश्चारुसटान्वितः ॥"

Verses quoted in Prameya-ratnamālā.

Commentary

From this aphorism, begins the most important subject of inference which attracted the subtle brains of all the Jain, Hindu and Buddhist logicians. In this aphorism Vyāptijñāna (the knowledge of universal concomitance) which is the basis of all inference is defined. It should be remembered that in Hindu Nyāya philosophy Tarka is defined as a special kind of knowledge (Sambhāvanā). Vātsyāyana and Uddyotakara have followed this interpretation in their commentaries on the Nyāyasūtra of Gautama. The later writers like Udayana also define Tarka as a special kind of objection. But in Jain logic Tarka is defined as knowledge of universal concomitance. In Nyāya-dıpikā we find "The knowledge of universal concomitance is Tarka"[1].

Vyāpti (universal concomitance) is a kind of relation-ship between the middle term and the major term. The middle term is technically called(as will be seen later on) Hetu, Liṅga or Sādhana. The major term is known as Sādhya or Vyāpaka· The minor term is known as Pakṣa. Vyāpti is also called Avinābhāva[2]. The example given universally to explain Vyāpti is this : 'Where there is smoke, there is fire'.

In other words, Tarka is a separate Pramāṇa which is instrumental in producing a knowledge of Vyāpti or Abinābhāva[3]. In Śloka-vārttika it is mentioned "Tarka is the instrumental cause of the result consisting of cessation of ignorance regarding the relationship of the major term and the middle term"[4].

Ūha is another name of Tarka[5].

---

1. "व्याप्तिज्ञानं तर्कः ।" Nyāya-dīpikā.

2. "साध्यसाधनयोर्गम्यगमकभावप्रयोजको व्यभिचारगंधासहिष्णुः संबंधविशेषो व्याप्तिरविनाभाव इति च व्यपदिश्यते ।" Nyāya-dīpikā.

3. "तस्याश्चाविनाभावापरनाम्न्या व्याप्तेः प्रमितौ यत् साधकतमं तदिदं तर्काख्यं पृथक् प्रमाणम् ।" Nyāya-dīpikā.

4. "साध्यसाधनसंबंध्यज्ञाननिवृत्तरूपे हि फले साधकतमस्तर्कः ।"
Śloka-vārttika.

5. "ऊह इति तर्कस्यैव व्यपदेशान्तरम् ।" Nyāya-dīpikā.

Tarka or Ūha concludes the presence or absence of one thing in connection with another in all places and times. We find fire when we see smoke. After constant knowledge of this kind we conclude that in all places and at all times smoke is inseparable from fire. This Tarka Pramāṇa is different from Pratyakṣa in which the relationship of fire and smoke is perceived only in a place which is near but no knowledge of universal concomitance arises from Pratyakṣa[1].

In Pramāṇanayatattvālokālaṅkāra, it has been mentioned "Tarka which is also called Ūha is knowledge produced from finding and not finding, dependant on the relationship of the major term and the middle term in the past, present and future viz. that this happens on that. As for example, wherever there is some smoke, this must be on account of the existence of fire and when it (i.e. fire) does not exist, this (smoke) does not exist"[2].

Hemachandra's definition of Tarka or Ūha is identical with that in Parīkṣā-mukhaṃ[3].

In the relation of two things like smoke and fire, one object (e. g. smoke) is called Vyāpya, and the other (e. g. fire) is known as Vyāpaka. Hemachandra therefore defines Vyāpti thus : "Vyāpti is existence of Vyāpaka whenever there is Vyāpya or the existence of Vyāpya whenever there is Vyāpaka"[4].

---

1. "अत्र हि धूमे सति भूयोऽग्न्युपलंभे, सर्वत्र सर्वदा धूमोऽग्निं न व्यभिचरति, एवं सर्वोपसंहारेणाविनाभावविज्ञानं पश्चादुत्पन्नं तर्काख्यं प्रत्यक्षादेः पृथगेव। प्रत्यक्षस्य सन्निहितदेश एव धूमाग्निसंबंधप्रकाशनान्न व्याप्तिप्रकाशकत्वम्।" Nyāya-dīpikā.

2. "उपलंभानुपलंभसंभवं त्रिकालीकलितसाध्यसाधनसंबध्याद्यालंवनमिदमस्मिन्सत्येव भवतीत्याद्याकारं संवेदनमूहापरनामा तर्कः ॥

"यथा यावान् कश्चिद् धूमः स सर्वो वह्नौ सत्येव भवतीति तस्मिन्नसत्यौ न भवत्येवेति ॥" Pramāṇanayatattvālokālaṅkāra. III. 7. 8.

3. "उपलंभानुपलंभनिमित्तं व्याप्तिज्ञानमूहः।" Pramāṇa-mimāṃsā. I. 2. 5.

4. "व्याप्तिर्व्यापकस्य व्याप्ये सति भाव एव व्याप्यस्य वा तत्रैव भावः।" Pramāṇa-mimāṃsā. 1. 2. 6.

साधनात् साध्यविज्ञानमनुमानम् ॥१४॥

14. Sādhanāt sādhyavijñānamanumānam.

14. Anumāna (inference) is the knowledge of Sādhya (the major term) from Sādhana (the middle term).

Commentary

A definition of Sādhana will be given in the next aphorism and Sādhya will be defined in aphorism 20.

Sādhana as we have already mentioned is the middle term and Sādhya the major term. In inference we have a knowledge of Sādhya (e. g. fire) from Sādhana (e. g. smoke). The syllogism will be detailed later on.

It may be mentioned here that in Hindu philosophies like the Nyāya and Vaiśeṣika systems, the knowledge derived from Anumāna Pramāṇa is called Anumiti but in Jain logic, the knowledge itself is called Anumāna. The result of Anumāna, according to Jain logic, is the cessation of ignorance. Māṇikya-nandī has devoted a separate chapter (Samuddeśa V) where the result of Pramāṇas is discussed in detail. We shall deal with this subject there.

Hemachandra and Dharma-bhūṣaṇa's definition of Anumāna is the same as mentioned in this aphorism[1]. In Śloka-vārttika it is mentioned "The wise know Anumāna to be the knowledge of Sādhya from sādhana"[2]. The Sādhana must be Jñāyamāna (in a knowing state) to produce Anumāna. Otherwise no inference can arise. For example, to a sleeping man, smoke cannot give rise

1. "साधनात् साध्यविज्ञानमनुमानम् ।"

Pramāṇa-mīmāṃsā I. 2. 7 and Nyāya-dīpikā.

2. "साधनात् साध्यविज्ञानमनुमानं विदुर्बुधाः ।" Śloka-vārttika.

to an inference of fire[1]. Sādhana is also known as Liṅga or Hetu. Vātsyāyana in his Bhāṣya on Nyāya-sūtras of Gautama (I. 1. 3) has mentioned "Anumāna is the subsequent knowing of the Liṅgī (e. g. fire) by the Liṅga (e. g. smoke) in its knowing state"[2]. Udayanāchārya while explaining "Talliṅgamanu-māpakaṃ" of the Praśastapādabhāṣya has mentioned that Jñāyamāna liṅga is the instrumental cause of Anumāna[3].

It appears from the Vaiśeṣika Sūtra of Kaṇāda[4] and the statement of Praśastapāda the writer of the Bhāṣya on the Vaiśeṣika Sūtras[5] that they also admit that inference results from Jñāyamāna Liṅga.

साध्याविनाभावित्वेन निश्चितो हेतुः ॥१५॥

15. Sādhyāvinābhāvitvena niśchito hetuḥ.

15. Hetu (or Sādhana or Liṅga) is that which is fixed in concomitance with Sādhya.

Commentary

In this aphorism Sādhana is defined. That which cannot be without Sādhya is Sādhana or Hetu, e. g. smoke which can never

---

1. "साधनाज्ज्ञायमानाद् धूमादेः साध्येऽग्न्यादौ लिंगिनि यद्विज्ञानं तदनुमानम्। अज्ञायमानस्य तस्य साध्यज्ञानजनकत्वे हि सुप्तादीनामप्यग्न्यादिज्ञानोत्पत्तिप्रसंगः।" Nyāya-dīpikā.

2. "मितेन लिंगेन लिंगिनोऽर्थस्य पश्चान्मानमनुमानम्।"

Vātsyāyana-Bhāṣya.

3. "अनुमितिरूपप्रमाकरणम्। एतेन परामृष्यमाणं लिंगमनुमानम्।"

Guṇa-Kiraṇāvali.

4. "हेतुरपदेशो लिंगं प्रमाणं करणमित्यनर्थान्तरम्।"

Vaiśeṣika Sūtra. 9. 2. 4.

5. "अनुमेयेन संबंधं प्रसिद्धं च तदन्विते।
तदभावे च नास्त्येव तल्लिंगमनुमापकम्॥" Praśastapāda.

be without fire. This is also known as Liṅga (sign or mark) and is the same as the middle term of a syllogism.

Kumāranandi Bhaṭṭāraka has mentioned "A Liṅga has the characteristic of being non-existent otherwise" ("अन्यथानुपपत्त्येकलक्षणं लिंगमभ्येत ।") e. g. smoke is non-existent otherwise than with fire. In Pramāṇa-naya-tattvālokālaṅkāra the same view is expressed[1]. In other words, a Sādhana can exist only in relation with Sādhya. It is therefore the determinant of Sādhya.

सहक्रमभावनियमोऽविनाभावः ॥ १६ ॥

16. Sahakramabhāvaniyamo a-vinābhāvaḥ.

16. Avinābhāva (or Vyāpti) is the rule of co-existence or the existence of one following the other (being related as cause and effect).

Commentary

Vyāpti, which has already been explained before, is here described as being of two kinds being connected in co-existence or in existence of one after another as in the case of a cause and its effect. These are being elucidated in the aphorisms which follow. Hemachandra also defines Avinābhāva in a similar manner[2].

सहचारिणोर्व्याप्यव्यापकयोश्च सहभावः ॥ १७ ॥

17. Sahachārinorvyāpyavyāpakayośca sahabhāvaḥ.

17. Sahabhāva exists in objects co-existent or in objects Vyāpya and Vyāpaka.

---

1. "निश्चितान्यथानुपपत्त्येकलक्षणो हेतुः ॥"

Pramāṇa-nayatattvālokālaṅkāra III. 11.

2. "सहक्रमभाविनोः सहक्रमभावनियमोऽविनाभावः ।"

Pramāṇa-mimāṃsā 1. 2. 10.

Commentary

The universal concomitance as exemplified by Sahabhāva can be seen in the form and colour in a fruit or being a tree and being a Śiṃśapā (a kind of tree). The former is an example of co-existence and the latter a relationship of Vyāpya and Vyāpaka[1].

पूर्वोत्तरचारिणोः कार्यकारणयोश्च क्रमभावः ॥ १८ ॥

18. Pūrvottaracharinoḥ kāryakāraṇayośchа kramabhāvaḥ.

18. Krama-bhāva exists in cases when one follows the other or in the case of cause and effect.

Commentary

The example commonly given in Jain logic of one following the other is : the constellation Krittikā is followed by the constellation Rohiṇī. The example of cause and effect is given as smoke following fire[2].

तर्कात्तन्निर्णयः ॥ १९ ॥

19. Tarkāt tannirṇayaḥ.

19. This is ascertained by Tarka.

Commentary

We have already explained that by Tarka (universal concomitance) inference is caused. The Jain philosophers sometimes hold that cause and effect are the same (Abheda) and according to such a view though universal concomitance itself is called Tarka, it is mentioned in this aphorism that Tarka determines universal concomitance. Hemachandra also holds this view[3].

---

1. "सहचारिणोः रूपरसयोः व्याप्यव्यापकयोश्च वृक्षत्वशिंशपात्वयोरिति ।" Prameya-ratna-mālā.

2. "पूर्वोत्तरचारिणोः कृत्तिकोदयशकटोदययोः कार्यकारणयोश्च धूमधूमध्वजयोः क्रमभावः ।" Prameya-ratna-mālā.

3. "ऊहात्तन्निश्चयः ।" Pramāṇa-mimāṃsā I. 2. 11.

इष्टमबाधितमसिद्धं साध्यम् ॥ २० ॥

20. Iṣṭamabādhitamasiddhaṃ sādhyaṃ.

सन्दिग्धविपर्यस्ताव्युत्पन्नानां साध्यत्वं यथा स्यादित्यसिद्धपदम् ॥ २१ ॥

21. Sandigdhaviparyastāvyutpannānāṃ sādhyatvaṃ yathā syādityasiddhapadaṃ.

अनिष्टाध्यक्षादिबाधितयोः साध्यत्वं माभूदितीष्टाबाधितवचनम् ॥ २२ ॥

22. Aniṣṭādhyakṣādivādhitayoḥ sādhyatvaṃ mā bhūditiṣṭāvādhitavachanaṃ.

न चासिद्धवदिष्टं प्रतिवादिनः ॥ २३ ॥

23. Na chāsiddhavadiṣṭaṃ prativādinaḥ.

प्रत्यायनाय हीच्छा वक्तुरेव ॥ २४ ॥

24. Pratyāyanāya hīchchhā vaktureva.

20. Sādhya is what is desired and what is Abādhita (i. e. opposed to Pratyakṣa etc.) and what is not Siddha (already established).

21. The word "Asiddha" has been used in defining Sādhya so that the doubtful, the false and the not understood may become Sādhya.

22 The words "Iṣṭa" and "Abādhita" have been used so that what is not desired and what is opposed to Pratyakṣa etc. might not be (included in the definition of) Sādhya.

23. In the case of an adversary, "Iṣṭa" is not required like "Asiddha".

24. The intention to explain exists only in the speaker.

Commentary

Sādhya (the major term) is defined in Aphorism 20. That which one wishes to establish is Sādhya. For example, we want to establish fire when we see smoke. So fire is Sādhya. But it should be noted that there should not be any Bādhā (hindrance). Hemachandra has mentioned that Bādhā is of six kinds (i) that which is opposed to Pratyakṣa (ii) that which is opposed to Anumāna (iii) that which is opposed to Āgama (iv) that which is opposed to popular belief (v) that which is opposed to one's own words and (vi) that which is opposed to belief[1]

That which is opposed to Pratyakṣa is thus illustrated. If one says that fire is cold, honey is not sweet, jasmine flowers are not sweet-scented, a pitcher is invisible etc. we have examples of Pratyakṣabādhā. The instance of Bādhā by Anumāna is : "The palm of the hand is hairy". Āgama-bādhā is what is against the injunctions of scriptures, for example, "Dharma does not produce happiness after death". It is enjoined in the scriptures that Dharma leads to happiness after death. Loka-bādhā is what is against popular belief. For example, "The skull of a human being is a clean object". The popular belief in this case is that skulls of human beings are unclean objects. Bādhā regarding one's own words are exemplified in "My mother is barren." That which is against belief is Pratīti-bādhā e. g. Chandra (the moon) is not Śaśī (the moon) We know that Chandra and Śaśī are synonyms signifying the moon[2].

---

1. "प्रत्यक्षानुमानागमलोकस्ववचनप्रतीतयो बाधाः ॥"

Pramāṇa-mīmāṃsā I. 2. 14.

2. "तत्र प्रत्यक्षबाधा यथा अनुष्णोऽग्निः, न मधु मधुरं, न सुगंधि विदलन्-मालतीमुकुलं, अचाक्षुषो घटः, अश्रावणः शब्दः, नास्ति बहिरर्थ इत्यादि। अनुमान-बाधा यथा, सरोम हस्ततलं, नित्यः शब्द इति वा।...आगमबाधा यथा प्रेत्यासुखप्रदो धर्म इति, परलोके सुखप्रदत्वं धर्मस्य सर्वागमसिद्धम्। लोकबाधा यथा, शुचि नरशिरः-कपालमिति, लोके हि नरशिरःकपालादीनां अशुचित्वं सुप्रसिद्धं। स्ववचनबाधा

Śadhya again should be one not previously established. Objects in cases of doubt e. g. when we are not certain whether this is a post or a man, cases of mistake e. g. when we mistake nacre to be silver and cases where we have no clear knowledge as when we merely touch a thing while going without clearly perceiving what it is, can become Sādhya. For, in these cases we establish by inference what the real thing is.

The three adjectives "Iṣṭa", "Abādhita" and "Asiddha" are therefore necessary. These have been termed "Abhīpsita", "Anirākrita" and "Apratīta" in Prameya-naya-tattvālokālaṅkāra[1] and "Sisādhayiṣita", "Abādhya" and "Asiddha" by Hemachandra[2].

Some may say, you have mentioned that what is desired is Sādhya. The desire of human beings is to sit, lie down, eat, go etc. So these should be Sādhya. In Prameyaratnamālā this is refuted by saying that by desire is meant the desire in connection with Sādhana. The meaning is to be understood according to the context. When we see a Sādhana (e. g. smoke) we desire to know of what this is a sign and the desired object inferred from the Sādhana (e. g. fire) is the Sādhya[3].

यथा माता मे बन्ध्येति। प्रतीतिबाधा यथा, अचन्द्रः शशीति, अत्र शशिनश्चन्द्रशब्द-वाच्यत्वं प्रतीतिसिद्धम् इति प्रतीति-बाधा।" Pramāṇa-Mīmāṃsā Bhāṣya to 1. 2. 14.

1. "अप्रतीतमनिराकृतमभीप्सितं साध्यम्॥ शंकितविपरीतानध्यवसितवस्तूनां साध्यताप्रतिपत्त्यर्थमप्रतीतवचनम्॥ प्रत्यक्षादिविरुद्धस्य साध्यत्वं मा प्रसज्यता-मित्यनिराकृतग्रहणम्॥ अनभिप्रेतस्यासाध्यत्वप्रतिपत्तयेऽभीप्सितपदोपादानम्॥"

Pramāṇanayatattvālokālaṅkāra. III. 14-17

2. "सिसाधयिषितमसिद्धमबाध्यं साध्यं पक्षः॥"

Pramāṇa-mīmāṃsā I. 1. 13.

3. "अत्रापरे दूषणमाचक्षते, आसनशयनभोजनयाननिधुवनादेरपीष्टत्वात्तदपि साध्यमनुषज्यत इति। तेऽप्यतिवालिशा अप्रस्तुतप्रलापित्वात्। अत्र हि साधनमधि-क्रियते। तेन साधनविषयत्वेनेप्सितमिष्टमुच्यते।" Prameya-ratna-mālā.

This adjective "Iṣṭa" (desired) is to be taken in connection with one's own intention. For, the person wishing to know fire from the smoke has this desire. When the inference of fire from smoke is explained to another person (who is technically called Prativādī), the Sādhya (fire) is not "Iṣṭa" to the latter. All the adjectives are not applicable to all parties but some to some parties according to use[1]. Hemachandra has used the word "सिसाधयिषितम्" explaining it as "साधयितुमिष्टं" (i. e. desired to establish) to evade this controversy in his definition of Sādhya.

Akalaṅka Deva in Nyāya-viniśchaya has thus defined Sādhya :—

"साध्यं शक्यमभिप्रेतमप्रसिद्धं ततोऽपरं ।
साध्याभासं विरुद्धादि साधनाविषयात्वतः ॥"

i. e. "Sādhya is Śakya (fit to be established not being opposed to Pramāṇa etc.), Abhipreta or Iṣṭa (desired) and Aprasiddha or Asiddha (like objects in cases of doubt, mistake or non-distinction). The opposite to Sādhya is Sādhyābhāsa. These are Viruddha (opposed to Pratyakṣa etc) etc. because these cannot be made known by Sādhana."

In Śloka-vārttika Sādhana and Sādhya have been similarly defined :

"अन्यथानुपपत्त्येकलक्षणं तत्र साधनं ।
साध्यं शक्यमभिप्रेतमप्रसिद्धमुदाहृतं ॥"

i. e. "the characteristic of Sādhana is that it does not arise otherwise and "Sādhya is Śakya, Abhipreta and Aprasiddha."

Dharmabhūṣaṇa also has followed these definitions[2].

---

1. "न हि सर्वं सर्वापेक्षया विशेषणम्, अपि तु किंचित् कमप्युद्दिश्य भवतीति।...यथा असिद्धं प्रतिवाद्यपेक्षया न तथेष्टम् इत्यर्थः।"

Prameyaratnamālā.

2. "शक्यमभिप्रेतमप्रसिद्धं साध्यं। यत्प्रत्यक्षादिप्रमाणाबाधितत्वेन साधयितुं शक्यं, वाद्यभिमतत्वेनाभिप्रेतं, संदेहाद्याक्रान्तत्वेनाप्रसिद्धं तदेव साध्यम्।" Nyāyadīpikā.

साध्यं धर्मः क्वचित्तद्विशिष्टो वा धर्मी ॥२५॥

25. Sādhyaṃ dharmaḥ kvachittadviśiṣṭo vā dharmī.

25. Sādhya is a Dharma and sometimes it is Dharmi in which there is the abode of the Dharma.

Commentary

In our familiar example we have seen that fire is the Sādhya (or the major term). Now, a distinction is being made. It is urged that when we have a knowledge of universal concomitance, Sādhya is a Dharma. For in such cases we hold : wherever there is smoke there is fire. Here Sādhya is fire. But after the inferential process we have the Dharmī (e.g. the mountain in which the fire is) which is the abode of the Dharma (Sādhya) as described above. This Dharmī is technically called the Pakṣa (the minor term) as will be mentioned in the next aphorism. When Sādhya is merely Dharma, there is no knowledge of Dharmī. For example, whenever we see smoke, we have an idea of fire but not of mountain or other object containing the fire. It is only when Sādhya is Dharmī, that we have the idea of the thing which is the abode of Dharma which is technically called Pakṣa[1].

पक्ष इति यावत् ॥ २६ ॥

26. Pakṣa iti yāvat.

26. This is also known as Pakṣa (the minor term).

Commentary

It has been explained in the previous aphorism that the Dharmī containing the Dharma of Sādhya is called Pakṣa. For

---

1. "साध्यं साध्यधर्मविशिष्टो धर्मी क्वचित्तु धर्मः ।" Pramāṇa-mīmāṃsā I. 2. 15

"व्याप्तिग्रहणसमयापेक्षया साध्यं धर्म एवान्यथा तदनुपपत्तेः ॥
न हि यत्र यत्र धूमस्तत्र चित्रभानोरिव धरित्रीधरस्याप्यनुवृत्तिरस्ति ॥
आनुमानिकप्रतिपत्त्यवसरापेक्षया तु पक्षापरपर्यायस्तद्विशिष्टः प्रसिद्धो धर्मी ॥"

Pramāṇanayatattvālokālaṅkāra III. 19-21

example, a mountain is Pakṣa as in it there is fire (Sādhya). In other words when we want to separate Dharma and Dharmī, we say that Sādhya is Dharma (viz. in the case of fire) but when we do not want to separate Dharma from Dharmī, we say that Sādhya is Dharmī or Pakṣa (e. g. the mountain in which there is abode of fire).

प्रसिद्धो धर्मी ॥ २७ ॥

27. Prasiddho dharmī.

27. Dharmi is well known.

Commentary

A Dharmī is known sometimes by Pramāṇa, sometimes by Vikalpa (imagination) and sometimes both by Vikalpa and Pramāṇa[1]. Hemachandra writes that a Dharmī is Pramāṇa-siddha as well as Buddhi-siddha[2].

The example of knowledge of a Dharmī by Vikalpa is : "There exists an omniscient being". The example of knowledge of a Dharmī by Pramāṇa is : "This mountain has fire." The example of knowledge of a Dharmī both by Pramāṇa and Vikalpa is "Sound is not eternal"[3].

विकल्पसिद्धे तस्मिन् सत्तेतरे साध्ये ॥ २८ ॥

28. Vikalpa-siddhe tasmin sattetare sādhye.

अस्ति सर्वज्ञो नास्ति खरविषाणम् ॥ २९ ॥

29. Asti sarvajño nāsti kharaviṣāṇaṃ.

---

1. "प्रसिद्धत्वं च धर्मिणः क्वचित् प्रमाणात्, क्वचिद्विकल्पात्, क्वचित्-प्रमाणविकल्पाभ्याम् ।" Nyāyadīpikā.

"क्वचिद्विकल्पतः कुत्रचित् प्रमाणतः क्वापि विकल्पप्रमाणाभ्याम् ।"

Pramāṇanayatattvālokālaṅkāra III. 21

2. "धर्मी प्रमाणसिद्धः ॥ बुद्धिसिद्धोऽपि ॥"

Pramāṇa-mimāṃsā. I. 2. 16-17

3. "यथा समस्ति समस्तवस्तुवेदी, क्षितिधरकंधरेयं धूमध्वजवती, ध्वनिः परिणतिमान् ॥" Pramāṇanayatattvālokālaṅkāra III. 22

28. When it (Dharmī) is established by Vikalpa, the Sādhya consists of existence and non-existence.

29. The omniscient exists. Horns of the ass do not exist.

Commentary

When we see smoke and infer fire, the object in which the fire is (e. g. the mountain) is known by Pratyakṣa Pramāṇa. But in the case of our belief in the existence and non-existence viz. "the omniscient exists" or "Horns of the ass do not exist" the Sādhya consisting of existence or non-existence is preceded by our such belief. So these are cases of Vikalpa-siddhi of the Dharmī[1].

प्रमाणोभयसिद्धे तु साध्यधर्मविशिष्टता ॥ ३० ॥

30. Pramāṇobhayasiddhe tu sādhyadharmaviśiṣṭatā.

अग्निमानयं देशः परिणामी शब्द इति यथा ॥ ३१ ॥

31. Agnimānayaṃ deśaḥ pariṇāmī śabda iti yathā.

30. When (a Dharmī) is established by Pramāṇa or by both (i. e. by Pramāṇa and Vikalpa), it is characterised by having the Dharma as Sādhya.

31. As for example, this place has fire ; sound is transient.

Commentary

In a Dharmī which is establihed by Pramāṇa, the Sādhya exists as Dharma. For example, we see by Pratyakṣa a place

---

1. "विकल्पसिद्धो यथा, सर्वज्ञः अस्ति सुनिश्चितासंभवबाधकप्रमाणत्वात् इत्यस्तित्वे साध्ये सर्वज्ञः। अथवा खरविषाणं नास्तीति नास्तित्वे साध्ये खरविषाणं। सर्वज्ञो ह्यस्तित्वसिद्धेः प्राङ् न प्रत्यक्षादिप्रमाणसिद्धः। अपि तु प्रतीतिमात्र-सिद्ध इति विकल्पसिद्धोऽयं धर्मी। तथा खरविषाणमपि नास्तित्वसिद्धेः प्राग् विकल्प-सिद्धं ॥" "विकल्पसिद्धे तु धर्मिणि सत्तासत्तयोरेव साध्यत्वमिति नियमः।"
Nyāyadīpikā.

containing fire and the place (which is Dharmī or Pakṣa) has the Dharma (or Sādhya) e. g. fire. The example of a Dharmī established by Pramāṇa as well as by Vikalpa is this : Sound is transient because it is caused (by some). Here sound can be established by Pramāṇa as well as by Vikalpa[1].

व्याप्तौ तु साध्यं धर्म एव ॥ ३२ ॥

32. Vyāptau tu sādhyaṃ dharma eva.

अन्यथा तदघटनात् ॥ ३३ ॥

33. Anyathā tadaghaṭanāt.

32. In universal concomitance, the Sādhya is only Dharma (and not Dharmī)

33. Otherwise, it (i. e. universal concomitance) cannot happen.

Commentary

It is not possible to find an universal concomitance seeing smoke that all mountains contain fire[2]. So in such a case the Sādhya viz. the fire is only Dharma and not Dharmī or Pakṣa viz. mountain. In other words, the universal concomitance is between fire and smoke but not between smoke and the object which is the abode of fire. So, a distinction should be made in this case by saying that here the Sādhya is only a Dharma and not a Dharmī.

साध्यधर्माधारसंदेहापनोदाय गम्यमानस्यापि पक्षस्य वचनम् ॥ ३४ ॥

34. Sādhyadharmādhārasandehāpanodāya gamyamānasyāpi pakṣasya vachanaṃ.

---

1. 'तत्र प्रमाणसिद्धो धर्मी यथा धूमवत्वादग्निमत्वे साध्ये पर्वतः खलु प्रत्यक्षेणानुभूयते ।....उभयसिद्धो धर्मी यथा शब्दो परिणामी कृतकत्वात् इत्यत्र शब्दः ।" Nyāya-dīpikā.

2. "न हि धूमदर्शनात् सर्वत्र पर्वतोऽग्निमानिति व्याप्तिः शक्या कर्तुं प्रमाणविरोधात् ॥" Prameyaratnamālā.

साध्यधर्मिणि साधनधर्मावबोधनाय पक्षधर्मोपसंहारवत् ॥ ३५ ॥

35. Sādhyadharmiṇi sādhanadharmāvavodhanāya pakṣadharmopasaṃhāravat.

को वा त्रिधा हेतुमुक्त्वा समर्थयमानो न पक्षयति ॥ ३६ ॥

36. Ko vā tridhā hetumuktvā samarthayamāno na pakṣayati.

34. The Pakṣa is used though it is understood (from Pratyakṣa) to dispel doubts regarding the abode of Sādhya when it is a Dharma.

35. As for example, Upanaya is used to explain the Dharma of Sādhana (the middle term, sign or mark) in the Dharmī containing Sādhya.

36. Is there any one who does not use a Pakṣa to substantiate after mentioning the three kinds of Hetu ?

Commentary

It may be urged that in inference, there is no necessity of a Pakṣa. For in the case of inference of fire in a mountain by seeing smoke, the mountain (Pakṣa) is established by Pratyakṣa. So it is not necessary to establish it again by inference (Anumāna). It is redundant to establish by inference, what we get by Pratyakṣa.

In answer to this, it is urged, that mention of Pakṣa is necessary to localize the Sādhya. Smoke may be in the mountain or in kitchens or in other places. To remove doubts as to where the smoke exists, the use of Pakṣa is necessary. Excluding the Pakṣa, we will only get a mention of the abstract relationship between smoke and fire. It may in such a case reduce Anumāna to Tarka e. g. 'where is this fire which is indicated by smoke ?' Or it may lead to an absurd inference e. g. existence of fire in a lake.

"Some philosophers hold that the minor term (Pakṣa) is not an essential part of an inference. But this view according to the Jainas, is untenable, it being absolutely necessary to state the minor term (Pakṣa) in the inference[1]."

---

1. Dr. Satischandra Vidyābhūṣan : Nyāyāvatāra. p. 15

Siddhasena Divākara has mentioned in his Nyāyāvatāra :

"It (i. e. Pakṣa) is to be used here (in an inference for the sake of others), as exhibiting an abode of the reason (i. e. the middle term called Hetu).

Otherwise owing to a misconception as to the abode of reason (i. e. Pakṣa or the minor term) as intended by the disputant his reason (Hetu or the middle term) may appear to his opponent as absurd.

A man who has come to behold the excellence of an archer will have to behold the opposite of it, if the archer hits without fixing an aim[1]."

Dr. Vidyābhūṣaṇa has amplified this as below :

"If any disputant does not explicitly state the minor term (Pakṣa) his reason might be misunderstood by his opponent e. g.

(1) This hill (the minor term) is full of fire (the major term);

(2) Because it is full of smoke (the middle term).

The above inference, if the minor term is omitted, will assume the following form :—

(1) Full of fire (the major term)

(2) because full of smoke (the middle term)

Here the opponent might not at once recollect any abode or place (the minor term, Pakṣa) in which the fire and smoke abide in union, and might mistake a lake for such an abode. In such a case the whole argument will be misunderstood.

Just as a clever archer, with a view to preventing his arrow from going to a wrong direction, fixes his aim before hitting, so a

---

1. "तत्प्रयोगोऽत्र कर्त्तव्यो हेतोर्गोचरदीपक : ।"
"अन्यथा वाद्यभिप्रेतहेतुगोचरमोहित: ।
प्रत्यायस्य भवेद्धेतुर्विरुद्धारेकितो यथा ॥
धानुष्कगुणसंप्रेक्षि जनस्य परिविध्यत: ।
धानुष्कस्य विना लक्ष्यनिर्देशेन गुणेतरौ ॥" Nyāyāvatāra 14-16

skilful disputant, in order to avoid being misunderstood, should, in stating an inference, mention the minor term (Pakṣa) with which the major term (Sādhya) and the middle term (Hetu) are both connected.

In Pramāṇanayatattvālokālaṅkāra the same is mentioned as follows : "The use of Pakṣa must be adopted as we always mention as conclusion by word expressing Dharmī (Pakṣa or the minor term e. g. mountain) Dharma (Sādhya or the major term e. g. fire) and Hetu (the middle term). Who will not agree to the use of Pakṣa in support of the Sādhana (the middle term) after mentioning the three varieties of the same[1].

The three kinds of Hetu will be described later on.

Hemachandra has mentioned the subject of this aphorism in a similar language[2].

एतद्द्वयमेवानुमानाङ्गं नोदाहरणम् ॥ ३७ ॥

37. Etaddvayamevānumānāṅgaṃ nodāharaṇaṃ.

37. These two only are the limbs of Anumāna, and not the Udāharaṇa.

Commentary

In Prameyaratnamālā, it is mentioned that this Aphorism refutes the view of the Sāṅkhya philosophy which holds that Anumāna has three limbs viz. Pakṣa, Hetu and Dṛiṣṭānta or Udāharaṇa, that of the Mīmāṃsā philosophy according to which there are four limbs of Anumāna viz. Pratijñā, Hetu, Udāharaṇa and Upanaya and that of the Nyāya-vaiśeṣika philosophies which hold

1. "साध्यस्य प्रतिनियतधर्मिधर्महेतोरुपसंहारवचनवत् पक्षप्रयोगोऽप्यवश्यमाश्रयितव्यः ।" "त्रिविधं साधनमभिधायैव तत्समर्थनं विदधानः कः खलु न पक्षप्रयोगमंगीकुरुते ।" [प्रमाणनयतत्वालोकालंकारः । ३।२४।२५ ।]

2. "गम्यमानत्वेऽपि साध्यधर्मा-धार-सन्देहापनोदाय धर्मिणि पक्षधर्मोपसंहारवत्तदुत्पत्तिः ।" Pramāṇa-mīmāṃsā 2. 1. 8.

that there are five limbs of Anumāna viz. Pratijñā, Hetu, Udāharaṇa, Upanaya and Nigamana[1].

It may be urged that the words "and not the Udāharaṇa" are redundant in this aphorism, as the word 'only' in the aphorism is sufficient for the purpose. The commentator Anantavīrya says that these words have been used to refute the views of others[2].

In the Nyāya philosophy of Gautama, five limbs of syllogism are recognised. These are Pratijñā (proposition), Hetu, Udāharaṇa (illustration), Upanaya (application) and Nigamana (conclusion). The following is an example :—

(1) This hill is full of fire. (Pratijñā)

(2) Because it is full of smoke. (Hetu)

(3) Whatever is full of smoke is full of fire, as a kitchen (Dṛiṣṭānta)

(4) So is this hill full of smoke. (Upanaya)

(5) Therefore this hill is full of fire. (Nigamana)

According to the view of Jain logicians as propounded in Parikṣāmukhaṃ, only Pakṣa and Hetu are the two limbs of Anumāna.

In Pramāṇanayatattvālokālaṅkāra, it is mentioned : "Inference derived from the speech of another has only two parts viz. Pakṣa and Hetu and not Dṛiṣṭānta etc[3].

---

1. "ननु भवतु पक्षप्रयोगस्तथापि पक्षहेतुदृष्टान्तभेदेन त्र्यवयवमनुमानमिति सांख्यः। प्रतिज्ञाहेतूदाहरणोपनयभेदेन चतुरवयमिति मीमांसकः। प्रतिज्ञाहेतूदाहरणोपनयनिगमनभेदात् पंचावयवमिति यौगः। तन्मतमपाकुर्वन् स्वमतसिद्धमवयवद्वयमेवोपदर्शयन्नाह।" Prameyaratnamālā.

2. "एवकारेणै"वोदाहरणादिव्यवच्छेदे सिद्धेऽपि परमतनिरासार्थं पुनर्नोदाहरणमित्युक्तम्।" Prameyaratnamālā.

3. "पक्षहेतुवचनलक्षणमवयवद्वयमेव परप्रतिपत्तेरंगं न दृष्टान्तादिवचनम्।" Pramāṇanayatattvālokālaṅkāra III. 28

This aphorism is amplified in the aphorisms which follow.

न हि तत् साध्यप्रतिपत्त्यङ्गं तत्र यथोक्तहेतोरेव व्यापारात् ॥ ३८ ॥

38. Na hi tat sādhyapratipatyaṅgaṃ tatra yathoktahetoreva vyāpārāt.

तदविनाभावनिश्चयार्थं वा विपक्षे बाधकादेव तत् सिद्धेः ॥ ३९ ॥

39. Tadavinābhāvaniśchayārthaṃ vā vipakṣe vādhakādeva tat-siddheḥ.

38. That (Udāharaṇa) is not the cause of understanding the Sādhya because, the aforesaid Hetu works there (as the cause)

39. (That Udāharaṇa) also is (not necessary) for establishing the universal concomitance (with the Sādhya). That (universal concomitance) is established from the opposition to its adverse (character).

Commentary

When we give the example of a kitchen to illustrate the universal concomitance 'where there is smoke, there is fire,' we cannot say that the illustration is of any help in the understanding of the Sādhya viz. fire, for the knowledge of fire is derived from the Hetu (viz. 'Because it is full of smoke'). The Udāharaṇa therefore is not a part of inference. It cannot also be said that Udāharaṇa causes a belief of universal concomitance with the Sādhya, because the universal concomitance is established when we get proof opposed to its adverse character.

व्यक्तिरूपं च निदर्शनं सामान्येन तु व्याप्तिस्तत्रापि तद्वि-प्रतिपत्तावनवस्थानं स्यात् दृष्टान्तान्तरापेक्षणात् ॥ ४० ॥

40. Vyaktirūpaṃ cha nidarśanaṃ sāmānyena tu vyāptistatrāpi tadvipratipattāvanavasthānaṃ syāt dṛṣṭāntāntarāpekṣanāt.

40. A Udāharaṇa deals only with particular but Vyāpti deals with universal concomitance. If that is not understood, the fault of Anavasthā will arise, as recourse to another example will have to be made,

Commentary

The existence of smoke in a kitchen is a particular instance of the concomitance of smoke and fire. It cannot establish universal concomitance of smoke and fire. If we doubt the example of the kitchen, another example will have to be cited and even if the latter again be disbelieved, a third illustration will be necessary. So the Udāharaṇa cannot be said to be the cause of the knowledge of universal concomitance. At the utmost it can be said to yield a knowledge of concomitance in a particular instance. The fault of Anavasthā (no final settlement) arises when we seek one instance after another to come at the idea of universal concomitance from particular instances.

This aphorism in another language is given in the Pramāṇa-nayatattvālokālaṅkāra III. 36[1].

नापि व्याप्तिस्मरणार्थं तथाविधहेतुप्रयोगादेव तत्स्मृतेः ॥ ४१ ॥

41. Nāpi vyāpti-smaraṇārthaṃ tathāvidhahetuprayogādeva tatsmriteḥ.

41. (This Udāharaṇa) cannot remind the universal concomitance, because such a reminiscence arises from the use of Hetu of that kind (which is connected with previously understood knowledge of the connection between smoke and fire).

Commentary

The knowledge of relationship between Sādhya and Sādhana (e. g. fire and smoke) must exist before there can be any Anumāna. Udāharaṇa gives an example of this relationship or Vyāpti (universal concomitance) and only tends to establish the validity of Vyāpti. It cannot be said to be of any real help in reminding us about the universal concomitance. This Vyāpti is reminded by the Hetu "where there is smoke, there is fire" and not by the Udāharaṇa viz. "As in the kitchen". Only a thing which had been

1. "नियतैकविशेषस्वभावे च दृष्टान्ते साकल्येन व्याप्तेरयोगतो विप्रतिपत्तौ सत्यां तदन्तरापेक्षायामनवस्थितेर्दुर्निवारः समवतारः ।"

experienced before, can be remembered. So universal concomitance can be reminded only by the Hetu and not by hundreds of examples[1]. This is also mentioned in Pramāṇanayatattvālokālaṅkāra III. 37[2].

तत्परमभिधीयमानं साध्यधर्मिणि साध्यसाधने सन्देहयति ॥४२॥

42. Tatparamabhidhīyamānaṃ sādhyadharmiṇi sādhyasādhane sandehayati.

42. This (Udāharaṇa) only raises a doubt in establishing Sādhya (e. g. fire) in the Dharmī (e. g. mountain) containing Sādhya (e. g. fire).

Commentary

Udāharaṇa is not the cause of universal concomitance. On the contrary, it raises a doubt whether fire is really in the mountain or not for we are given an illustration where fire may exist without the mountain which we see. It is after we remember the universal concomitance through Hetu that we come to the conclusion that the mountain is full of fire. Udāharaṇa therefore is not an essential part of inference.

कुतोऽन्यथोपनयनिगमने ॥४३॥

43. Kutohnyathopanaya-nigamane.

43. Otherwise, why should there be Upanaya and Nigamana ?

Commentary

We have already mentioned the five parts of the inference as accepted in the Nyāya philosophy of Gautama. The fourth and the fifth parts are Upanaya and Nigamana, viz. 'So is this hill full of smoke' (Upanaya) and 'Therefore this hill is full of

1. "गृहीतसम्बन्धस्य हेतुप्रदर्शनेनैव व्याप्तिसिद्धिरगृहीतसम्बन्धस्य दृष्टान्तशतेनापि न तत्स्मरणमनुभूतविषयत्वात् स्मरणस्येति भावः ।" Prameyaratnamālā.

2. "नाप्यविनाभावस्मृतये प्रतिपन्नप्रतिबन्धस्य व्युत्पन्नमतेः पक्षहेतु-प्रदर्शनेनैव तत्प्रसिद्धेः ।"

fire' (Nigamana). Māṇikyanandi urges that acceptance of these two presupposes some doubt about the existence of fire in the mountain owing to the use of the Udāharaṇa. Otherwise, what is the use of having these two parts Upanaya and Nigamana ?

The modern syllogism of European philosophy following the same of Aristotle is of three propositions.

1. All things which are full of smoke are full of fire,
2. This mountain is full of smoke,
3. Therefore this mountain is full of fire.

It will be seen that in the first proposition, Vyāpti or universal concomitance is laid down. In the second proposition the Hetu is mentioned and in the third the Pratijñā is given. The Upanaya, Nigamana ann Dṛiṣṭānta are not accepted in modern syllogism. Really speaking, the Upanaya and Nigamana (which will be defined in Aphorisms 50 and 51 which follow) are merely repetitions of what is stated in the Pratijñā and Hetu. So these are not necessary parts of Anumāna. This is laid down in the next aphorism.

न च ते तदंगे । साध्यधर्मिणि हेतुसाध्ययोर्वचनादेवासंशयाद् ॥४४॥

44. Na cha te tadaṅge. Sādhyadharmiṇi hetu-sādhyayorvachanādevāsaṃśayāt.

44. These (Upanaya and Nigamana) are not parts of that (Anumāna) because by mentioning the Sādhya and the Hetu in the Dharmī containing the Sādhya, no doubt exists.

Commentary

When we mention the Hetu (the middle term e. g. smoke) and the Sādhya (the major term e. g. fire) in the Dharmī (e. g. mountain) which contains the Sādhya (e. g. fire), we have no kind of doubt in the knowledge of the Sādhya (e. g. fire) or in other words the existence of the Hetu (smoke) and Sādhya (fire) is ascertained by their mention without there being any kind of doubt. So it is redundant to repeat them again in the form of Upanaya and Nigamana. So these two parts should not be considered as necessary limbs of Upamāna.

"There is no power of Upanaya and Nigamana to produce a knowledge in the mind of others as this knowledge arises from the use of the Pakṣa and the Hetu." Pramāṇanayatattvālokālaṅkāra. III. 40.

समर्थनं वा वरं हेतुरूपमनुमानावयवो वाऽस्तु साध्ये तदुपयोगात् ॥ ४५ ॥

45. Samarthanaṃ vā varaṃ heturūpamanumānāvayavo vāhstu sādhye tadupayogāt.

45. (The establishment e. g. fire) is got from the support of the limb of Anumāna named Hetu (e. g. smoke) as this (Hetu e. g. smoke) is connected with the Sādhya (e. g. fire).

Commentary

The purport of this aphorism is that there is no necessity of the parts of Anumāna, Dṛiṣṭānta, Upanaya and Nigamana because the Sādhya (e. g. fire) is established by Hetu (e. g. smoke). As we have knowledge of the Sādhya without the help of Dṛiṣṭānta, Upanaya and Nigamana these cannot be said to be essential parts of Anumāna.

When faults of Hetu are dispelled and it is supported, it is said to have samarthana. If you say that that which is not supported can never be a Hetu, and so after mentioning Dṛiṣṭānta etc. a support should be given to the same, we reply that it is the very Hetu which is a part of Anumāna which establishes the Sādhya and it is not at all necessary to give any other support by mentioning Udāharaṇa etc. first[1].

1. "किं चाभिधायापि दृष्टान्तादिकं समर्थनमवश्यं वक्तव्यम्, असमर्थितस्य अहेतुत्वात्, इति ; तदेव वरं हेतुरूपम् अनुमानावयवो वाऽस्तु साध्यसिद्धौ तस्यैवोपयोगान्नोदाहरणादिकम् ।" Prameyaratnamālā.

Pramāṇanayatattvālokālaṅkāra mentions the same in another language[1].

बालव्युत्पत्त्यर्थं तत्त्रयोपगमे शास्त्र एवासौ न वादे, अनुपयोगात् ॥ ४६ ॥

46. Bālavyutpattyarthaṃ tattrayopagame śāstra evāsau na vāde, anupayogāt.

46. These (Dṛiṣṭānta) etc. may be for understanding of those who have little knowledge and for this purpose may be discussed only in the Śāstra, but these are quite unfit to be used in logical discussions.

Commentary

When we try to teach others who have no full knowledge of inference, we may use Dṛiṣṭānta etc. and for this purpose in works on logic, we may treat this subject. Such words may be of use to students. But in logical discussions between trained men, these are useless.

"The statement of Pakṣa···and Hetu are alone needed in an inference at the instance of another. It is obvious that the true basis of Anumāna is always the force of Vyāpti (logical connection), so that the moment this relationship is asserted by mentioning the Sādhana, smoke and the like, mind is immediately led to that which is inseparably connected therewith, and discovers the Sādhya··· Upanaya and Nigamana besides serving no useful purpose, are also objectionable as pure repetition of what is already stated in the Pratijñā and Hetu ; and Udāharaṇa would reduce logic to a child's play. For while it may be necessary to cite an actual instance of Vyāpti (logical connection) in a Vītarāgakathā (lecture to a pupil) to enable little children to familiarize themselves with the basis of inference it is bad rhetoric to do so in the course of a

---

1. "समर्थनमेव वरं परप्रतिपत्त्यंगमास्तां तदन्तरेण दृष्टान्तादिप्रयोगेऽपि तदसंभवात् ।" Pramāṇanayatattvālokālaṅkāra III. 41.

Vijigīsukathā (logical discussion) with a clever and presumably learned opponent. And after all Udāharaṇa only tends to establish the validity of Vyāpti and may be useful in showing the necessary relationship between the Sādhana and its Sādhya ; it is of no real help in Anumāna which presupposes the knowledge of this relationship.

The modern syllogism of three steps, or propositions, as they are called, is also open to objection for similar reasons. It is the culmination of a highly elaborate system of ratiocination, it is true, but it is no less true that the system of which it is the outcome is not a natural but a highly artificial one. The practical value of modern logic, as a science, is to be judged from the fact that its inferential processes, though suitable to a certain extent, for the purposes of the school room, are never actually resorted to by men —not even by lawyers, philosophers and logicians—in their daily life, nor can they be carried out without first bending the current of thought from its natural channel, and forcing it into the artificial and rigid frame-work of an Aristotelian syllogism.

The syllogism that answers the practical requirements of life and is natural to rational mind, then, consists of two and only two steps—Pratijñā and Hetu[1]."

दृष्टान्तो द्वेधा, अन्वयव्यतिरेकभेदात् ॥ ४७ ॥

47. Dristānto dvedhā anvayavyatirekabhedāt.

47. The Dristānta is of two kinds, being with Anvaya and Vyatireka.

Commentary

It has been mentioned that Dristānta, Upanaya and Nigamana are not parts of Anumāna. But in the previous aphorism it was stated that these may be discussed in the Śāstras

---

1. The Science of Thought by C. R. Jain Pp. 42, 43, Foot note.

for teaching students. So in this and the next two aphorisms the two kinds of Driṣṭānta, and in aphorisms 50 and 51 Upanaya and Nigamana are explained.

साध्यव्याप्तं साधनं यत्र प्रदर्श्यते सोऽन्वयदृष्टान्तः ॥ ४८ ॥

48. Sādhyavyāptaṃ sādhanaṃ yatra pradarśyate sohnvaya-driṣṭāntaḥ.

साध्याभावे साधनाभावो यत्र कथ्यते स व्यतिरेकदृष्टान्तः ॥४९॥

49. Sādhyābhāve sādhanābhāvo yatra kathyate sa vyatireka-driṣṭāntaḥ.

49. Where the Sādhana is shown as always concomitant with Sādhya, that is (an example) of Anvaya Driṣṭānta.

50. Where the absence of Sādhana is mentioned through the absence of Sādhya, that is (an example) of Vyatireka Driṣṭānta.

Commentary.

The Driṣṭānta or illustration which states a connection between the Sādhya (fire) and Sādhana (smoke) affirmatively e. g. 'where there is smoke, there is fire as in a kitchen' is Anvaya Driṣṭānta. The Driṣṭānta which mentions the same connection negatively e. g. 'where there is no smoke, there is no fire as in a lake' is Vyatireka Driṣṭānta.

This is propounded in another language in the Nyāyāvatāra as follows :

"Where the inseparable connection of the major term (Sādhya) and the middle term (Sādhana or Hetu) is shown by homogeneousness (Sādharmya) the example is called a homogeneous one, on account of the connection (between those terms) being recollected.

The heterogeneous example is that which shows that the absence of the major term (Sādhya) is followed by the absence of the middle term." Verses 18 and 19[1].

---

1. "साध्यसाधनयोर्व्याप्ति-र्यत्र निश्चीयतेतराम् ।
साधर्म्येण स दृष्टान्तः सम्बन्धस्मरणान्मतः ॥

Dr. Satischandra Vidyābhūṣaṇa has commented on the above thus :

"An example (Driṣṭānta) is a familiar case which re-assures the inseparable connection (Vyāpti) between the major term (Sādhya) and the middle term (Hetu). It is of two kinds : 1. homogeneous (Sādharmya) and 2. heterogeneous (Vaidharmya). The homogeneous example is that which re-assures the connection (Vyāpti) by homogeneousness (Sādharmya) thus :

1. This hill is full of fire (major term) ;
2. Because it is full of smoke (middle term) ;
3. Just as the kitchen (homogeneous example).

Here the fire and smoke abide homogeneously in the kitchen.

The heterogeneous example re-assures the connection (Vyāpti) by contrariety, that is, by showing that absence of the major term (Sādhya) is attended by the absence of the middle term (Hetu) thus :

1. This hill has no smoke (major term) ;
2. Because it has no fire (middle term) :
3. Just as a lake (heterogeneous example)[1]."

In Pramāṇanayatattvālokālaṅkāra (III. 43-46) we find : "Illustration (Driṣṭānta) consists of knowledge of obstruction. It is of two kinds being connected with homogeneousness or heterogeneousness. Homogeneous example is that where the existence of the quality of the Sādhya is invariably revealed with the existence of the quality of Sādhana. Heterogeneous example is that where the invariable absence of Sādhana is shown on account of the absence of the Sādhya[2]."

साध्ये निवर्त्तमाने तु साधनस्याप्यसंभवः ।
ख्याप्यते यत्र दृष्टान्ते वैधर्म्येणेति स स्मृतः ॥"

1. Nyāyāvatāra by Dr. S. C. Vidyābhūṣaṇa p. 17.
2. "प्रतिबंधप्रतिपत्तेरास्पदं दृष्टान्तः ।
स द्वेधा साधर्म्यतो वैधर्म्यतश्च ।
यत्र साधनधर्मसत्तायामवश्यं साध्यधर्मसत्ता प्रकाश्यते स साधर्म्यदृष्टान्तः ।
यत्र तु साध्याभावे साधनस्यावश्यमभावः प्रदर्श्यते स वैधर्म्यदृष्टान्तः ।"

The Naiyāyikas following Gautama also mention "Udāharaṇa is illustration following a mention of universal concomitance, e. g. whatever is full of smoke is full of fire as a kitchen. This is Sādharmya Udāharaṇa. Whatever is not full of fire is not full of smoke as a lake. This is an example of Vaidharmya Udāharaṇa[1]."

हेतोरुपसंहार उपनयः ॥ ५० ॥

50. Hetorupasaṃhāra upanayaḥ.

50. Upanaya is the application (asserting the existence) of the Hetu (in the Dharmī after a knowledge of concomitance).

Commentary

Upanaya is the description of the undoubted existence of the Hetu (e. g. smoke) in the Pakṣa (e. g. mountain) in concomitance[2].

We have already mentioned the five parts of Anumāna as adopted by Gautama viz. Pratijñā, Hetu, Udāharaṇa, Upanaya and Nigamana[3]. Upanaya or application is used after Driṣṭānta e. g. "So is this hill full of smoke."

प्रतिज्ञायास्तु निगमनम् ॥ ५१ ॥

51. Pratijñāyāstu nigamanaṃ.

51. Nigamana is the (conclusion) of the Pratijñā.

---

1. "व्याप्तिपूर्वकदृष्टान्तवचनमुदाहरणम्। यथा यो यो धूमवानसावसावग्निमान् यथा महानसः। इति साधर्म्योदाहरणम्। यो योऽग्निमान्न भवति स स धूमवान्न भवति यथा महाह्रदः। इति वैधर्म्योदाहरणम्।" Nyāya-dīpikā. Prakaśa III.

2. "हेतोः साध्यधर्मिणि उपसंहरणमुपनयः।"

Pramāṇa-naya-tattvālokālaṅkāra, III. 47.

3. "प्रतिज्ञाहेतूदाहरणोपनयनिगमनान्यवयवाः।"

Nyāyasūtra of Gautama.

Commentary

Pratijñā is the proposition to be proved. In other words the statement of the Pakṣa is the Pratijña[1], e. g. this hill (minor term) is full of fire (the major term). This proposition is the Pratijñā.

After setting out the Pratijñā, we mention the Hetu, Udāharaṇa and Upanaya. Last of all we come to the conclusion as already set forth in the Pratijñā. This conclusion is the fifth part of Anumāna and is called Nigamana.

It may be urged that as according to the Jain logicians Udāharaṇa, Upanaya and Nigamana are not accepted as parts of inference, why have these been described in this work ? In answer to this, it may be said that we have already mentioned that in works on Logic, these may be described for teaching students. According to the different manners of exposition, the parts of Anumāna in Vītarāgakathā (lecture to pupils) may be two (Pratijñā and Hetu), three (Pratijñā, Hetu and Udāharaṇa), four (Pratijñā, Hetu, Udāharaṇa and Upanaya) or five (Pratijñā, Hetu, Udāharaṇa, Upanaya and Nigamana)[2]. This use of different parts depends upon the suitability of persons to whom the subject is explained[3].

तदनुमानं द्वेधा ॥ ५२ ॥

52. Tadanumānaṃ dvedhā.

---

1. "साध्यधर्मस्य पुनर्निगमनम् ।"

Pramāṇanayatattvālokālaṅkāra, III. 48.

2. "वीतरागकथायां तु प्रतिपाद्याशयानुरोधेन प्रतिज्ञाहेतू द्वाववयवौ, प्रतिज्ञाहेतूदाहरणानि त्रयः, प्रतिज्ञाहेतूदाहरणोपनयाश्चत्वारः, प्रतिज्ञाहेतूदाहरणोपनय-निगमनानि वा पंचेति यथायोग्यं प्रयोगपरिपाटी ।" Nyāya-dīpikā. Prakāśa III.

3. "प्रयोगपरिपाटी तु प्रतिपाद्यानुरोधतः ।"

Kumaranandī Bhattāraka, quoted in Nyāya-dīpikā.

स्वार्थ-परार्थभेदात् ॥ ५३ ॥

53. Svārtha-parārthabhedāt.

स्वार्थमुक्तलक्षणम् ॥ ५४ ॥

54. Svārthamuktalakṣaṇaṃ.

परार्थं तु तदर्थपरामर्शिवचनाज्जातम् ॥ ५५ ॥

55. Parārthaṃ tu tadarthaparāmarśivachanājjātaṃ.

52. This Anumāna is of two kinds :

53. Svārtha and Parārtha.

54. Svārtha (Anumāṇa) has already been defined.

55. Parārtha (Anumāna) arises from words touching that (Svārthāṇumāna)*.

Commentary

Anumāna is of two kinds, Svārthānumāna and Parārthānumāna. The former variety has been defined in aphorism 14 of the third samuddeśa of this work viz. "the knowledge of Sādhya (the major term e. g. fire) from Sādhana or Hetu (the middle term e. g. smoke) is Anumāna." Parārthānumāna arises through words of another.

"Inference is of two kinds : 1. Svārthānumāna, inference for one's own self, and 2. Parārthānumāna, inference for the sake of others. The first kind is the inference drawn in one's own mind after having made repeated observations. Suppose that having repeatedly seen in the kitchen and other places, that where there is smoke there is fire, and having realised in his mind that there is a universal antecedence of fire in respect of smoke, a man after-

* "तद्द्विधा स्वार्थं परार्थं च ।" "स्वार्थं स्वनिश्चितसाध्याविनाभावैकलक्षणात् साधनात् साध्यज्ञानम् ॥" "यथोक्तसाधनाभिधानजः परार्थं ।"

Pramāṇamimāṃsā, 1. 2. 8, 1, 2, 9, and II, 1, 1,

wards goes to a hill and entertains a doubt as to whether or not there is fire in it. Instantly when he observes smoke on it, he recollects the inseparable connection between fire and smoke, and concludes in his mind that the hill has fire in it, as it has smoke on it. This is an inference for one's own self[1]."

Parārthānumāna has thus been defined in Nyāyāvatāra :

"A statement expressive of the reason (i. e. mark or the middle term, called Hetu) which is inseparably connected with that which is to be proved (i. e. the major term, called Sādhya) having been composed of the minor term (called Pakṣa, signifying a side or place) etc., is called an inference for the sake of others (Parārthānumāna)[2]."

This is amplified by Dr. Satischandra Vidyābhūṣaṇa as follows :

"In an 'inference for the sake of others' the minor term (pakṣa) etc. must be explicity set forth. The major term or 'proven' (Sādhya) is that which is to be proved. The middle term or reason (hetu, liṅga or sādhana) is that which cannot exist except in connection with the major term or 'proven' (sādhya or liṅgī). The minor term or abode (Pakṣa) is that with which the reason or middle term (hetu) is connected, and whose connection with the major term (Sādhya) is to be proved. In a proposition the subject is the minor term (pakṣa) and the predicate the major term (sādhya). The following is an inference for the sake of others :

1. This *hill* (minor term) is full of *fire* (major term)—Proposition (pratijñā),

2. Because it is full of *smoke* (middle term),

---

1. Nyāyāvatāra by Dr. S. C. Vidyābhūṣaṇa, p. 9.

2. "साध्याविनाभुवो हेतोर्वचो यत् प्रतिपादकम् ।
परार्थमनुमानं तत् पक्षादिवचनात्मकम् ॥"

Nyāyāvatāra. verse 10.

3. Whatever is full of smoke is full of fire, just as the kitchen (example, *driṣṭānta*),

4. So is this hill full of smoke (application, upanaya),

5. *Therefore*, this hill is full of fire (conclusion, nigamana)[1]."

The example given above consists of five parts as acknowledged in the Nyāya philosophy of Gautama. But Jain logicians accept only two parts. So according to them "Parārthānumāna means the knowledge of Sādhya from its Sādhana arising in the mind in consequence of the speech of another. It consists of two parts, Pratijñā and Hetu. Pratijñā means the proposition to be proved and Hetu is the statement of the logical connection called Vyāpti advanced in proof thereof. Illustration : There is fire in this hill (Pratijñā), because there is smoke on it (Hetu)"[2].

तद्वचनमपि तद्धेतुत्वात् ॥ ५६ ॥

56. Tadvachanamapi taddhetutvāt.

56. The words expressing this (Parārthānumāna) is also Parārthānumāna as these (words) are the cause of that (knowledge arising in Parārthānumāna)[3].

Commentary

Anantavīrya says that though really the knowledge is Parārthānumāna, the words in a secondary sense are also called so. In such cases the cause is taken as the effect or the effect is taken as the cause[4].

---

1. Nyāyāvatāra by Dr. S. C. Vidhyābhūṣaṇa, pp. 13-14.

2. The Science of Thought by C. R. Jain pp. 41-43.

3. "वचनमुपचारात्।" Pramāṇa-mimāṃsā. II. 1. 2.

4. "परार्थानुमानप्रतिपादकवचनमपि परार्थानुमानम् .... । कारणे कार्यस्योपचारात्। अथवा तत्प्रतिपादकानुमानं हेतुर्यस्य तत्-तद्धेतुस्तस्य भावस्तत्त्वं ततस्तद्वचनमपि तथा....अस्मिन् पक्षे कार्ये कारणस्योपचारः।"

Prameyaratnamālā.

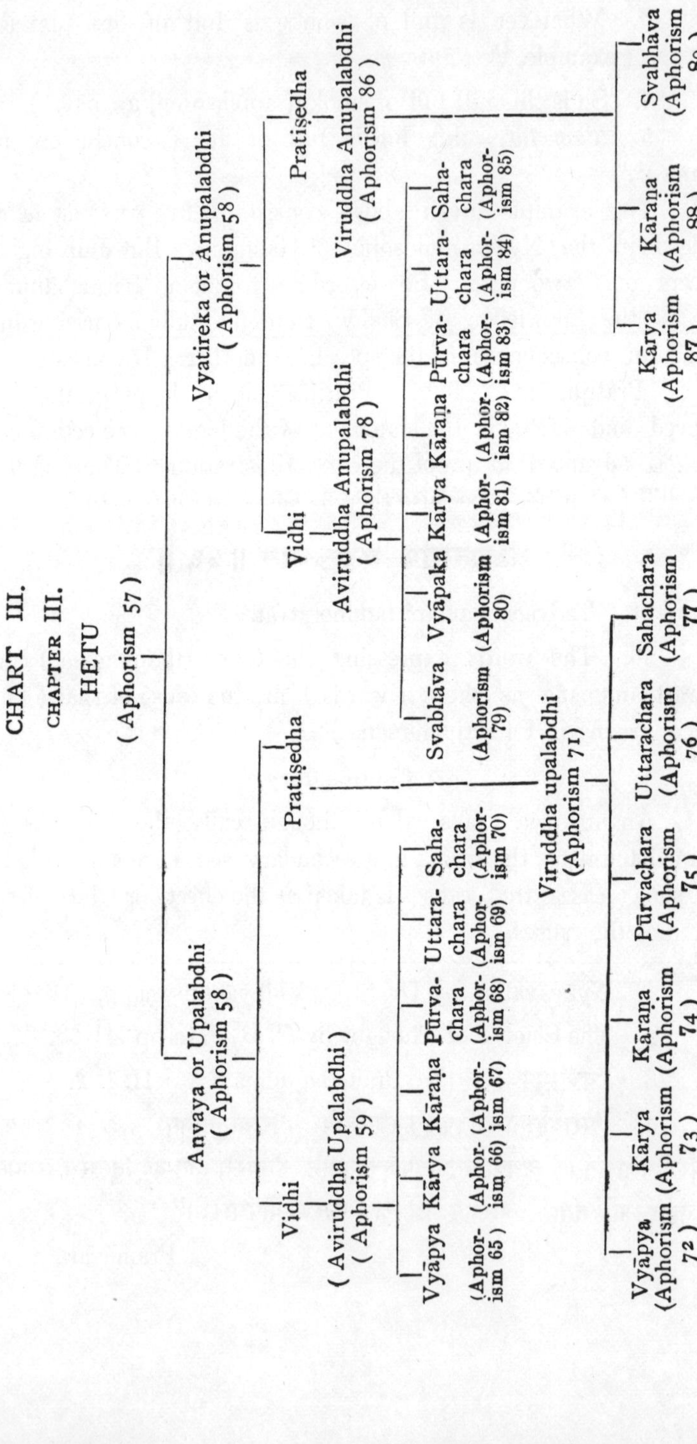

CHART III.
CHAPTER III.
HETU
(Aphorism 57)
Anvaya or Upalabdhi
(Aphorism 58)
Vyatireka or Anupalabdhi
(Aphorism 58)
Vidhi
Pratiṣedha
Vidhi
Pratiṣedha
(Aviruddha Upalabdhi)
(Aphorism 59)
Viruddha upalabdhi
(Aphorism 71)
Aviruddha Anupalabdhi
(Aphorism 78)
Viruddha Anupalabdhi
(Aphorism 86)
Vyāpya (Aphorism 65)
Kārya (Aphorism 66)
Kāraṇa (Aphorism 67)
Pūrva-chara (Aphorism 68)
Uttara-chara (Aphorism 69)
Saha-chara (Aphorism 70)
Vyāpya (Aphorism 72)
Kārya (Aphorism 73)
Kāraṇa (Aphorism 74)
Pūrvachara (Aphorism 75)
Uttarachara (Aphorism 76)
Sahachara (Aphorism 77)
Svabhāva (Aphorism 79)
Vyāpaka (Aphorism 80)
Kārya (Aphorism 81)
Kāraṇa (Aphorism 82)
Pūrva-chara (Aphorism 83)
Uttara-chara (Aphorism 84)
Saha-chara (Aphorism 85)
Kārya (Aphorism 87)
Kāraṇa (Aphorism 88)
Svabhāva (Aphorism 89)

स हेतुर्द्वेधोपलब्ध्यनुपलब्धिभेदात् ॥ ५७ ॥

57. Sa heturdvedhopalabdhyanupalabdhibhedāt.

57. That Hetu is of two kinds: Upalabdhi and Anupalabdhi.

Commentary

We have already mentioned that universal concomitance can be expressed in two ways viz. affirmatively called Anvaya e. g. 'wherever there is smoke there is fire' or negatively called Vyatireka e. g. 'where there is no fire there is no smoke.' The first kind of Hetu is known as Upalabdhi and the second Anupalabdhi[1].

उपलब्धिर्विधिप्रतिषेधयोरनुपलब्धिश्च ॥ ५८ ॥

58. Upalabdhirbidhipratiṣedhayoranupalabdhiścha.

58. Upalabdhi is subdivided into Vidhi and Pratiṣedha. Anupalabdhi also (is subdivided into the same two kinds).

Commentary

In Upalabdhi Hetu, the Sādhya may be of two kinds, Vidhi and Pratiṣedha. These two kinds of Sādhya also can exist in Anupalabdhi Hetu. It should not be said that in Upalabdhi the Sādhya is only in the form of Vidhi and in Anupalabdhi, it is in the form of Pratiṣedha.

The Upalabdhi and Anupalabdhi Hetus are subdivided into two kinds each: those which prove the existence of a fact (Vidhi) and those that prove the non-existence of a fact (Niṣedha).

A Hetu may also be of Viruddha (contradictory) nature implying existence of a fact which is incompatible with the Sādhya e. g. there is no fire in this pitcher, because it is full of water; or it may be of Aviruddha (non-contradictory) nature such as in an argument which is not based on any fact incompatible with the

---

1. "तद् द्वेधा ।" "तथोपपत्त्यन्यथानुपपत्तिभेदात् ।"
Pramāṇa-mīmāṃsā II. 1. 3 and II. I. 4.

existence of Sādhya e. g. there is fire in this hill, because there is smoke on it. (Vide The Science of Thought by C. R. Jain, p. 44).

अविरुद्धोपलब्धिर्विधौ षोढा व्याप्यकार्यकारणपूर्वोत्तर-सहचरभेदात् ॥ ५९ ॥

59. Aviruddhopalabdhirvidhau ṣoḍhā vyāpya-kārya-kāraṇa-pūrvo-ttara-sahachara-bhedāt.

59. Aviruddha Upalabdhi is of six kinds in Vidhi viz. Vyāpya, Kārya, Kāraṇa, Pūrvachara, Uttarachara and Sahachara.

Commentary

Upalabdhi in Vidhi will be explained in Aphorisms 65, 66, 67, 68, 69 and 70 respectively.

In Pramāṇanayatattvālokālaṅkāra III. 6. 4. it is mentioned that the Aviruddhopalabdhi in establishing a Vidhi is of six kinds[1].

In the Buddhist philosophy it is held that the inference proving the existence of a fact (Vidhi) is only of two kinds Svabhāva (own nature) and Kārya (effect)[2]. But in this aphorism, six varieties of Aviruddha Upalabdhi establishing Vidhi have been mentioned. So in the following five aphorisms the view of the Buddhist logicians is refuted and that of the Jain logicians established.

The next aphorism lays down why Kāraṇa should be accepted as a Hetu.

रसादेकसामग्र्यनुमानेन रूपानुमानमिच्छद्भिरिष्टमेव किञ्चित् कारणं हेतुर्यत्र सामर्थ्याप्रतिबन्धकारणान्तरावैकल्ये ॥ ६० ॥

60. Rasādekasāmagryanumānena rūpānumānamichchhad-bhiriṣṭameva kiñchit kāraṇaṃ heturyatra sāmarthyāprativandha-kāraṇāntarā-vaikalye.

---

1. "तत्राविरुद्धोपलब्धिर्विधेः सिद्धौ षोढा ।"

2. "अत्राह सौगतः, विधिसाधनं द्विविधमेव, स्वभावकार्यभेदात् ।"
Prameyaratnamālā.

60. From Rasa (juice), one thing is inferred and from that, Rūpa (form) is inferred Those who accept this, accept also some Kāraṇa as Hetu where there is no other Kāraṇa to obstruct the potency of (the Kāraṇa or cause).

Commentary

Kāraṇa (cause) is not accepted by all logicians as a true Hetu because according to their view, a Kāraṇa (cause) is not always followed by its appropriate Kārya (effect). Dharmabhūṣaṇa says "An effect may preclude a cause for without a cause no effect can take place. But a cause can exist without any effect[1] e. g. we see fire though there is no smoke. So a fire cannot be said to indicate smoke. To this argument, the following is the reply. Whenever there is a cause having potency, we invariably find its effect".[2] There may be cases in which a cause is opposed by some other cause by which the potency of the first cause is lost. In such cases the first cause may not cause any effect but where this potency is not obstructed, we are certain to find a result. By accepting Kāraṇa as a Hetu, we mean a Kāraṇa having potency. "The true Kāraṇa always implies an active, potent (having Sāmarthya) cause which nothing can prevent from producing its effect. In the instance of rain-clouds, the absence of all those causes which prevent them from giving rain is presumed and implied."[3]

In this aphorism an illustration is given. There is juice in some fruit. Suppose a man in the dark tastes juice of a mango. He

---

1. "कारणस्य तु कार्याविनाभावाभावादलिंगत्वम्। नावश्यं कारणानि कार्यवन्ति भवन्तीति वचनात्।" Prameyaratnamālā.

2. "ननु कार्यं कारणानुमापकमस्तु कारणाभावे कार्यस्यानुपपत्तेः। कारणं तु कार्याभावेऽपि संभवति। यथा धूमाभावेऽपि संभवन् वह्निः सुप्रतीतः। अतएव न वह्निर्धूमं गमयति इति चेत्, तन्न। उन्मीलितशक्तिकस्य कारणस्य कार्याव्यभिचारित्वेन कार्यं प्रति हेतुत्वाविरोधात्।" Nyāyadipikā.

3. The Science of Thought by C. R. Jain, P. 47.

infers its form from the juice arising from previous experience that such a juice is connected with such a fruit. In this case as there is no obstruction to the inference and existence of another cause one must accept the Kāraṇa (cause)[1]. So the view of the Buddhists that there are only Svabhāva-Hetu and Kārya-Hetu is not correct.

न च पूर्वोत्तरचारिणोस्तादात्म्यं तदुत्पत्तिर्वा
कालव्यवधाने तदनुपलब्धेः ॥ ६१ ॥

61. Na cha pūrvottarachāriṇostādātmyaṃ tadutpattirvā kālavyavadhāne tadanupalabdheḥ.

61. In the case of antecedence and consequence, there is no identity or its appearance, for there is no knowledge of these after an interval of time.

Commentary

In this aphorism, it is asserted that the Pūrvachara and Uttarachara Hetus (i. e. Hetus concerned with antecedence and consequence) cannot be said to be included within the Svabhāva-Hetu or Kārya-Hetu as accepted by the Buddhists. Svabhāva Hetu is concerned with identity and in Kārya-Hetu, one thing arises from another. So in both these cases the two things exist at the same time. But in antecedence and consequence, the two things do not exist together[2]. The example of identity is as follows :—There is no jar in this room, because its Svabhāva (identity) is not to be found (that is, nothing resembling its identity is present in it). The example of Kārya is : There is fire

1. "तमस्विन्यामास्वाद्यमानादाम्रादिफलरसादेकसामग्रयानुमित्या रूपाद्यनुमितिमभिमन्यमानैरभिमतमेव किमपि कारणं हेतुतया यत्र शक्तेरप्रतिस्खलनमपरकारणसाकल्यं च ।" Pramāṇanayatattvālokālaṅkāra III. 66.

2. "पूर्वोत्तरचरयोर्न स्वभावकार्यकारणभावौ तयोः कालव्यवहितावनुपलम्भात ।" Ibid, III. 67.

in this hill, because there is smoke on it. Now these illustrations will show that Svabhāva or Kārya Hetu cannot include Pūrvachara (antecedent) or Uttarachara (consequent) Hetus in which cases there is an interval between two things e. g. It will be Sunday tomorrow because it is Saturday to-day (antecedence), or yesterday was a Sunday, because it is Monday to-day (consequence).

भाव्यतीतयोर्मरणजाग्रद्बोधयोरपि नारिष्टोद्बोधौ प्रति हेतुत्वम् ॥ ६२ ॥

62. Bhābyatītayormaraṇajāgradbodhayorapi nāriṣṭodbodhau prati hetutvaṃ.

62. The future and the past, death and the knowledge of waking are not the causes of Ariṣṭas (omens of death) or of rising (in the morning).

Commentary

The Buddhist logicians hold that a relationship of cause and effect can exist though there be an interval of time, as the death which will occur in the future is the cause of the Ariṣṭas (signs preceding and foretelling death) or the past knowledge of waking is the cause of rising in the morning after sleep. Jain logicians say that death which will occur in future is not the cause of omens of death and the past knowledge of waking is not the cause of our rising in the morning for the existence of an effect when there is a cause depends on the cause. In the aforesaid examples, causes do not exist up to the happening of the effect. So there cannot be any Kāraṇa Hetu in these instances. This has been propounded in another language in Pramāṇanayatattvālokālaṅkāra III. 68[1].

तद्व्यापाराश्रितं हि तद्भावभावित्वम् ॥ ६३ ॥

63. Tadvyāpārāśritaṃ hi tadbhāvabhāvitvaṃ.

63. Because that (Kārya) happens with the existence of that (Kāraṇa) as that is connected with this.

---

1. "न चातिक्रान्तानागतयोर्जाग्रद्दशासंवेदनमरणयोः प्रबोधोत्पत्तौ प्रति कारणत्वं व्यवहितत्वेन निर्व्यापारत्वात् ।"

Commentary

As a potter is the cause of a pot having connection with the latter, so the causality of a thing depends on its connection with the thing. So where there is no such connection, it is not proper to infer the relation of cause and effect[1].

सहचारिणोरपि परस्परपरिहारेणावस्थानात् सहोत्पादाच्च ॥ ६४ ॥

64. Sahachāriṇorapi parasparaparihāreṇābasthānāt sahotpādāchcha.

64. Co-existence (is also a separate Hetu) because the things exist independently of each other and arise together.

Commentary

The Sahachāri (co-existent) Hetu is also not included within Kārya Hetu, Kāraṇa Hetu or Svabhāva Hetu. As the things have separate and independent existence, this Sahachāri Hetu cannot be said as the same as Svabhāva Hetu which signifies identity. Also, as these arise simultaneously, it cannot be said to be Kārya Hetu or Kāraṇa Hetu[2].

---

1. "स्वव्यापारापेक्षिणी हि कार्यं प्रति पदार्थस्य कारणत्वव्यवस्था कुलालस्येव कलसं प्रति।"

"न च व्यवहितयोस्तयोर्व्यापारपरिकल्पनं न्याय्यमतिप्रसक्तेः।"

"परंपराव्यवहितानां परेषामपि तत्कल्पनस्य निवारयितुमशक्यत्वात्॥"

Pramāṇanayatattvālokālaṅkāra III. 69, 70, 71

2. "परस्परपरिहारेणोपालंभात् तादात्म्यासंभवात् स्वभावहेतावनन्तर्भावः। सहोत्पादाच्च न कार्ये कारणे वा इति। न च समानसमयवर्त्तिनोः कार्यकारणभावः सव्येतरगोविषाणवत्। कार्यकारणयोः प्रतिनियमाभावप्रसंगाच्च।"

Prameyaratnamālā

"सहचारिणोः परस्परस्वरूपपरित्यागेन तादात्म्यानुपपत्तेः सहोत्पादेन तदुत्पत्तिविपत्तेश्च सहचरहेतोरपि प्रोक्तेषु नानुप्रवेशः।"

Pramāṇanayatattvālokālaṅkāra III. 72

Example of Vyāpya Hetu :—

परिणामी शब्दः कृतकत्वात् ।
य एवं स एवं दृष्टो, यथा घटः ।
कृतकश्चायं तस्मात् परिणामीति ।
यस्तु न परिणामी स न कृतको दृष्टो, यथा बन्ध्यास्तनंधयः ।
कृतकश्चायं तस्मात् परिणामीति ॥ ६५ ॥

65. Pariṇāmi śabdaḥ kritakatvāt.

Ya evaṃ sa evaṃ driṣṭo yathā ghataḥ.

Kritakaśchāyaṃ tasmāt pariṇāmīti.

Yastu na pariṇāmi sa na kritako driṣṭo, yathā vandhyāstanandhayaḥ.

Kritakaśchāyaṃ tasmāt pariṇāmiti.

65. Sound is subject to modification, because it is a product.

All products are seen as liable to modifications e. g. a pitcher.

This is a product, so this is subject to modification.

That which is not a product is not seen as liable to modifications as the son of a barren woman.

This is a product, so this is subject to modification[1].

Commentary

In Aphorism 59, it has been mentioned that there are six kinds of Aviruddha Upalabdhi in Vidhi. In the present aphorism an example of the first variety viz., Aviruddha Vyāpyopalabdhi is given.

---

1. "Here sound falls in the larger category of products which is characterised by the quality of being subject to modification. Therefore being Vyāpya (included) in the larger class Vyāpaka it is liable to have the whole class predicated of itself."

The Science of Thought by C. R. Jain, P. 47, footnote.

In this aphorism all the parts of the inference are given in detail showing Sādharmya and Vaidharmya, In subsequent aphorisms only the example in short will be given. It may be expanded like the present aphorism in all its parts.

Example of Kārya Hetu (effect) :—

अस्त्यत्र देहिनि बुद्धिर्व्याहारादेः ॥ ६६ ॥

66. Astyatra dehini buddhirbyāhārādeḥ.

66. There is intelligence in this animal as it shows activities like speech etc.

Commentary

The familiar example 'There is fire in this hill, because there is smoke on it' is also an illustration of Kārya Hetu.

Example of Kāraṇa Hetu (cause) :—

अस्त्यत्र छाया छत्रात् ॥ ६७ ॥

67. Astyatra chhāyā chhatrāt.

67. There is shade here, as there is an umbrella.

Commentary

Another example is this : "There will be rain, as potent rain-clouds are seen"

Example of Purvachara (antecedent) Hetu :—

उदेष्यति शकटं कृत्तिकोदयात् ॥ ६८ ॥

68. Udeṣyati śakataṃ krittikodayāt.

68. The Rohiṇī (constellation) will appear (after a muhūrta) as the Krittikā (constellation) has arisen.

Commentary

There are twenty seven Nakṣatras which rise one after the other. The first four are the Aśvinī, the Bharaṇī, the Krittikā and the Rohiṇī. Now as the time of the Krittikā is going to pass, we infer that the Rohiṇī will now arise. Similarly, we infer from the existence of the Krittikā, that the Bharaṇī had arisen before. This is an example of consequence which is mentioned in the next aphorism,

Example of Uttarachara (consequence) Hetu :—

उदगाद् भरणिः प्राक्तत एव ॥ ६९ ॥

69. Udagād bharaṇiḥ prāktata eva.

69. The Bharaṇi had already risen before this.

Example of Sahachara Hetu (co-existence) :—

अस्त्यत्र मातुलिंगे रूपं रसात् ॥ ७० ॥

70. Astyatra mātuliṅge rūpaṃ rasāt.

70. There is colour in this Mātuliṅga (fruit) as there is juice (in it)[1].

We have finished the description of the six varieties of Aviruddha Upalabdhi. Now follows the illustrations of six kinds of Viruddha Upalabdhi after its definition.

विरूद्धतदुपलब्धिः प्रतिषेधे तथा ॥ ७१ ॥

71. Viruddhatadupalabdhiḥ pratiṣedhe tathā.

71. Viruddha Upalabdhi is also the same (i. e. of six varieties) implying a Sādhya of a non-existent nature (or which is refuted).

Example of Viruddha Vyāpya Upalabdhi :—

नास्त्यत्र शीतस्पर्श औष्ण्यात् ॥ ७२ ॥

72. Nāstyatra śitasparśa auṣṇyāt.

72. There is no feeling of cold here, as it is hot.

Commentary

By refuting (Pratiṣedha) the feeling of cold, its antithesis (Viruddha) fire and the heat pervading (vyāpya) the same is inferred.

---

1. "This illustration proceeds on the principle of concomitance or co-existence of colour and taste, so that the presence of the one is an index to the existence of the other." The Science of Thought by C. R. Jain, P. 48, footnote.

Example of Viruddha Kāryopalabdhi :—

नास्त्यत्र शीतस्पर्शो धूमात् ॥ ७३ ॥

73. Nāstyatra śitasparśo dhūmāt.

73. There is no feeling of cold here, because there is smoke.

Commentary

Here cold is the antithesis of heat the Kārya of which is smoke. So this is an example of inference of a Kārya (effect) of the antithesis.

Example of Viruddha Kāraṇopalabdhi :—

नास्मिन् शरीरिणि सुखमस्ति हृदयशल्यात् ॥ ७४ ॥

74. Nāsmin śarīriṇi sukhamasti hridayaśalyāt.

74. There is no happiness in this creature because it has grief (the antithesis of happiness)

Example of Viruddha Pūrvachara Upalabdhi :—

नोदेष्यति मुहूर्त्तान्ते शकटं रेवत्युदयात् ॥ ७५ ॥

75. Nodeṣyati muhūrtānte śakataṃ revatyudayāt.

75. The Rohiṇī will not rise after the end of a Muhūrta as the Revatī has arisen.

Commentary

The constellation of the Rohiṇī will not appear after a Muhūrta (two ghatikās = 48 minutes) as now the constellation Revatī which succeeds the constellation Aśvinī (which as opposed to the Rohiṇī) has arisen.

Another example is this : Tomorrow will not be a Sunday, because it is Friday today.

Example of Viruddha Uttarachara Upalabdhi :—

नोदगाद् भरणिर्मुहूर्त्तात् पूर्वं पुष्योदयात् ॥ ७६ ॥

76. Nodagād Bharaṇirmuhūrttāt pūrvaṃ puṣyodayāt.

76. The Bharaṇī (constellation) did not appear before the Muhūrta because (now) the constellation Puṣyā has arisen.

Commentary

The constellations up to Puṣyā according to sequence are these: The Aśvinī, the Bharaṇī, the Krittikā, the Rohiṇī, the Mrigaśirā, the Ādrā, the Punarvasu, and the Puṣyā. So when there is the Puṣyā constellation which follows the Punarvasu, it follows that the Bharaṇi did not rise one Muhūrta before it as it was Punarvasu which rose in that time.

Another example of this is: "Yesterday was not a Friday, because it is Tuesday to-day".

Example of Viruddha Sahachara upalabdhi :—

नास्त्यत्र भित्तौ परभागाभावोऽर्वाग्भागदर्शनात् ॥ ७७ ॥

77. Nāstyatra bhittau parabhāgābhāvo'rvāgbhagadarśanāt.

77. This wall is not devoid of an outside, because it has an inside [the Sahachara (coexistent) of the outside].

Six varieties of each of Aviruddha and Viruddha upalabdhi have now been described. Next we proceed to describe the (seven) varieties of Aviruddha Anupalabdhi and (three) varieties of Viruddha Anupalabdhi.

अविरुद्धानुपलब्धिः प्रतिषेधे सप्तधा स्वभावव्यापककार्यकारण-पूर्वोत्तरसहचरानुपलम्भभेदात् ॥ ७८ ॥

78. Aviruddhānupalabdhiḥ pratiṣedhe saptadhā svabhāva-vyāpakakāryakāraṇa-pūrvottarasahacharānupalambhabhedāt.

78. When (the Sādhya consists of) Pratiṣedha (non-existence of some fact), Aviruddha Anupalabdhi is of seven kinds viz. non-finding of Svabhāva, Vyāpaka, Kārya, Kāraṇa, Pūrvachara, Uttarachara and Sahachara

Commentary

There are seven kinds of Aviruddha Anupalabdhi which cause knowledge of nonexistence of some fact. Not finding the antithesis consists of Aviruddha Anupalabdhi and when this establishes non-existence of some fact, we call it Aviruddha Anupalabdhi in Pratiṣedha. This is of seven kinds, examples of which will be given in the following seven aphorisms 79-85[1].

Example of Aviruddha Svabhāva Anupalabdhi :—

नास्त्यत्र भूतले घटोऽनुपलब्धेः ॥ ७९ ॥

79. Nāstyatra bhūtale ghato'nupalabdheḥ.

79. There is no pitcher in this place because (its Svabhāva or identity) is not to be found (i. e. nothing resembling its identity is present here).

Example of Aviruddha Vyāpaka Anupalabdhi :—

नास्त्यत्र शिंशपा वृक्षानुपलब्धेः ॥ ८० ॥

80. Nāstyatra śinśapā vrikṣānupalabdheḥ.

80. There is no Sinśapā (tree) here, because no tree is found here.

Example of Aviruddha Kāryānupalabdhi :—

नास्त्यत्राप्रतिबद्धसामर्थ्योऽग्निर्धूमानुपलब्धेः ॥ ८१ ॥

81. Nāstyatrāpratibaddhasāmarthyo'gnirdhūmānupalabdheḥ.

81. There is no fire whose potency (Sāmarthya) has not been obstructed here, because we do not find smoke.

Example of Aviruddha Kāraṇānupalabdhi :

नास्त्यत्र धूमोऽनग्नेः ॥ ८२ ॥

82. Nāstyatra dhūmo'nagneḥ.

82. There is no smoke here because there is no fire.

---

1. "तत्राविरुद्धानुपलब्धिः प्रतिषेधावबोधे सप्तप्रकाराः ।"

Pramāṇanayatattvālokālaṅkāra, III. 90.

"प्रतिषेध्येनाविरुद्धानां स्वभावव्यापककार्यकारणपूर्वचरोत्तरसहचाराणामनुपलब्धिः ।" Ibid. III. 91.

Example of Aviruddha Pūrvachara Anupalabdhi :

न भविष्यति मुहूर्त्तांते शकटं कृत्तिकोदयानुपलब्धेः ॥ ८३ ॥

83. Na bhaviṣyati muhūrtānte śakataṃ krittikodayānupalabdheḥ.

83. There will be no rise of the Rohiṇī after a Muhūrta as we have no knowledge of the rise of the Krittikā.

Commentary

Another Example is this : It will not be Sunday tomorrow because it is not Saturday to-day.

Example of Aviruddha Uttarachara Anupalabdhi :

नोदगाद् भरणिर्मुहूर्त्तात् प्राक्तत एव ॥ ८४ ॥

84. Nodagād Bharaṇirmuhūrttāt prāktata eva.

84. The Bharaṇi had not risen before a Muhūrta because now the Krittikā is not up.

Example of Aviruddha Sahachara Anupalabdhi :

नास्त्यत्र समतुलायामुन्नामो नामानुपलब्धेः ॥ ८५ ॥

85. Nāstyatra samatulāyāmunnāmo nāmānupalabdheḥ.

85. One pan of this pair of scales does not touch beam as the other one is on the same level with it.

Now, the varieties of Viruddha Anupalabdhi (nonfinding of antithesis) establishing a Sādhya of Vidhi (existence of a fact) are being described.

विरुद्धानुपलब्धिर्विधौ त्रेधा विरुद्धकार्यकारणस्वभावानुपलब्धिभेदात् ॥ ८६ ॥

86, Viruddhānupalabdhirvidhau tredhā viruddhakāryakāraṇasvabhāvānupalabdhibhedāt.

86. Viruddha Anupalabdhi in Vidhi is of three kinds :— Viruddha Kārya Anupalabdhi, Viruddha Kāraṇa Anupalabdhi and Viruddha Svabhāva Anupalabdhi.

Example of Viruddha Kārya Anupalabdhi :—

यथाऽस्मिन् प्राणिनि व्याधिविशेषोऽस्ति निरामयचेष्टानुपलब्धेः ॥ ८७ ॥

87. Yathāsmin prāṇini vyādhiviśeṣosti nirāmayacheṣṭānupalabdheḥ.

87. As for example, some disease exists in this animal, because the actions of a healthy body are not found.

Example of Viruddha Kāraṇa Anupalabdhi :—

अस्त्यत्र देहिनि दुःखमिष्टसंयोगाभावात् ॥ ८८ ॥

88. Astyatra dehini duḥkhamiṣṭasaṅyogābhāvāt.

88. There is grief in this creature, because it has no connection with its dear ones.

Example of Viruddha Svabhāva Anupalabdhi :—

अनेकान्तात्मकं वस्त्वेकांतस्वरूपानुपलब्धेः ॥ ८९ ॥

89. Anekāntātmakaṃ vastvekāntasvarūpānupalabdheḥ.

89. All things are Anekāntika (posessed of different aspects) because we do not find that these have only one aspect.

Commentary

In Pramāṇanayatattvālokālaṅkāra, five varieties[1] (instead of three as described in the Parikṣāmukhaṃ) of Viruddha Anupalabdhi in Vidhi have been described. The first three are the same as described in aphorisms 87, 88 and 89. The additional ones are Viruddha Vyāpaka Anupalabdhi e. g. "There is wind here because there is no heat" and Viruddha Sahachara Anupalabdhi e. g. 'He has false knowledge because we do not find perfect knowledge in him'[2].

---

1. "विरुद्धानुपलबधिस्तु विधिप्रतीतौ पंचधा ।"

Pramāṇanayatattvālokālaṅkāra, III. 99.

2. "विरुद्धव्यापकानुपलब्धिर्यथा अस्त्यत्र छाया औष्ण्यानुपलब्धेः ।"

"विरुद्धसहचारानुपलब्धिर्यथा अस्त्यस्य मिथ्याज्ञानं सम्यग्दर्शनानुपलब्धेः ।"

Ibid III. 104, 105

परंपरया संभवत् साधनमत्रैवान्तर्भावनीयम् ॥ ९० ॥

90. Paramparayā saṃbhavat sādhanamatraivāntarbhāvanīyaṃ.

90. The Hetus which arise one after the other should be included within those (which have been described).

Commentary

There are cases where a Hetu is not the direct cause of anything but it leads to another and that leads to a third etc. In such cases there is no necessity of accepting these as separate Hetus, but we should include these within the proper Hetus already defined and illustrated. Examples of such Hetus are given in the following aphorism.

अभूदत्र चक्रे शिवकः स्थासात् ॥ ९१ ॥

91. Abhūdatra chakre śivakaḥ sthāsāt.

कार्यकार्यमविरुद्धकार्योपलब्धौ ॥ ९२ ॥

92. Kāryakāryamaviruddhakāryopalabdhau.

91. There was Śivaka (a clod of earth resembling a Śivaliṅga) on this potter's wheel because we see *Sthāsa* there.

92. (This Hetu showing) effect of an effect will be included within Aviruddha Kārya upalabdhi (as already defined).

Commentary

To manufacture a pitcher, a clod of earth is necessary. This clod resembling a Śivaliṅga is placed on the potter's wheel. *Chhatraka* (mushroom) may grow on it and after that *Sthāsa* (signs of mushroom) may be found on the earth. As *Sthāsa* is now seen, we infer Śivaka though the intervening Hetu *Chhatraka* is not seen or mentioned. Sthāsa is therefore the effect of Chhatraka which is an effect of Śivaka. This can be included within Aviruddha Kāryopalabdhi as already defined.

नास्त्यत्र गुहायां मृगक्रीडनं मृगारिसंशब्दनात् ।
कारणविरुद्धकार्यं विरुद्धकार्योपलब्धौ यथा ॥ ९३ ॥

93. Nāstyatra guhāyāṃ mrigakrīḍanaṃ mrigārisaṃśabdanāt.
Kāraṇaviruddhakāryaṃ viruddhakāryopalabdhau yathā.

93. There is no play of deer in this cave because there is a roar of lion. Here there is an effect opposed to a cause. This should be (included) within Viruddha Kārya Upalabdhi.

Commentary

In the example given, deer (Kāraṇa) are the causes of play (Kārya). A lion is the antithesis (Viruddha) of deer for no deer can play in the presence of a lion. The Kārya of lion is the roaring. So we have Kāraṇa Viruddha Kārya in this place. This should be included within Viruddha Kārya Upalabdhi and not recognized as a separate inference.

व्युत्पन्नप्रयोगस्तु तथोपपत्त्याऽन्यथानुपपत्त्यैव वा ॥ ९४ ॥

94. Vyutpannaprayogastu tathopapattyānyathānupapattyaiva vā.

94. The use by those who are conversant (with the process of inference) is from existence or non-existence of that universal concomitance (between the Sādhya and the Sādhana).

Commentary

It has already been mentioned (Aphorism 46) that though five parts of Anumāna are used for teaching students, really there are only two parts of an inference (Aphorism 37). But those who are conversant with processes of reasoning employ inference through the knowledge of the existence of Sādhya (e. g. fire) always along with Sādhana (e. g. smoke) or the nonexistence of Sādhya where Sādhana is absent. This is amplified in the four aphorisms which follow.

अग्निमानयं देशस्तथैव धूमवत्त्वोपपत्तेर्धूमवत्त्वान्यथानुपपत्तेर्वा ॥९५॥

हेतुप्रयोगे हि यथा व्याप्तिग्रहणं विधीयते सा च तावन्मात्रेण व्युत्पन्नैरवधार्यते ॥ ९६ ॥

95. Agnimānayaṃ deśastathaiva dhūmavattvopapatter-dhūmavattvānyathānupapatterva.

96. Hetuprayoge hi yathā vyāptigrahaṇaṃ vidhīyate sā cha tāvanmātreṇa vyutpannairavadhāryate.

तावता च साध्यसिद्धिः ॥ ९७ ॥

97. Tāvatā cha sādhyasiddhiḥ.

तेन पक्षस्तदाधारसूचनायोक्तः ॥ ९८ ॥

98. Tena pakṣastadādhārasūchanāyoktaḥ.

95. This place is full of fire, for existence of smoke is only possible if there be fire here or (this place is not full of fire) as smoke does not exist here.

96. In the employment of Hetu, the use of Vyāpti (universal concomitance) is made. That (Vyāpti) is understood by the persons conversant (with the process of inference) from it (viz. Hetu) (without use of Udāharaṇa etc.).

97. The Sādhya is established from this (viz. Hetu) only.

98. So it has been mentioned that it is necessary to mention Pakṣa to indicate the Ādhāra (abode) of Hetu consisting of universal concomitance.

Commentary

The subjectmatter of these four aphorisms has already been discussed in connection with the establishment of the principle that Driṣṭānta etc. are not necessary in inference by logicians conversant with the processes of reasoning, though these may be used in lectures to pupils for their better understanding (vide Aphorisms 37, 43, 44 and 46).

आप्तवचनादिनिबंधनमर्थज्ञानमागमः ॥ ९९ ॥

99. Āptavachanādinivandhanamarthajñānamāgamaḥ.

99. Āgama is knowledge derived from words etc. of a reliable person.

Commentary

The characteristics of Anumāna have been described. Now the same of Āgama are mentioned. Knowledge derived from interpretation of signs, symbols, words etc. is called Śruta Jñāna. Now the words, signs etc. of a person who has no motive for deceiving or misleading any one, are reliable. Such a person is known as Āpta. The knowledge derived from words etc. of an Āpta is called Āgama.

This is the same as Śabda Pramāṇa of Hindu philosophers. Knowledge may be derived from words of living beings or from scriptures. In Nyāyāvatāra, the Śabda Pramāṇa with its subdivision scriptural knowledge is thus described :—

"Knowledge arising from words, which taken in their proper acceptance express real objects not inconsistent with what are established by perception, is known as *Śabda* (the verbal testimony).

The scripture (Śāstra) is that which was invented (or first known) by a competent person, which is not such as to be passed over by others, which is not incompatible with the truths derived from perception, which imparts true instructions and which is profitable to all men and is preventive of the evil path[1]."

Dr. S. C. Vidyābhūṣana in his notes to these verses has written : "*Śabda* (the word or verbal testimony) is of two kinds, viz. (1) Laukika (the knowledge derived from a reliable person), and (2) Śāstraja (the knowledge derived from scripture). This definition sets aside the view of those (Mimāmsakas) who maintain that the scripture (such as the Veda) is eternal and was not composed by any human being. The scripture could not have

---

1. "दृष्टेष्टाव्याहतत्वाद् वाक्यात् परमार्थाभिधायिनः ।
तत्त्वग्राहितयोत्पन्नमानं शाब्दं प्रकीर्त्तितम् ॥
आप्तोपज्ञमनुल्लङ्घ्यमदृष्टेष्टविरोधकम् ।
तत्त्वोपदेशकृत् सार्वं शास्त्रं कापथघट्टनम् ॥" Nyāyāvatāra 8. 9.

Tr. by Dr. S. C. Vidyābhūṣana. The latter verse appears as verse 9 in Ratnakaraṇḍaśrāvakāchāra by Samantabhadra (2nd century).

been called a verbal testimony (Śabda or word) unless it embodied the words of any particular person or persons[1]."

In Pramāṇanayatattvālokālaṅkāra it is mentioned : "Āgama is knowledge derived from words etc. of an Āpta. The words themselves are also called Āgama in a secondary sense. For example, there is a mine of jewels in this place. Hills etc. containing jewels exist. An Āpta is a person who knows the real nature of a thing about which he speaks and who speaks according to his correct knowledge. Only words of such a person are established without any opposition. Such an Āpta is of two kinds Laukika or Lokottara. A Laukika person is (an ordinary human being) like Janaka. Lokottara persons are like the Tirthankaras[2]." In the Hindu Nyāya philosophy also Śabda (Pramāṇa) is said to be derived from the speech of one worthy of confidence and a person who speaks the truth becomes worthy (Āpta) of such confidence[3].

An Āpta is free from eighteen faults viz. hunger, thirst, senility, disease, birth, death, fear, pride, attachment, aversion, infatuation, worry, conceit, hatred, uneasiness, sweat, sleep and

---

1. Nyāyāvatāra Edited by S. C. Vidyābhuṣana, Pp. 11-12.
2. "आप्तवचनादाविर्भूतमर्थसंवेदनमागमः ॥"
"उपचारादाप्तवचनश्च ॥"
"समस्त्यत्र प्रदेशे रत्ननिधानं, सन्ति रत्नसानुप्रभृतयः ॥"
"अभिधेयं वस्तु यत्रावस्थितं यो जानीते यथाज्ञानं चाभिधत्ते स आप्तः ॥"
"तस्य हि वचनम् अविसंवादि भवति ।"
"स च द्वेधा लौकिको लोकोत्तरश्च ।"
"लौकिको जनकादिर्लोकोत्तरस्तु तीर्थंकरादितः ॥"
Pramāṇanayatattvālokālaṅkāra IV. 1—7
3. "आप्तवाक्यं शब्दः । आप्तस्तु यथार्थवक्ता ।"
Tarkasaṅgraha by Annaṃ Bhatta 48.

surprise[1]. He is the knower of all things. Being free from faults, he reveals the scriptures[2]. He is of the highest status and of unsurpassed splendour. He is free from attachment and void of impurities. He has omniscience and has no beginning, middle or end and is a friend of all living beings and their teacher[3]. Just as a drum sounds being struck by the hands of the drummer without any desire of its own, so an Āpta reveals the Truth for the benefit of people without any personal motive[4]. Revelation comes out of an Āpta spontaneously to remove sufferings of people.

सहजयोग्यतासंकेतवशाद्धि शब्दादयो वस्तुप्रतिपत्तिहेतवः ॥१००॥

100. Sahajayogyatāsaṃketavaśāddhi śabdādayo vastu-pratipattihetavaḥ.

यथा मेर्वादयः सन्ति ॥ १०१ ॥

101. Yathā mervādayaḥ santi.

100. Words etc. (signs, symbols and other things of like nature) are causes of knowledge of things through their inherent power in connoting things.

101. As for example "The Meru etc. exist."

Commentary

A question may arise, how do we have knowledge derived from words ? In Hindu Nyāya philosophy it is mentioned "The

---

1. "क्षुत्पिपासाजरातङ्कजन्मान्तकभयस्मयाः ।
न रागद्वेषमोहाश्च यस्याप्तः स प्रकीर्त्तितः ॥"

Ratnakaraṇḍaśrāvakāchāra, Verse 6

2. "आप्तेनोच्छिन्नदोषेण सर्वज्ञेनागमेशिना ।
भवितव्यं नियोगेन नान्यथा ह्याप्तता भवेत् ॥" Ibid Verse 5

3. "परमेष्ठी परंज्योतिर्विरागो विमलः कृती ।
सर्वज्ञोऽनादिमध्यान्तः सार्वः शास्तोपलाल्यते ॥" Ibid Verse 7

4. "अनात्मार्थं विना रागैः शास्ता शास्ति सतो हितम् ।
ध्वनन् शिल्पिकरस्पर्शान्मुरजः किमपेक्षते ॥" Ibid Verse 8

cause of the knowledge of the sense of a sentence is the inter-dependance, Compatibility and Juxta-position (of the words). Inter-dependance means the inability of a word to indicate the intended sense in the absence of another word. Compatibility consists in (a word's) not rendering futile the sense (of a sentence). Juxta-position consists in the enunciation of the words without a (long) pause between each.

A collection of words devoid of interdependance etc. is no valid sentence. For example 'cow, horse, man, elephant' gives no information, the words not looking out for one another. The expression 'He should irrigate with fire' is no cause of right knowledge, for there is no compatibility (between fire and irrigation). The words 'Bring-the-cow' not pronounced close together but with an interval of some three hours between each, are not a cause of correct knowledge, from the absence of (the requisite closeness of) juxta-position[1]."

"A speech is a collection of significant sounds as for example, Bring the cow. A significant sound is that which is possessed of power (to convey a meaning)[2]."

Now, if we ask, who decides that such and such a word means such and such a thing, the answer given by some Hindu logicians is that it is God's will which decides this. "The power (of a word) is the appointment, in the shape of God's will that such and

---

1. "आकाङ्क्षा योग्यता संनिधिश्च वाक्यार्थज्ञानहेतुः। पदस्य पदान्तर-व्यतिरेकप्रयुक्तान्वयाननुभावकत्वमाकांक्षा। अर्थाबाधो योग्यता। पदानामविलंबेनोच्चारणं संनिधिः।

आकांक्षादिरहितं वाक्यमप्रमाणम्। यथा गौरश्वः पुरुषो हस्तीति न प्रमाण-माकांक्षाविरहात्। अग्निना सिञ्चेदिति न प्रमाणं योग्यताविरहात्। प्रहरे प्रहरे-ऽसहोच्चारितानि गामानयेत्यादिपदानि न प्रमाणं सांनिध्याभावात्॥" Tarka-saṅgraha, 49-50.

2. "वाक्यं पदसमूहः। यथा गामानयेति। शक्तं पदम्।" Tarka-saṅgraha, 48.

such an import should be recognizable from such and such a significant sound[1]. Or, we may hold that we take the meaning of words from its use in a particular sense by previous users[2].

In this connection we may remember the conclusions arrived at by scholars dealing with the science of language regarding sematology or the science of meaning of words. "The phenomena with which sematology deals are too complicated, too dependent on psychological conditions ; the element of chance or conscious exertion of will seems to enter into them, and it is often left to the arbitrary choice of an individual to determine the change of meaning to be undergone by a word. Still this meaning must be accepted by the community before it can become part of language; unless it is so accepted it will remain a mere literary curiosity in the pages of a technical dictionary. And since its acceptance by the community is due to general causes, influencing many minds alike, it is possible to analyze and formulate these causes, in fact, to refer significant change to certain definite principles to bring it under certain definite generalizations. Moreover, it must be remembered that the ideas suggested by most words are what Locke calls 'mixed modes.' A word like *just* or *beauty* is but a shorthand note suggesting a number of ideas more or less associated with one another. But the ideas associated with it in one mind cannot be exactly those associated with it in another ; to one man it suggests what it does not to another. So long as we move in a society subjected to the same social influences and education as ourselves we do not readily perceive the fact, since the leading ideas called up by the word will be alike for all ; but it is quite otherwise when we come to deal with those whose education has been imperfect as compared with our own. A young speaker often imagines that he makes himself intelligible to an uneducated

---

1. "अस्मात् पदात् अयमर्थो बोद्धव्य इतीश्वरेच्छासंकेतः शक्तिः ।"
Tarkasaṅgraha, 48.

2. "संकेतस्य ग्रहः पूर्वं वृद्धस्य व्यवहारतः ।" Śabdaśaktiprakāśikā

audience by using short and homely words ; unless he also suits his ideas to theirs, he will be no better understood than if he spoke in the purest Johnsonese. If we are suddenly brought into contact with experts in a subject we have not studied, or dip into a book on an unfamiliar branch of knowledge, we seem to be listening to the meaningless sounds of a foreign tongue. The words used may not be technical words ; but familiar words and expressions will bear senses and suggest ideas to those who use them which they will not bear to us. It is impossible to convey in a translation all that is meant by the original writer. We may say that the French *juste* answers to the English *just*, and so it does in a rough way ; but the train of thoughts associated with *juste* is not that associated wih *just*, and the true meaning of a passage may often depend more on the associated thoughts than on the leading idea itself. Nearly every word, in fact, may be described as a complex of ideas, which is not the same in the minds of any two individuals, its general meaning lying in the common ideas attached to it by all the members of a particular society. The significations, therefore, with which the comparative philologist has to concern himself are those unconsciously agreed upon by a body of men, or rather the common group of ideas suggested by a word to all of them alike. Here again some general causes must be at work which may yet be revealed by a careful analysis. The comparative philologist has not to trouble himself, like the classical philologist, with discovering the exact ideas connected with a word by some individual author ; it is the meaning of words as they are used in current speech, not as they illustrate the idiosyncrasies of a writer, which it is his province to investigate.[1]."

We must also remember that analogy lends new senses to words. The original meaning is forgotten and metaphorical senses come to be used in its place. A dead meaning may again be

---

1. Introduction to the Science of Language (Sayce) Vol. I Pp. 336-338.

revived. There are also metaphors, variation of meaning according to their application to persons or things, to what is good or bad, great or small. Words change their signification according to their use as active or passive, as subjects or as objects. An idea may also be expressed either by a compound or periphrasis or by a single word. The same word may also be applied in a variety of senses, the particular sense which it bears being determined by the context. Change of meaning may also follow from change of pronunciation or the introduction of new words[1].

In aphorism 99 it has been mentioned that knowledge can be derived from "words etc." of an Āpta. We have mentioned that by 'etc.' it is implied that signs, symbols etc. can also impart knowledge. The modern science of language also recognises that thoughts can be expressed by other symbols than words. Writing consisting of hieroglyphics or mathematical symbols and gesture language are examples of this. Onomatopaeia, interjectional or instinctive cries also of men whose language we do not know are intelligible to us.

End of Samuddeśa 3.

1. Ibid Pp. 338-343.

CHART IV.

[CHAPTER IV.]

- Viṣaya (Aphorism 1)
  - Sāmānya (or Dravya) (Aphorism 3)
    - Tiryak (Aphorism 4)
    - Ūrddhvatā (Aphorism 5)
  - Viśeṣa (or Paryāya) (Aphorism 6)
    - Paryāya (Aphorism 8)
    - Vyatireka (Aphorism 9)

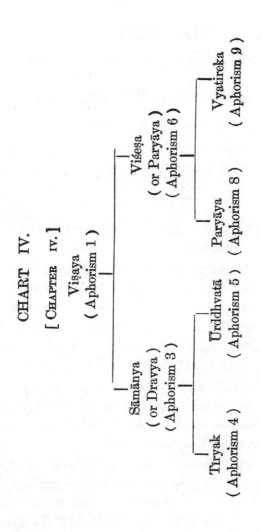

चतुर्थः समुद्देशः

SAMUDDEŚA IV.

This samuddeśa deals with the object of Pramāṇa.

सामान्यविशेषात्मा तदर्थो विषयः ॥ १ ॥

1. Sāmānyaviśeṣatmā tadartho viṣayaḥ.

1. The subject matter of it (Pramāṇa) is viṣaya of two kinds characterised by sāmānya and viśeṣa.

Commentary

The subject matter of this samuddeśa is summarised in the Chart which faces this page.

"Things in nature are characterised by many-sidedness. Each of them presents a number of aspects which have to be known before we can be said to have exact knowledge of their nature.

The different points of view for studying things are called Nayas of which the Dravyārthika (the natural) and the Paryāyārthika (changing or conditional) are the most important.

The Dravyārthika point of view only takes into consideration the nature of the substance of material of a thing, while the Paryāyārthika confines itself to the study of the form or forms in which substances manifest themselves[1]."

"Jainism aims, from the very commencement, at a systematic classification of the subject-matter of knowledge, and divides the philosophical standpoint into two main heads, the Niśchaya and the Vyavahāra. Of these, the former deals with the permanent qualities, hence, the essential nature of things about which there can be no possibility of doubt, and which remains true under all

---

1. The Science of Thought by C. R. Jain, Pp. 21-22.

circumstances, conditions and states. For this reason, it is called the Niśchaya i. e. the natural or certain. The latter, however, only deals with things not with reference to their real or essential nature, but with respect to their utility or non-natural states and conditions. The statement 'This is a jar of clay' is an illustration of the Niśchaya Naya, while 'This is a jar of butter' is true only from the Vyavahāra or the practical point of view[1]."

In Naya-karṇikā by Vinaya-vijaya we have: "All objects possess two kinds of properties, viz. 1. Sāmānya or the generalizing (general) and 2. Viśeṣa or the differentiating (specific) properties; the general expressing the genus (*jāti*) etc. and the specific expressing the species, differences and distinctions. By means of general properties in each of a hundred ('hundred' here means 'all') jars, one idea (that of jarness is recognised and by means of specific properties, people distinguish each individual particular jar as their own[2]."

Hemachandra writes: "The objects of Pramāṇa are things characterised by Dravya or Paryāya[3]." Dravya and Paryāya are the same as Sāmānya and Viśeṣa or Niśchaya and Vyavahāra.

अनुवृत्तव्यावृत्तप्रत्ययगोचरत्वात् पूर्वोत्तराकारपरिहारावाप्तिस्थितिलक्षणपरिणामेनार्थक्रियोपपत्तेश्च ॥ २ ॥*

2. Anuvritta-vyāvritta-pratyaya-gocharatvāt pūrvottarākāra-parihārāvāpti-sthiti-lakṣaṇa-pariṇāmenārtha-kriyopapatteścha.

---

* "पूर्वोत्तराकारपरिहारस्वीकारस्थितिलक्षणपरिणामेनास्यार्थक्रियोपपत्तिः ।"
Pramāṇamīmāṃsā I. I. 34

1. The Nayakarṇikā by M. D. Desai. Introduction Pp. 5-6.

2. "अर्थाः सर्वेऽपि सामान्यविशेषा उभयात्मकाः ।
सामान्यं तत्र जात्यादि विशेषश्च विभेदकाः ॥
ऐक्यबुद्धिर्घटशते भवेत् सामान्यधर्मतः ।
विशेषाच्च निजं निजं लक्षयन्ति घटं जनाः ॥"
Nayakarṇikā 3 and 4

3. "प्रमाणस्य विषयो द्रव्यपर्यायात्मकं वस्तु ।"
Pramāṇa-mīmāṃsā I. 1. 31.

2. As there is attainment of the object (as a result of knowledge) from signs of changes from its original state to a later state preserving its essential characteristics and from our idea of general and special characteristics.

Commentary

In every substance, there is knowledge of its general and special characteristics. For example, we have a general knowledge of a man and a special knowledge whether he is a Brahmin or not etc. Also, a thing changes its qualities for example a man grows up, leaving his childhood and youth and becomes old. But throughout his different ages, he maintains essential charcteristics of being a person.

This acceptance of change leading to the manysidedness of a thing is a peculiarity of Jain doctrine establishing the Anekāntavāda.

"Dravya means that which flows or changes. While changing through its different qualities and modifications, its essential nature persists. This kind of progressive development is associated with Dravya. But such development is also the characteristic of substance. Hence according to Jaina attitude, Dravya is not entirely different from Sattā or substance···

According to this view there is no unchanging substance or Sattā in Jaina system···Here···the similarity between the Hegelian concept of 'thing' and the Jaina concept of Dravya is worth noticing. Sattā is not 'a thing in itself' behind Dravya. Sattā and Dravya are one and the same as Hegel mentioned. Thing in itself and experience are not absolutely distinct. Dravya refers to facts of experience. Sattā refers to existence or reality. One may be abstracted from the other but it is not different from the other as a fact[1]."

---

1. "दवियदि गच्छदि ताइं ताइं सब्भाव पज्जयाइं जं ।
दवियं तं भण्णंति अणण्णभूदं तु सत्तादो ॥"

Pañchāstikāyasamayasāra. Verse 9.

This changing nature of the substance is mentioned in the Tattvārthādhigama Sūtra as "Sat (the dravya) consists of utpāda, vyaya and dhrauvya[1]." Utpada is appearance i. e., assuming new modification. This does not mean creation out of nothing. Creation by the fiat of a will is not recognised by the Jainas. Utpāda therefore means that phase of the process of the development when a new form is assumed. Vyaya is losing the previous form. Here also it is different from absolute disappearance. It only means that phase in the process of development where the earlier form is replaced by the succeeding one. Dhrauvya refers to the persistence of the essential nature of dravya which undergoes development and which makes both utpāda and vyaya simultaneously possible. In fact the process of development includes all the three phases. This fact is not only recognised by scientists like Darwin and Spencer, but by the great French philosopher Bergson who has raised it to an important philosophical principle[2]."

Hemachandra says that from the fact that only a thing characterised by Dravya and Paryāya is capable of producing the result of Pramāṇa viz. acceptance of things desirable and non-acceptance of undesirable things or indifference to the latter, we say that merely a Dravya or a Paryāya or both of them independantly of the thing cannot be the object of Pramāṇa[3].

---

1. "सत् द्रव्यलक्षणम् ।"
"उत्पादव्ययध्रौव्ययुक्तं सत् ।"
Tattvārtha Sūtra V. 29 and 30.

2. Sacred Books of the Jainas Vol. III. P. 9.

3. "कुतः पुनर्द्रव्यपर्यायात्मकमेव वस्तु प्रमाणानां विषयो, न द्रव्यमात्रं पर्यायमात्रमुभयं वा स्वतन्त्रमित्याह, अर्थक्रियासामर्थ्यात् । अर्थस्य हानोपादानादि-लक्षणस्य क्रियानिष्पत्तिस्तत्र सामर्थ्यात् द्रव्यपर्यायात्मकस्यैव वस्तुनोऽर्थक्रियासमर्थत्वादित्यर्थः ।" Pramāṇa-mīmāṃsā 1. 1. 32.

सामान्यं द्वेधा तिर्यगूर्ध्वताभेदात् ॥ ३ ॥

3. Sāmānyaṃ dvedhā tiryagūrdhvatābhedāt.

3. Sāmānya is of two kinds being divided into Tiryak (sāmānya) and ūrdhvatā (sāmānya).

सदृशपरिणामस्तिर्यक् खंडमुंडादिषु गोत्ववत् ॥ ४ ॥

4. Sadriśapariṇāmastiryak khandamuṇḍādiṣu gotvavat.

4. Tiryak (sāmānya) is the same modification such as Khaṇda Muṇda etc. in the condition of a cow.

परापरविवर्त्तव्यापिद्रव्यमूर्ध्वंता मृदिव स्थासादिषु ॥ ५ ॥

5. Parāparavivartavyāpidravyamūrddhvatā mridiva sthāsādiṣu.

5. Ūrdhvatā sāmānya is a thing which remains the same through changes such as earth in its (modifications) sthāsa etc.

विशेषश्च ॥ ६ ॥

6. Viśeṣascha.

पर्यायव्यतिरेकभेदात् ॥ ७ ॥

7. Paryāyavyatirekabhedāt.

6. Viśeṣa (is) also (of two kinds).

7. Being divided into Paryāya and Vyatireka.

एकस्मिन् द्रव्ये क्रमभाविनः परिणामाः पर्याया आत्मनि हर्षविषादादिवत् ॥ ८ ॥

8. Ekasmin dravye kramabhāvinaḥ pariṇāmāḥ paryāyā ātmani harṣaviṣādādivat.

8. Paryāyās are modifications in sequence in a single substance e. g. joy and grief in oneself.

अर्थान्तरगतो विसदृशपरिणामो व्यतिरेको गोमहिषादिवत् ॥ ९ ॥

9. Arthāntaragato visadriśa-pariṇāmo vyatireko go-mahiṣādivat.

9. Vyatirekas are different modifications in different objects such as a cow and a buffalo etc.

Commentary

With this aphorism, the description of the subject matter of Pramāṇa ends. In the next samuddeśa the result of Pramāṇa will be discussed.

End of Samuddeśa IV.

पञ्चमः समुद्देशः

SAMUDDEŚA V.

अज्ञाननिवृत्तिर्हानोपादानोपेक्षाश्च फलम् ॥ १ ॥

1. Ajñāna-nivrittirhānopādānopekṣāścha phalaṃ.

1. The result is the dispelling of false knowledge and leaving (the undesirable things), acquirement (of desirable things) and indifference (to other things).

Commentary

The result of Pramāṇa primarily consists of correct knowledge dispelling false knowledge, secondarily it leads to the acquirement of desirable objects, discarding of undesirable objects and indifference to other objects. This secondary result arises after we ascertain an object correctly by Pramāṇa[1].

Hemachandra mentions : when Pramāṇa arises in a person, the correct knowledge of an object is established. The immediate result is therefore the destruction of false knowledge[2], or the idea of leaving (the undesirable) etc. The following verse of Nyāyāvatāra is quoted in the commentary by Hemachandra.

"प्रमाणस्य फलं साक्षादज्ञानविनिवर्त्तनम् ।
केवलस्य सुखोपेक्षे शेषस्यादानहानधीः ॥"

---

1. "द्विविधं हि फलं साक्षात् पारम्पर्येणेति । साक्षादज्ञाननिवृत्तिः पारम्पर्येण हानादिकमिति । प्रमेयनिश्चयोत्तरकालभावित्वात् तस्येति ।"

Prameyaratnamālā.

2. "तस्यां सत्यामर्थप्रकाशसिद्धेः ।"

Pramāṇa-mimāṃsā I. 1. 38.

"अज्ञाननिवृत्तिर्वा ।" Ibid. I. 1. 39.

"हानादिबुद्धयो वा ।" Ibid. I. 1. 41.

That is to say, the immediate result of Pramāṇa is the removal of ignorance. So the mediate effect is happiness and indifference or equanimity to a Kevali (one possessed of absolute knowledge) and to others, a desire to accept (desirable objects) and leave (undesirable objects).

In Āpta Mīmāṃsā also the same has been mentioned :

"उपेक्षा फलमाद्यस्य शेषस्यादानहानधीः ।
पूर्वा वाऽज्ञाननाशो वा सर्वस्यास्य स्वगोचरे ॥"

In Sarvārtha-siddhi while explaining the aphorism "Tat Pramāṇe" of Tattvārthādhigama Sūtra, the result of Pramāṇa is mentioned as **"अन्धकारकल्पाज्ञानाभावः अज्ञाननाशो वा फलमित्युच्यते ।"** i. e. "the result is said to be the want of false knowledge resembling darkness or the destruction of false knowledge."

We have discussed while dealing with the definition of Pramāṇa that the Jain logicians have accepted the result of Pramāṇa to be the same as Pramāṇa. In Hindu philosophical systems like the Nyāya and Vaiśeṣika systems, the knowledge is mentioned as a result of Pramāṇa. For example Gautama in his Nyāya Sūtras has propounded that the knowledge of fire from smoke is the result known as Anumiti from Anumāna Pramāṇa (inference). But in Jain logic, this result itself has been called Anumāna and the dispelling of false knowledge is said to be the result of Pramāṇa.

It will be laid down in the two aphorisms which follow that in one sense a result is indentical with Pramāṇa and in another sense it is different.

In the different stages of knowledge Avagraha, Īhā, Avāya Dhāraṇā, Smriti, Pratyabhijñāna, Ūha, and Anumāna, the first is Pramāṇa and the second is the result of the first. Again the second becomes Pramāṇa and the third becomes the result of the second and so on[1].

---

1. **"अवग्रहादीनां वा क्रमापेक्षजननधर्माणां पूर्वं पूर्वं प्रमाणमुत्तरमुत्तरं फलम् ।"**
Pramāṇa-mīmāṃsā I. 1. 40.

प्रमाणादभिन्नं भिन्नं च ॥ २ ॥

2. Pramāṇādabhinnaṃ bhinnaṃ cha.

2. (The result) is different and not different (in another sense) from the Pramāṇa.

यः प्रमिमीते स एव निवृत्ताज्ञानो जहात्यादत्त उपेक्षते चेति प्रतीतेः ॥ ३ ॥

3. Yaḥ pramimīte sa eva nivrittājñāno jahātyādatta upekṣate cheti pratīteḥ.

3. He who takes cognizance, becomes free from false knowledge and rejects (undesirable objects), selects (desirable objects) or becomes indifferent.

Commentary

The self which is changed in the form of a Pramāṇa is also changed in the form of the result. In this sense Pramāṇa is not different from its result. But if we take that Pramāṇa is the instrumental cause (Kāraṇa) of the action (Kriyā) viz. the result, we can say in this sense, that Pramāṇa is different from the result[1].

"अवग्रहेहावायधारणास्मृतिप्रत्यभिज्ञानोहानुमानानां क्रमेणोपजायमानानां यद् यत् पूर्वं तत्त१ प्रमाणं यद्यदुत्तरं तत्तत्फलरूपं प्रतिपत्तव्यम् । अवग्रहपरिणामवान् ह्यात्मा ईहारूपफलतया परिणमति इतीहाफलापेक्षया अवग्रहः प्रमाणम्, ततोपीहा प्रमाणमवायः फलं, पुनरवायः प्रमाणं धारणा फलम्, ईहाधारणयोर्ज्ञानोपादानत्वात् ज्ञानरूपतोन्नेया, ततो धारणा प्रमाणं स्मृतिः फलम्, ततोऽपि स्मृतिः प्रमाणं प्रत्यभिज्ञानं फलं, ततोऽपि प्रत्यभिज्ञा प्रमाणमूहः फलं, ततोऽप्यूहः प्रमाणमनुमानं फलमिति प्रमाणफलविभाग इति ।" Bhāṣya to Ibid.

1. "यस्यैवात्मनः प्रमाणाकारेण परिणतिस्तस्यैव फलरूपतया परिणाम इत्येकप्रमात्रपेक्षया प्रमाणफलयोरभेद । करणक्रियापरिणामभेदाद् भेदः ।"

Prameyaratnamālā.

This is also laid down in Pramāṇa-mimāṃsā[1].

It is mentioned in Prameyaratnamālā that the propounders of Nyāyavaiśeṣika philosophies maintain that Pramāṇa is different from its result and the Buddhists say that the result is identical with the Pramāṇa. Refuting these views, it is laid down by Māṇikyanandi that result is in one sense different from Pramāṇa and in another, identical with it[2].

End of Samuddeśa V.

---

1. "प्रमाणाद् भिन्नाभिन्नम् ।" Pramāṇa-mimāṃsa. I. I. 24.

"करणरूपत्वात् क्रियारूपत्वाच्च प्रमाणफलयोरभेदः ।···तस्यैवात्मनः प्रमाणाकारेण परिणतिस्तस्यैव फलरूपतया परिणाम इत्येकप्रमात्रपेक्षया प्रमाणफलयोरभेदः ।" Ibid. Bhāṣya.

2. "तद्विविधमपि फलं प्रमाणाद्भिन्नमेवेति यौगाः । अभिन्नमेवेति सौगताः । तन्मतद्वयनिरासेन स्वमतं व्यवस्थापयितुमाह ।" Prameyaratnamālā.

षष्ठः समुद्देशः

SAMUDDEŚA VI.

ततोऽन्यत्तदाभासम् ॥ १ ॥

1. Tatonyattadābhāsaṃ

1. The opposite of it, is Ābhāsa of the same.

Commentary

In this Chapter, the fallacies will be taken up and described. We have mentioned before hand the nature, number, object and result of Pramāṇa. The opposite of these will be fallacies of these. The fallacies of Pramāṇa are described in Aphorisms 2-54, those of number are described in aphorism 55 ; those of object are described in aphorism 61 and those of result in aphorism 66.

अस्वसंविदितगृहीतार्थदर्शनसंशयादयः प्रमाणाभासाः ॥ २ ॥

2. Asvasaṃviditagrihītārthadarśanasaṃśayādayaḥ pramāṇābhāsāḥ.

2. Pramāṇābhāsas (fallacies of Pramāṇa) are non-cognizance by one's own-self, knowledge of what has already been known, doubt etc.

स्वविषयोपदर्शकत्वाभावात् ॥ ३ ॥

3. Svaviṣayopadarśakatvābhāvāt.

3. Because (such knowledge) does not establish its own object.

पुरुषान्तरपूर्वार्थगच्छत्तृणस्पर्शस्थाणुपुरुषादिज्ञानवत् ॥ ४ ॥

4. Puruṣāntarapūrvārthagachchattriṇa-sparśa-sthāṇupuruṣādijñānavat.

4. As (for example), the knowledge of another person, the knowledge of a thing previously known, the knowledge of touching

grass of a person moving, the knowledge whether this is a post ʳ ᵈ man etc.

Commentary

That which is not cognized by one's own self does not establish one's own knowledge ; so it is not fit to establish the object of knowledge. Consequently knowledge of others is not Pramāṇa but only a fallacy.

Again Nirvikalpaka Darśana is a fallacy as the Vikalpa caused by it (and not itself) shows the object.

Knowledge of what has already been known is a fallacy as it does not establish the object (being already known by previous experience).

By the word "doubt etc." in the aphorism, Samśaya (doubt), Anadhyavasāya and Viparyaya are meant. These have been thoroughly described in the commentary on Aphorism 3 Samuddeśa I of this work.

चक्षू रसयोर्द्रव्ये संयुक्तसमवायवच्च ॥ ५ ॥

5. Chakṣū rasayordravye saṃjuktasamavāyavachcha.

5. Like Saṃjukta Samavāya of eye and juice in a thing.

Commentary

According to the view of Hindu Nyāya philosophy, knowledge of colour etc. arises in Samavāya Samvandha (intimate relation or co-inherence). Seven categories viz. substance (Dravya), quality (Guṇa), action (Karma), genus (Sāmānya), difference (Viśeṣa). co-inherence (Samavāya) and non-existence (Abhāva) are recognized in Hindu Nyāya philosophy[1]. Samavāya is thus described : "Intimate relation is co-inherence (Samavāya). It exists in things which cannot exist separately. Two things which cannot exist separately are those of which two, the one exists only as lodged in the other. Such pairs are, parts and what is made up of the parts,

---

1. "द्रव्यगुणकर्मसामान्यविशेषसमवायाभावाः सप्तपदार्थाः ।" Tarkasaṅgraha.

qualities and the thing qualified, action and agent, species and individual, and difference and eternal substances[1]." "It exist, between the whole and its parts, the class and the individual, substance and qualities, agent and action, the ultimate atom and its viśeṣa[2]." When the eye sees a pitcher, the colour which is co-inherent in the pitcher is cognized by the eye. So according to Hindn Naiyāyikas, the relationship of Saṃjukta Samavāya can be the cause of the knowledge of colour.

In Jain Nyāya philosophy this view is not accepted and is refuted by this aphorism. It is urged that when we see a fruit, we do not cognise its taste though the taste has co-inherence in the fruit. So it cannot be said that knowledge arises from Saṃjukta Samavāya Saṃvandha. Though in a thing (fruit) there is co-inherence of sight and taste, Pramāṇa of taste cannot arise from the sight. In the same manner coinherence of sight and colour also cannot be accepted as Pramāṇa. So the Pramāṇa called Sannikarśa in Hindu Nyāya philosophy is not accepted by Jain logicians.

अवैशद्ये प्रत्यक्षं तदाभासं बौद्धस्याकस्माद्
धूमदर्शनाद्वह्निविज्ञानवत् ॥ ६ ॥

6. Avaiśadye pratyakṣaṃ tadābhāsaṃ bauddhasyākasmāt dhūma-darśanādvanhivijñānavat.

6. When Pratyakṣa is accepted in (things) not clear, we have its fallacy e. g. cognizance of fire by the followers of the Buddhist philosophy from sudden vision of smoke.

Commentary

In this aphorism, fallacy of Pratyakṣa (Pratyakṣābhāsa) is described.

---

1. Dr. Ballantyne's Translation of the following passage from Tarkasaṅgraha : "नित्यसंवन्धः समवायोऽयुतसिद्धवृत्तिः । ययोर्द्वयोर्मध्य एकमपराश्रितमेवावतिष्ठते तावयुतसिद्धौ ॥ अवयवावयविनौ गुणगुणिनौ क्रिया-क्रियावन्तौ जातिव्यक्ती विशेषनित्यद्रव्ये च ।"

2. Arthur Venis. Notes on Vedānta-Paribhāṣā.

Acceptance of Pratyakṣa knowledge without clearness is fallacy of Pratyakṣa. This happens in the case of the followers of the Buddhist Nyāya philosophy who hold that from a sudden vision of smoke, a knowledge of fire arises by Pratyakṣa and not by inference (Anumāna). Clearness has already been defined in Samuddeśa II. Aphorism 4 as illumination without any other intermediate knowledge or illumination in details. In Anumāna or inference we have an intermediate knowledge of smoke before we have a knowledge of fire and from the smoke we infer that there is fire. In Pratyakṣa we see the fire with our own eyes or learn of its existence by words of a reliable person. The view of the Buddhist Nyāya philosophy that we have a Pratyakṣa knowledge of fire from the sudden vision of smoke is held to be faulty in this aphorism. It is said that such a knowledge wants clearness which is the characteristic of Pratyakṣa is Pratyakṣābhāsa. Details of Pratyakṣa knowledge have already been mentioned in Samuddeśa II. a reference to to which may be made. In a sudden vision of smoke, there is no definite ascertainment (Niśchaya) whether it is smoke or steam. So the knowledge of concomitance of fire and smoke cannot arise. For this uncertainty the knowledge of fire as derived from a sudden vision of smoke is Pratyakṣābhāsa. The Nirvikalpa Pratyakṣa as accepted by the Buddhists is for this reason Pratyakṣābhāsa (fallacy of Pratyakṣa)[1].

वैशद्येऽपि परोक्षं तदाभासं मीमांसकस्य करणस्य ज्ञानवत् ॥ ७ ॥

7. Vaiśadyehpi parokṣaṃ tadābhāsaṃ mīmāṃsakasya karaṇasya jñānavat.

7. In Parokṣa (accepted) in clearness, (we have) its fallacy (Parokśābhāsa) e. g. knowledge derived from the senses as accepted by the Mīmāsakas.

---

1. "यथा धुमवाष्पादिविवेकनिश्चयाभावाद् व्याप्तिग्रहणाभावाद् अकस्माद् धुमदर्शनाज्जातं यद्वह्विविज्ञानं तत्तदाभासं भवति कस्मादनिश्चयाद्। तथा वौद्धपरिकल्पितं यन्निर्विकल्पकप्रत्यक्षं तत् प्रत्यक्षाभासं भवति कस्मादनिश्चयात्।" Note on Prameyakamalamārtaṇda.

Commentary

Parokṣābhāsa (fallacy of Parokṣa) arises when we accept Parokṣa knowledge as clear. The followers of the Mīmāṃsā philosophy hold that knowledge derived from the senses is Parokṣa. This view is refuted in this aphorism which lays down that such knowledge is clear and hence cannot be Parokṣa. In Samuddeśa III of this work, Parokṣa knowledge has been described in detail and clearness has been described in Aphorism 3 Samuddeśa II. In knowledge derived from the senses, we have no intermediate knowledge (as in the case of inference e. g. of smoke before we cognise fire). So clearness exists in these cases[1] and to hold such cases to be Parokṣa will be fallacy of Parokṣa.

अतस्मिंस्तदिति ज्ञानं स्मरणाभासं जिनदत्ते स देवदत्तो यथा ॥ ८ ॥

8. Atasminstaditi jñānaṃ smaraṇābhāsaṃ jinadatte sa Devadatto yathā.

8. Smaraṇābhāsa (fallacy of memory) is the knowledge in one of another e. g. when we (falsely recognise) Jinadatta as Devadatta.

Commentary

Fallacies of each of the subdivisions of Pratyakṣa viz. Smriti, Pratyabhijñāna, Tarka, Anumāna and Āgama are described in Aphorisms 8, 9, 10, 11-50 and 51 of this Samuddeśa.

Smriti or Smaraṇa (recollection) has been defined in Aphorism 3 of Samuddeśa III. We see Jinadatta. Later on when we see him again, we recognise him to be that Jina-datta. This is Smriti or recollection. But if we have remembrance of Devadatta when we see Jinadatta, this will be a fallacy of recollection (Smaraṇābhāsa).

---

1. "न हि करणज्ञानेऽव्यवधानेन प्रतिभासलक्षणं वैशद्यमसिद्धं स्वार्थयोः प्रतीत्यन्तरनिरपेक्षतया तत्र प्रतिभासनात् ।" Prameyakamalamārtaṇda.

सदृशे तदेवेदं तस्मिन्नेव तेन सदृशं यमलकवदित्यादि प्रत्यभिज्ञानाभासम् ॥ ९ ॥

9. Sadriśe tadevedaṃ tasminneva tena sadriśaṃ yamalaka-vadityādi pratyavijñānābhāsaṃ.

9. Fallacy of Pratyabhijñāna is the knowledge of "this is that" in things bearing similarity or knowledge of similarity in the identical thing e. g. in the case of twins.

Commentary

In the case of twins, we may falsely take one of them as the other from the similarity or we may fail to recognise the real person wanted and say that he resembles the real man (without understanding that he is the real man). There are therefore two kinds of fallacy of Pratyabhijñāna one referring to identity (Ekatva Pratyabhijñānābhāsa) and the other to similarity (Sādriśya-pratyabhijñānābhāsa[1].

Pratyabhijñāna has already been defined and explained in Aphorisms 5-10 Samuddeśa III to which a reference may be made.

असम्बद्धे तज्ज्ञानं तर्काभासम् ॥ १० ॥

10. Asambaddhe tajjñānaṃ tarkābhāsaṃ.

10. Knowledge of concomitance in objects not related is fallacy of Tarka.

Commentary

Tarka or Ūha has been defined in Aphorism 11 of Samuddeśa III. In Tarka we have knowledge of universal concomitance viz. that of fire and smoke. Fallacy of Tarka occurs when we set up inseparable connection between objects which are independent of each other e. g. smoke and water.

---

1. "द्विविधं प्रत्यभिज्ञानाभासमुपदर्शितं ; एकत्वनिबंधनं, सादृश्यनिबंधनश्चेति । तत्रैकत्वं सादृश्यावभासः, सादृश्ये चैकत्वाभासस्तदाभासमिति ।" Prameyaratnamālā.

इदमनुमानाभासम् ॥ ११ ॥

11. Idamanumānābhāsaṃ.

11. The following are fallacies of Anumāna.

Commentary

Anumāna has been defined in Aphorism 14 of Samuddeśa III Anumāna is employed by using Pakṣa, Hetu and Dristānta. Fallacies of these viz Pakṣābhāsa, Hetvābhāsa and Driṣṭāntābhāsa with their subdivisions will be described in the following aphorisms.

तत्रानिष्टादि पक्षाभासः ॥ १२ ॥

12. Tatrāniṣṭādi pakṣābhāsaḥ.

अनिष्टो मीमांसकस्यानित्यः शब्दः ॥ १३ ॥

13. Aniṣṭo mīmāṃsakasyānityaḥ śabdaḥ.

सिद्धः श्रावणः शब्दः ॥ १४ ॥

14. Siddhaḥ śrāvaṇaḥ śabdaḥ.

वाधितः प्रत्यक्षानुमानागमलोकस्ववचनैः ॥ १५ ॥

15. Vādhitaḥ pratyakṣānumānāgamalokasvavachanaiḥ.

12. Among them Pakṣābhāsa (fallacy of the minor term or thesis) is Aniṣṭa (un-accepted) etc.

13. Aniṣṭa (un-accepted) is (the view of) Mīmāṃsakas that sound is momentary.

14. It is established that sounds can be heard by the ear.

15. Opposition (may exist) from Pratyakṣa, Anumāna, Āgama, popular acceptance and one's own words.

Commentary

The followers of Mīmāṃsā philosophy hold that sound is eternal. So in their case there will be Pakṣābhāsa if we establish that sound is momentary. In the definition of Pakṣa we have laid down that it must be Iṣṭa (acceptable or that what we want). Opposite of it will be Aniṣṭa and hence it will be a fallacy of Pakṣa.

Next, to establish by inference what is accepted (Siddha) is also Pakṣābhāsa e. g. 'Sound can be heard by the ear'.

There is also Pakṣābhāsa when it involves opposition to Pratyakṣa, Anumāna, Āgama, Loka-vachana and Sva-vachana. These will be illustrated in the following five aphorisms. (See Page 95).

Siddhasena Divākara has defined Pakṣābhāsa in his Nyāyāvatāra as follows :—

"If that of which the major term or predicate (Sādhya) is affirmed is opposed by evidence (Liṅga), the public understanding, one's own statement etc. we have that which is known as the fallacy of the minor term or thesis (Pakṣā-bhāsa) of which there are many varieties[1]".

तत्र प्रत्यक्षबाधितो यथाऽनुष्णोऽग्निर्द्रव्यत्वाज्जलवत् ॥ १६ ॥

16. Tatra pratyakṣavādhito yathānusṇognirdravyatvājjala-vat.

16. In these subdivisions, Pratyakṣa-vādhita (opposed to Pratyakṣa) may be exemplified by "Fire is not hot as it is a thing e. g. water".

Commentary

Any proposition laying down anything opposed to actual perception is an instance of Pratyakṣa-vādhita. We know by actual perception that fire is hot. If anyone tries to lay down in the shape of inference "Fire is not hot as it is a thing e. g. water", it will be an example of Pratyakṣa-vādhita.

अपरिणामी शब्दः कृतकत्वात् घटवत् ॥ १७ ॥

17. Apariṇāmī śabdaḥ kritakatvāt ghatavat.

---

1. "प्रतिपाद्यस्य यः सिद्धः पक्षाभासोऽस्ति लिंगतः ।
लोक-स्ववचनाभ्यां च बाधितोऽनेकधा मतः ॥" Nyāyāvatāra, 21.

17. Sound is without modification as it is something caused e. g. a pitcher.

Commentary

This aphorism gives an example of the fallacy Anumāna-vādhita. The following is the correct inference or Anumāna :

"Sound has modification.

Because it is caused.

Like a pitcher."

But if we try to establish an inference opposed to this inference as follows :

"Sound is without modification.

Because it is caused.

Like a pitcher."

It will be an instance of Anumāna-vādhita that is to say opposed by inference.

प्रेत्यासुखप्रदो धर्मः पुरुषाश्रितत्वादधर्मवत् ॥ १८ ॥

18. Pretyāsukhaprado dharmaḥ puruṣāśritatvādadharmavat.

18. Dharma will produce grief after death as it is subservient to beings like Adharma.

Commentary

This is an example of the fallacy Āgama-vādhita. In all śastras, it is accepted that pursuit of Dharma will produce happiness after death and Adharma will cause misery. If we try to establish by inference that Dharma will produce misery after death, it will be an example of Āgama-vādhita Anumana (i. e. inference as opposed to the śāstras).

शुचि नरशिरःकपालं प्राण्यंगत्वाच्छङ्खशुक्तिवत् ॥ १९ ॥

19. Śuchi naraśiraḥkapālaṃ praṇyaṅgatvāchchaṅkhaśuktivat.

19. A human skull is pure as it is a part of the body of an animal like a conch-shell or oyster.

Commentary

This is an example of Loka-vādhita Anumāna or inference opposed to public understanding. According to popular acceptance parts of bodies of some animals e. g. conch-shells and oysters are accepted as pure, while parts of bodies of other animals e. g. human skull are considered as impure. So if we try to establish by inference as mentioned in the aphorism that human skull is pure, it will be a fallacy of Loka-vādhita Anumāna.

माता मे बन्ध्या पुरुषसंयोगेऽप्यगर्भत्वात् प्रसिद्धबन्ध्यावत् ॥२०॥

20. Mātā me bandhyā puruṣasaṃyogepyagarbhatvāt prasiddhabandhyāvat.

20. My mother is barren because she does not conceive in spite of connection with a male like women famous as barren.

Commentary

This is an example of Sva-vachana-vādhita Anumāna (or inference opposed to one's own words). If a person says that his mother is barren and tries to establish this by an inference as shown in the aphorism, the inference will be opposed to his own words and will be a fallacy of Svavachana-vādhita Anumāna.

Dr. Satis Chandra Vidyābhuṣaṇa in his notes on the translation of Nyāyāvatāra has mentioned the following with reference to different kinds of Pakṣābhāsa which will further elucidate the aphorisms in Parīkṣāmukhaṃ regarding this subject.

"The semblance or fallacy of the minor term or thesis (Pakṣābhāsa) arises when one predicates of the minor term (Pakṣa) that which is yet to be proved to the opponent, or which is incapable of being proved, or when it is opposed to perception and inference, or inconsistent with the public understanding or incongruous with one's statement thus :—

(1) 'The jar is corporeal (Paudgalika)'—This is a conclusion which is yet to be proved to the opponent.

(2) 'Everything is nothing'. This is a Saugata (Buddhist) doctrine which according to the Jainas, is incapable of being proved.

(3) 'The general (Sāmānya) and particular (Viśeṣa) things are without parts, are distinct from each other and are like themselves alone'. This is opposed to perception.

(4) 'There is no omniscient being'. This is, according to the Jainas, opposed to inference.

(5) 'The sister is to be taken as wife'. This is inconsistent with the public understanding.

(6) "All things are non-existent'. This is incongruous with one's own statement.

हेत्वाभासा असिद्धविरुद्धानैकान्तिकाकिञ्चित्कराः ॥२१॥

21. Hetvābhāsā asiddhaviruddhānaikāntikākiñchitkarāḥ.

21. Hetvābhāsas are Asiddha, Viruddha, Anaikāntika and Akiñchitkara.

Commentary

Now the fallacies of Hetu are being described. Hetu has been defined in Aphorism 15 in Samuddeśa III. The opposites of this are fallacies of Hetu[1]. These are of four kinds : Asiddha, Viruddha, Anaikāntika and Akiñchitkara.

Siddhasena has laid down "The reason (i. e. the middle term called Hetu has been defined as that which cannot exist except in connection with the major term (Sādhya); the fallacy of the rea-

---

1. "साध्याविनाभावित्वेन निश्चितो हेतुरित्युक्तं प्राक् । तद्विपरीतास्तु हेत्वाभासाः ।" Prameya-kamala-mārtaṇḍa.

son (Hetvābhāsa) arises from non-conception, doubt or misconception about it (the middle term)"[1].

Siddhasena lays down that there are only three (and not four as mentioned in Parīkṣāmukhaṃ) varieties of Hetvābhāsa: " That which has not yet been established is called 'the unproved' (Asiddha) ; that which is possible only in the opposite way is called 'the inconsistent' (Viruddha); that which can be explained in one way as well as in the opposite way is called 'the uncertain' (Anaikāntika)"[2]

Hemachandra also in his Pramāṇa-mīmāṃsā lays down that there are only three kinds of Hetvābhāsa *viz.* Asiddha, Viruddha and Anaikāntika[3]. He rejects the view of those who maintain that there are two other forms of Hetvābhāsa viz. Kālātīta and Prakaraṇa-sama. According to Hemachandra, Kālātīta is included within the fallacy of Pakṣa and Prakaraṇa-sama is an impossibility as none but a madman can use it. In arguments between sane men this is an impossibility[4].

---

1. "अन्यथानुपपन्नत्वं हेतोर्लक्षणमीरितम् ।
तदप्रतीतिसन्देहविपर्यासैस्तदाभता ॥" Nyāyāvatāra 22.

2. "असिद्धस्त्वप्रतीतो यो योऽन्यथैवोपपद्यते ।
विरुद्धो योऽन्यथाप्यत्र युक्तोऽनैकान्तिकः स तु ॥" Nyāyāvatāra 23.

3. "असिद्धविरुद्धानैकान्तिकास्त्रयो हेत्वाभासाः ॥"
Pramāṇa-mimāṃsā II. 1. 16.

4. "त्रय इति संख्यान्तरव्यवच्छेदार्थम् । तेन कालातीत-प्रकरणसमयो-र्व्यवच्छेदः । तत्र कालातीतस्य पक्षदोषेष्वन्तर्भावः प्रत्यक्षागमबाधितधर्मिनिर्देशानन्तर-प्रयुक्तः कालात्ययापदिष्ट इति हि तस्य लक्षणम् इति, यथाऽनुष्णस्तेजोऽवयवी कृतकत्वाद् घटवदिति । प्रकरणसमस्तु न सम्भवत्येव नह्यस्ति सम्भवो यथोक्तलक्षणोऽनुमाने प्रयुक्तेऽदूषिते वानुमानान्तरस्य यत्तूदाहरणमनित्यः शब्दः पक्षसपक्षयोरन्यतरत्वादिति तदतीवासाम्प्रतम् । को हि चतुरंगसभायां बादी प्रतिबादी चैवंविधमसम्बद्धमनुन्मत्तोऽ-भिदधीत ?" Pramāṇa Mīmāṃsā. Bhāṣya to Aphorism II. 1. 16.

असत्सत्तानिश्चयोऽसिद्धः ॥ २२ ॥

22. Asatsattāniśchayo'siddhaḥ.

22. Asiddha is that whose existence is wanting in Paksa and which is not definitely established.

Commentary

Asiddha Hetvābhāsa is of two kinds : Svarūpāsiddha and Sandigdhāsiddha.

These will be described in the aphorisms which follow.

अविद्यमानसत्ताकः परिणामी शब्दश्चाक्षुषत्वात् ॥ २३ ॥

23. Avidyamānasattākaḥ pariṇāmī śabdaśchakṣuṣatvāt.

स्वरूपेणासत्वात् ॥ २४ ॥

24. Svarūpeṇāsatvāt.

23. " Sound is perishable because it can be seen by the eyes." This is (an example of) non-existence of itself.

24. Because it does not exist at all in its self.

Commentary

Sound is heard by the ear and not seen by the eye. So in the Pakṣa 'Sound,' Hetu in its real nature does not exist. So this is an example of Svarūpāsiddha Hetvābhāsa where the falsehood is a matter of certainty.

अविद्यमाननिश्चयो मुग्धबुद्धिं प्रति, अग्निरत्र धूमात् ॥ २५ ॥

25. Avidyamānaniśchayo mugdhabuddhiṃ prati agniratra dhūmāt.

तस्य वाष्पादिभावेन भूतसंघाते संदेहात् ॥ २६ ॥

26. Tasya vāṣpādibhāvena bhūtasaṃghāte sandehāt.

25. When there is uncertainty, if one says to a man of inferior intellect 'Here is fire because there is smoke.'

26. He has doubt owing to the existence of vapour etc. in the collection of many elements (earth, water, etc. and he cannot definitely ascertain whether it it is smoke or vapour.)

Commentary

Sandigdhāsiddha is described in these aphorisms. This fallacy arises where there is an uncertainty of the Hetu itself. For example, where there is no certainty whether what is seen is smoke or vapour, if one infers 'there is fire because there is smoke', the inference will not be sound as the very existence of the Hetu viz. smoke is involved in doubt.[1] A person who is not thoroughly conversant with the major term (Sādhya) or the middle term (Hetu or Sādhana) will not be able to ascertain 'this is smoke' and 'this is vapour'[2] So there is absence of certainty in these cases which is the criterion of the fallacy of Sandigdhāsiddha.

सांख्यं प्रति परिणामी शब्दः कृतकत्वात् ॥ २७ ॥

27. Sāṅkhyaṃ prati pariṇāmī śabdaḥ kritakatvāt.

तेनाज्ञातत्वात् ॥ २८ ॥

28. Tenājñātatvāt.

27. To (the follower of) the Sāṅkhya (philosophy) : 'Sound is perishable, because it is caused (by some one).

28. Because he does not know (or accept) it.

Commentary

In Sāṅkhya philosophy, appearance and disappearance (and not creation and destruction) of things are accepted. So the inference 'Sound is perishable because it is created' by a follower of the Sāṅkhya philosophy is an example of Sandigdhāsiddha because he does not accept creating of a sound as creation is unknown (Ajñāta) to him.

---

1. "सत्वस्य संदेहेऽप्यसिद्धो हेत्वाभासः संदिग्धासिद्ध इत्यर्थः यथा बाष्पादिभावेन संदिह्यमाना धूमलताग्निसिद्धावुपदिश्यमाना ।" Pramāṇa-mimāṃsā. Bhāṣya on II. 1. 17.

2. "कुतोऽस्याविद्यमाननियततेत्याह । मुग्धबुद्धेर्बाष्पादिभावेन भूतसंघाते संदेहात् । न खलु साध्यसाधनयोरव्युत्पन्नप्रज्ञो धूमादिरीदृशो बाष्पादिश्चेदृश इति विवेचयितुं समर्थः ।" Prameyakamala-mārtaṇḍa,

Hemachandra has mentioned that Asiddha Hetvābhāsa may be Svarūpāsiddha or Sandigdhāsiddha.[1] The first should not be held to arise from not having the quality of a Pakṣa (minor term) because the definition of a Hetu has no connection with the quality of a Pakṣa. This fallacy arises from the fact that it wants the essence of Hetu viz. that it cannot arise otherwise. Hemachandra quotes the following verse from Kumārila Bhatta :—

"To infer the son of a Brahmin, to be a Brahmin is not universally accepted as it depends on the quality of Pakṣa". (For the mother might be unchaste).[2]

Hemachandra has mentioned three subdivisions of Asiddha Hetvābhāsa viz Asiddha regarding Vādī, that regarding Prativādī and that regarding both.[3] The illustration of the first of these is the same as given in Aphorism 27 of this Samuddeśa of Parīkṣāmukham.[4]

Some Jain logicians have laid down that there are other varieties of Asiddha Hetvābhāsa viz. Viśeṣyāsiddha, Viśeṣaṇā-

---

1. "नासन्ननिश्चितसत्वो वान्यथानुपपन्न इति सत्वस्यासिद्धौ सन्देहे वाऽसिद्धः ।" Pramāṇa-mīmāṃsā. II. 1. 17.

2. "अपक्षधर्मत्वादयमसिद्ध इति न मन्तव्यमित्याह नान्यथानुपपन्न इति, अन्यथानुपपंत्तिरूपहेतुलक्षणविरहात् अयमसिद्धो नापक्षधर्मत्वात् । नहि पक्षधर्मत्वं हेतोर्लक्षणं तदभावेऽप्यन्यथानुपपत्तिबलाद्धेतुत्वोपपत्तेरित्युक्तप्रायम् । भट्टोऽप्याह—

पित्रोश्च ब्राह्मणत्वेन पुत्रब्राह्मणतानुमा ।
सर्वलोकप्रसिद्धा न पक्षधर्ममपेक्षते ॥"

Pramāṇa-mīmāṃsā II. 1. 17.

3. "वादिप्रतिवाद्युभयभेदाच्चैतद्भेदः ॥"

Pramāṇa-mīmāṃsā II. 1. 18.

4. "तत्र वाद्यसिद्धो यथा परिणामी शब्द उत्पत्तिमत्त्वात् अयं सांख्यस्य स्वयंवादिनोऽसिद्धः । तन्मते उत्पत्तिमत्त्वस्यानभ्युपेतत्वात् नासदुत्पद्यते नापि सद्विनश्यत्युत्पादविनाशयोराविर्भावतिरोभावरूपत्वादिति तत्सिद्धान्ताच्च ।" Pramāṇa-mīmāṃsā. II. 1. 18.

siddha, Bhāgāsiddha, Āśrayāsiddha, Aśraiyakādeśasiddha, Vyartha-viśeṣyāsiddha, Vyarthaviśeṣaṇāsiddha, Sandigdhaviśeṣyāsiddha and Sandigdha-viśeṣaṇāsiddha[1]. Hemachandra says that all these are included within Vādyasiddha, Prativādyasiddha and Ubhayāsiddha as defined by him[2].

In Prameyakamala-mārtaṇda also it is mentioned "Others accept varieties of Asiddha viz. Viśeṣyāsiddha etc. These are mere varieties of Asiddha Hetvābhāsa (as defined in Parikṣāmukham) because they bear the criterion of non-existence of itself. So these are not separate varieties, for there is no separate characteristics of these"[3].

विपरीतनिश्चिताविनाभावो विरुद्धोऽपरिणामी शब्दः कृतकत्वात् ॥ २९ ॥

29. Viparītaniśchitāvinābhāvo viruddhopariṇāmī śabdaḥ kritakatvāt.

---

1. "तत्र विशेष्यासिद्धादय उदाह्रियन्ते। विशेष्यासिद्धो यथाऽनित्यः शब्दः सामान्यवत्वे सति चाक्षुषत्वात्। विशेषणासिद्धो यथाऽनित्यः शब्दश्चाक्षुषत्वे सति सामान्यविशेषवत्वात्। भागासिद्धो यथानित्यः शब्दः प्रयत्नानन्तरीयकत्वात्। आश्रयासिद्धो यथास्ति प्रधानं विश्वपरिणामित्वात्। आश्रयैकदेशासिद्धो यथा नित्याः प्रधान-पुरुषेश्वराः अकृतकत्वात्। व्यर्थविशेष्यासिद्धो यथा नित्यः शब्दः कृतकत्वे सति सामान्यवत्वात्। संदिग्धविशेष्यासिद्धो यथा अद्यापि रागादियुक्तः कपिलः पुरुषत्वे सत्यद्याप्यनुत्पन्नतत्वज्ञानत्वात्। संदिगधविशेषणासिद्धो यथा अद्यापि रागादियुक्तः कपिलः सर्वदा तत्वज्ञानरहितत्वे सति पुरुषत्वात्।" Pramāṇa-mimāṃsā. Bhāṣya to II. 1. 19.

2. "एते असिद्धभेदा यदान्यतरवाद्यसिद्धत्वेन विवक्ष्यन्ते तदा वाद्यसिद्धाः प्रतिवाद्यसिद्धा वा भवन्ति, यदोभयवाद्यसिद्धत्वेन विवक्ष्यन्ते तदोभयसिद्धा भवन्ति।" Ibid.

3. "ये च विशेष्यासिद्धादयोऽसिद्धप्रकाराः परैरिष्टास्तेऽसत्सत्ताकत्व-लक्षणासिद्ध-प्रकारान्नार्थान्तरं, तल्लक्षणभेदाभावात्।" Prameyakamala-mārtaṇda.

29. Viruddha (Hetvābhāsa) is concomitance with the opposite of the major term e. g. sound is not perishable because it is caused.

Commentary

In this aphorism, Viruddha Hetvābhāsa is defined and illustrated. Where the universal concomitance (Avinābhāva or Vyāpti) is ascertained with the opposite of the major term, we get the fallacy of Viruddha Hetvābhāsa. In this case the inseparable connection (Vyāpti) of the middle term is not with the major term but with its antithesis. The example given is "Sound is eternal because it is an effect". Now there is universal connection of an effect with perishability, but if we try to establish its opposite by the example given above, we get fallacy of Viruddha Hetvābhāsa.

Dr. S. C. Vidyābhūṣaṇa in his notes on Nyāyāvatāra gives another example : "The inconsistent (viruddha) such as 'This is fiery because it is a body of water'. Here the reason alleged is opposed to what is to be established".

Hemachandra defines Viruddha as that whose concomitance is the opposite or which is derived otherwise[1].

Some hold the view that there are eight kinds of Viruddha, but in Prameya-kamala-mārtaṇḍa it is mentioned that all of these come under the definition here given[2]. Hemachandra also is of the same view[3].

---

1. 'विपरीतनियमोऽन्यथैवोपपद्यमानो विरुद्धः ॥"

Pramāṇa-mīmāṃsā II. 1. 20.

2. "ये चाष्टौ विरुद्धभेदा परैरिष्टास्तेऽप्येतल्लक्षणलक्षितत्वाविशेषतोऽत्रैवान्तर्भवन्ति ।" Prameyakamala-mārtaṇḍa.

3. "अनेन येऽन्यैरन्ये विरुद्धा उदाहृतास्तेऽपि संगृहीता ।" Pramāṇa-mīmāṃsā Bhāṣya on II. 1. 20. These eight varieties of Viruddha are described as follows by Hemchandra. There are four varieties where Sapakṣa exists and there are four varieties when Sapakṣa

विपक्षेऽप्यविरुद्धवृत्तिरनैकान्तिकः ॥ ३० ॥

30. Vipakṣepyaviruddhavrittiranaikāntikaḥ

30. In Anaikāntika (Hetvābhāsa), (Hetu) resides also in Vipakṣa (in addition to being in Pakṣa and Sapakṣa).

निश्चितवृत्तिरनित्यः शब्दः प्रमेयत्वाद् घटवत् ॥ ३१ ॥

31. Niśchitavrittiranityaḥ śabdaḥ prameyatvād ghatavat.

31. Where it is certain that (Hetu) is in (Vipakṣa) (we have the fallacy of Niśchita vipakṣa vritti Hetvābhāsa), e. g. "Sound is perishable because it is knowable like a pitcher.

आकाशे नित्येऽप्यस्य निश्चयात् ॥ ३२ ॥

32. Ākāśe nityepyasya niśchayāt.

32. Because it (the quality of knowability) is ascertained in things like Ākāśa which are imperishable.

शंकितवृत्तिस्तु नास्ति सर्वज्ञो वक्तृत्वात् ॥ ३३ ॥

33. Śankitavrittistu nāsti sarvajño vaktritvāt.

---

does not exist. : "सति सपक्षे चत्वारो भेदाः। (1) पक्षविपक्षव्यापको, यथा नित्यः शब्दः कार्यत्वात्। (2) पक्षव्यापको विपक्षैकदेशवृत्तिः, यथा नित्यः शब्दः सामान्यवत्वे सत्यस्मदादिवाह्येन्द्रियग्राह्यत्वात्। (3) पक्षैकदेशवृत्तिर्विपक्षव्यापको, यथा अनित्या पृथिवी कृतकत्वात्। (4) पक्षविपक्षैकदेशवृत्तिः, यथा नित्यः शब्दः प्रयत्नानन्तरीयकत्वात्।

असति सपक्षे चत्वारो विरुद्धाः। (5) पक्षविपक्षव्यापको, यथा आकाशविशेषगुणः शब्दः प्रमेयत्वात्। (6) पक्षव्यापको विपक्षैकदेशवृत्तिः, यथा आकाशविशेषगुणः शब्दो वाह्येन्द्रियग्राह्यत्वात्। (7) पक्षैकदेशवृत्तिर्विपक्षव्यापको, यथा आकाशविशेषगुणः शब्दोऽपदात्मकत्वात्। (8) पक्षविपक्षैकदेशवृत्तिः, यथा आकाश विशेषगुणः शब्दः प्रयत्नानन्तरीयकत्वात्। एषु च चतुर्षु विरुद्धता पक्षैकदेशवृत्तिषु चतुर्षु पुनरसिद्धता विरुद्धता च इत्युभयसमावेशः।" Ibid.

33. Where the matter is involved in doubt (we have the fallacy of Śaṅkita vipakṣa vritti e. g. an omniscient being does not exist for he can speak.

सर्वज्ञत्वेन वक्तृत्वाविरोधात् ॥ ३४ ॥

34. Sarvajñatvena vaktritvāvirodhāt.

34. Because there is no opposition of being able to speak with omniscience.

Commentary

When Hetu is found in Pakṣa, Sapakṣa and Vipakṣa we have the fallacy of Anaikāntika Hetvābhāsa. "The effect of the presence of the Hetu in Vipakṣa is to rob the conclusion of that logical validity which Anumāna (inference) directly aims at".

"Anaikāntika Hetvābhāsa is of two kinds (1) the Niśchita Vipakṣa vritti where it is certain that the Hetu resides in the Vipakṣa and (2) the Śaṅkita Vipakṣa vritti where the matter is involved in doubt."[1]

The following are illustrations :

(1) "Sound is perishable because it is knowledge".

This is an instance of the Niśchita Vipakṣa Vritti type, because it is certain that the quality of knowability resides not only in perishable things, but also in those that are imperishable e. g. space, souls and the like.

(2) Watches are fragile because they are manufactured with machinery.

This is an instance of the Śaṅkita Vipakṣa Vritti. The fallacy in this case lies in the fact that it is not certain whether the quality of being manufactured with machinery does or does not reside in things which are not fragile i. e. the Vipakṣa.[2]

---

1. The Science of Thought by C. R. Jain Page 55.

2. The Science of Thought by C. R. Jain Pages 55—56.

Dr. Vidyābhūsaṇa in his note on Verse 23 of Nyāyāvatāra already quoted says :

"The uncertain (Anaikāntika) such as 'All things are momentary, because they are existent'. Here the reason alleged is uncertain, because 'existence' may or may not be a proof of momentariness, for, an opponent may equally argue : 'all things are eternal, because they are existent'.[1] This example corresponds to the Śaṅkita Vipakṣa Vritti variety of Anaikāntika Hetvābhāsa mentioned above. The first variety is not described in Nyāyāvatāra.

Hemachandra defines and illustrates both the varieties and uses the same examples as given in Parīkṣāmukhaṃ.[2] He mentions that some logicians accept other varieties of Anaikāntika Hetvābhāsa but it is not necessary to accept these as all of these are included in the definition of the two varieties Niśchita Vipakṣa Vritti and Śaṅkita Vipakṣa Vritti varieties.[3]

---

1. Nyāyāvatāra by S. C. Vidyābhūṣaṇa Page 21.

2. "नियमस्यासिद्धौ संदेहे वाऽन्यथाप्युपपद्यमानोऽनैकान्तिकः ।"

Pramāṇamimāṃsā II. 1. 21.

"नियमोऽविनाभावस्तस्यासिद्धावनैकान्तिको यथाऽनित्यः शब्दः प्रमेयत्वात् प्रमेयत्वं नित्येप्याकाशादावस्तीति । संदेहे यथा सर्वज्ञः कश्चिद्रागादिमान् वा वक्तृत्वात् स्वभावविप्रकृष्टाभ्यां हि सर्वज्ञत्ववीतरागत्वाभ्यां हि न वक्तृत्वस्य विरोधः सिद्धः, न च रागादिकार्यम् वचनमिति संदिग्धोऽन्वयः ।" Bhāṣya to Ibid.

3. "ये चान्येऽन्यैरनैकान्तिकभेदा उदाहृतास्ते उक्तलक्षण एवान्तर्भवन्ति । (1) पक्षत्रयव्यापकः, यथानित्यः शब्दः प्रमेयत्वात् । (2) पक्षसपक्षव्यापको विपक्षैकदेशवृत्तिः, यथा गौरयं विषाणित्वात् । (3) पक्षविपक्षव्यापकः सपक्षैकदेशवृत्तिः यथा नायं गौरविषाणित्वात् । (4) पक्षव्यापकः सपक्षविपक्षैकदेशवृत्तिः, यथानित्यः शब्दः प्रत्यक्षत्वात् । (5) पक्षैकदेशवृत्तिः सपक्षविपक्षव्यापको, यथा न द्रव्याण्याकाशकालदिगात्ममनांसि क्षणिकविशेषगुणरहितत्वात् । (6) पक्षविपक्षैकदेशवृत्तिः सपक्षविपक्षव्यापकः, यथा न द्रव्याण्याकाशकालदिगात्ममनांसि क्षणिकविशेषगुणरहितत्वात् ।

सिद्धे प्रत्यक्षत्वादिवाधिते च साध्ये हेतुरकिंचित्करः ॥३५॥

35. Siddhe pratyakṣatvādivādhite cha sādhye heturakiñchitkaraḥ.

सिद्धः श्रावणः शब्दः शब्दत्वात् ॥ ३६ ॥

36. Siddhaḥ śrāvaṇaḥ śabdaḥ śabdatvāt.

किंचिदकरणात् ॥ ३७ ॥

37. Kiñchidakaraṇāt.

यथाऽनुष्णोऽग्निर्द्रव्यत्वादित्यादौ किंचित् कर्त्तुमशक्यत्वात् ॥३८॥

38. Yathānuṣṇo'gnirdravyatvādityādau kiñchit karttumaśakyatvāt.

लक्षण एवासौ दोषो व्युत्पन्नप्रयोगस्य पक्षदोषेणैव दुष्टत्वात् ॥३९॥

39. Lakṣaṇa evāsau doṣo vyutpannaprayogasya pakṣadoṣeṇaiva duṣṭatvāt.

35. Akiñchitkara (Hetvābhāsa) consists of (use of) Hetu (middle term) in connection with a Sādhya (major term) which had already been established and which is opposed by Pratyakṣa etc.

36. Capability of being heard by the ear is established regarding sound, as it is sound.

37. Because (Hetu) does not do anything (in such a case).

38. As for example, fire is cold as this a thing. In such cases (Hetu) cannot do anything.

39. This fault arises only in definition. For in use by those conversant with reasoning, the fault is proved by fault of Pakṣa (minor term).

---

(7) पक्षविपक्षैकदेशवृत्तिः सपक्षव्यापी, यथा न द्रव्याणि दिक्कालमनांस्यमूर्त्तत्वात्। (8) सपक्षपक्षैकदेशवृत्तिर्विपक्षव्यापी, यथा द्रव्याणि दिक्कालमनांस्यमूर्त्तत्वात्। (9) पक्षत्रयैकदेशवृत्तिर्यथा अनित्या पृथिवी प्रत्यक्षत्वात् ॥" Ibid.

Commentary

Akiñchitkara Hetvābhāsa is here defined. Really speaking, this is not a separate variety as this is included in the fallacy of Pakṣābhāsa as already defined being opposed to Pratyakṣa, Anumāna, Āgama, Loka-vachana and Sva-vachana (Aphorism 15). This fault is included in those varieties of fallacies. If you say, that it is redundant to lay down a separate definition of Akiñchitkara Hetvābhāsa, we reply (by Aphorism 39) that this fallacy is described only for the understanding of students in a treatise dealing with definitions though this is not used at the time of discussion by logicians[1].

As this is not really a different variety, it is not mentioned in works such as Nyāyāvatāra, Pramāṇa-mīmāṃsā etc.

Two examples of Akiñchitkara Hetvābhāsa are given in Parīkṣāmukhaṃ. The first is : "Sound is capable being heard by the ear, because it is a sound". Here the capability of being heard is established by itself. So it is useless to establish this by employing a Hetu. So this is an example of Akiñchitkara Hetvābhāsa where Sādhya (Major term) is Siddha (already established). The second example is "Fire is cold as this is a thing". Here coldness of fire is opposed to Pratyakṣa. So employment of such a reasoning cannot produce any result in such cases. This is an example of Akiñchitkara Hetvābhāsa where Sādhya is opposed by Pratyakṣa[2].

---

1. "ननु प्रसिद्धः प्रत्यक्षानुमानागमलोकस्ववचनैश्च वाधितः पक्षाभासः प्रतिपादितः। तद्दोषेनैव चास्य दुष्टत्वात्। पृथगकिंचित्कराभिधानमनर्थकमित्याशङ्क्य 'लक्षण एव' इत्यादिना प्रतिविधत्ते। लक्षणे लक्ष्यव्युत्पादनशास्त्रे एवासावकिंचित्करत्व-लक्षणो दोषो विनेयव्युत्पत्त्यर्थं व्युत्पाद्यते। न तु व्युत्पन्नानां प्रयोगकाले। कुत एत-दित्याह व्युत्पन्नप्रयोगस्य पक्षदोषेणैव दुष्टत्वात्।" Prameyakamala-mārtaṇḍa

2. "सिद्धे निर्णीते प्रमाणान्तरात् साध्ये प्रत्यक्षादिबाधिते च हेतुर्न किंचित् करोतीत्यकिंचित्करोऽनर्थको यथा श्रावणः शब्दः शब्दत्वात्। नह्यसौ स्वसाध्यं साधयति तस्याध्यक्षादेव प्रसिद्धेः। नापि साध्यान्तरं तत्रावृत्तेरित्यत आह 'किंचिद-

"Akiñchitkara Hetvābhāsa is the fallacy of redundancy. This is also of two kinds.

(a) The Siddhasādhana which means the establishing of that which has already been proved by some other kind of Pramāṇa. Illustration : Sound is heard by the ear, because it is sound.

(b) The Vādhita viṣaya which relates to a proposition inconsistent with Pratyakṣa (direct observation or jñāna), logical inference, scriptural text or its own sense. Illustrations : (i) Fire is not endowed with warmth, because it is a substance (inconsistent with Pratyakṣa). (ii) Sound is unchanging, because it is not an effect (inconsistent with Anumāna). (iii) Dharma (virtue or righteousness) is the cause of pain, because it resides in man (inconsistent with scripture according to which Dharma is the cause of happiness). (iv) Z is the son of a barren woman because she has never conceived (inconsistent with the proposition itself)".[1]

दृष्टान्ताभासा अन्वयेऽसिद्धसाध्यसाधनोभयाः ॥ ४० ॥

40. Driṣṭāntābhāsā anvaye'siddhasādhyasādhanobhayāḥ.

अपौरुषेयः शब्दोऽमूर्त्तत्वादिन्द्रियसुखपरमाणुघटवत् ॥४१॥

41. Apauruṣeyaḥ śabdo'mūrttatvādindriyasukhaparamāṇu-ghatavat.

विपरीतान्वयश्च यदपौरुषेयं तदमूर्त्तम् ॥ ४२ ॥

42. Viparītānvayaścha yadapauruṣeyaṃ tadamūrttaṃ.

विद्युदादिनातिप्रसंगात् ॥ ४३ ॥

43. Vidyudādinātiprasaṅgāt.

करणात्' प्रत्यक्षादिवाधिते च साध्येऽकिंचित्करोऽसौ अनुष्णोग्निर्द्रव्यत्वात् इत्यादौ यथा। कुतोऽस्याकिंचित्करत्वमित्याह 'किंचित्कर्त्तुमशक्यत्वात्।" Prameya-kamala-mārtaṇda.

1. The Science of Thought by C. R. Jain Pages 56—57

40. Fallacies of Driṣṭānta (illustration) in Anvaya consists of non-establishment of Sādhya, Sādhana or both of them.

41. Sound is unproduced by man because it has no form like sensual pleasure, atom or pitcher.

42. Viparītānvaya also : "That which is unproduced by man has no form".

43. Because this will be applied in lightening etc.

व्यतिरेके सिद्धतद्व्यतिरेकाः परमाण्विन्द्रियसुखाकाशवत् ॥४४॥

44. Vyatireke siddha-tadvyatirekāḥ paramāṇvindriyasukhā-kāśavat.

विपरीतव्यतिरेकश्च यन्नामूर्त्तत्वं तन्नापौरुषेयम् ॥ ४५ ॥

45. Viparīta-vyatirekaścha yannāmūrttatvaṃ tannāpauru-ṣeyaṃ.

44. In Vyatireka, Siddha and the Vyatirekas of the same, like atom, sensual pleasure and Ākāśa.

45. Viparīta Vyatireka : The quality of not being without form, is not unproduced by man.

Commentary

"Driṣṭāntābhāsa (fallacy of illustration) occurs when a Driṣṭānta is not an appropriate illustration. This is of two kinds : (i) Sādharmya or Anvaya Driṣṭāntābhāsa and (ii) Vaidharmya or Vyatireka Driṣṭāntābhāsa.

The Sādharmya fallacy arises when a negative illustration is given in place of an affirmative one. Illustration : There is no Sarvajña (omniscient being) because he is not apprehended by the senses, like a jar. [The illustration should have been of some thing not perceivable with the senses].

The Vaidharmya is the opposite of Sādharmya. Illustration : Kapila is omniscient, because he is beset with desires like the Arhanta (Tirthaṅkara). [Here the comparison should have been with some one who became omniscient without giving up his desires, not with the Arhanta who is absolutely desireless].

Every illustration has reference to either the Sādhya, or Sādhana or both. This gives us three forms of the Anvaya and three of the Vyatireka Driṣṭāntābhāsa. Illustrations : (i) Sound is Apauruṣeya (unproduced by man) because it is devoid of sensible qualities ; whatever is devoid of sensible qualities is Apauruṣeya, like (a) sensual pleasure (6) an atom or (c) a jar. [Here (a) is an instance of the wrong illustration of the Sādhya (because sensual pleasure is the opposite of Apauruṣeya) (b) of the Sādhana (an atom is not devoid of sensible qualities) and (c) of both, the Sādhya and Sādhana (for a jar is neither Apauruṣeya nor devoid of sensible qualities). These are instances of the Anvaya Driṣṭāntābhāsa. (ii) Sound is Apauruṣeya because it is Amūrttika (devoid of sensible qualities) ; whatever is not Apauruṣeya is not Amūrttika as (a) an atom (b) sense-gratification or (c) space. [This is a three-fold illustration of the Vyatireka Driṣṭāntābhāsa. The atom, being Apauruṣeya does not furnish an instance of the not Apauruṣeya quality ; sense-gratification is not not-Amūrttika, and space is neither not-Apauruṣeya nor not-Amūrttika].

Anvaya Driṣṭāntābhāsa also occurs where the order of the Sādhya and Sādhana is reversed in the exemplification of Hetu. Illustration : There is fire in this hill. Because there is smoke on it. Whereever there is fire there is smoke (Anvaya Driṣṭāntābhāsa). [The true form of the Anvaya exemplification here should be "Whereever there is smoke there is fire"].

Similarly, Vyatireka Driṣṭāntābhāsa also occurs when the Sādhya and Sādhana replace each other in Vyatireka exemplification. Illustration :

This hill is full of smoke.

Because it is full of fire.

Whatever is not full of smoke is also not full of fire.

[The fallacy is obvious, for there may be fire without smoke][1].

Siddhasena has defined Driṣṭāntābhāsa as follows : "Logicians have declared that fallacies of the example (Driṣṭāntābhāsa) in the homogeneous form, arise here from an imperfect middle term or from a defect in the major term etc.

Logicians have declared that fallacies of the example in the heterogeneous form arise when the absence of the major term (Sādhya) or the middle term (Sādhana or Hetu) or both, is not shown, or when there is a doubt about them"[2].

In the commentary to Nyāyāvatāra the varieties of Sādharmya and Vaidharmya Driṣṭāntābhāsa are thus described :

"Fallacies of the homogeneous example (Sādharmya Driṣṭāntābhāsa) arise from a defect in the major term (Sādhya) or middle term (Hetu) or both, or from doubt about them, thus :—

(1) Inference is invalid (major term) because it is a source of knowledge (middle term) like perception (homogeneous example). Here the example involves a defect in the major term (Sādhya) for perception is not invalid.

(2) Perception is invalid (major term) because it is a source of true knowledge (middle term) like a dream (homogeneous example). Here the example involves a defect in the middle term (Hetu) for a dream is not a source of true knowledge.

---

1. The Science of Thought Pages 57—58

2. "साधर्म्येणात्र दृष्टान्तदोषा न्यायविदीरिताः ।
अपलक्षणहेतूत्थाः साध्यादिविकलादयः ॥
वैधर्म्येणात्र दृष्टान्तदोषा न्यायविदीरिताः ।
साध्यसाधनयुग्मानामनिवृत्तेश्च संशयात् ॥"

Nyāyāvatāra. 24, 25. Translated by S. C. Vidyābhūṣaṇa. Pages, 21 and 23.

(3) The omniscient being is not existent (major term) because he is not apprehended by the senses (middle term) like a jar (homogeneous example). Here the example involves a defect in both the major and middle terms (Sādhya and Hetu) for the jar is both existent and apprehended by the senses.

(4) This person is devoid of passions (major term) because he is mortal (middle term) like a man in the street (homogeneous example). Here the example involves doubt as to the validity of the major term, for it is doubtful whether the man in the street is devoid of passions.

(5) This person is mortal (major term) because he is full of passions (middle term) like the man in the street (homogeneous example). Here the example involves doubt as to the validity of the middle term, for it is doubtful whether the man in the street is devoid of passions.

(6) This person is not omniscient (major term) because he is full of passions (middle term) like the man in the street (homogeneous example). Here the example involves doubt as to the validity of both the major and middle terms, for it is doubtful whether the man in the street is full of passions and not omniscient.[1]

---

1. "तत्र साध्यविकलो यथा, भ्रान्तमनुमानं प्रमाणत्वात् प्रत्यक्षवत्, प्रत्यक्षस्य भ्रान्तताविकलत्वात्। साधनविकलो यथा जाग्रत्संवेदनं भ्रान्तं प्रमाणत्वात् स्वप्नसंवेदनवत्, स्वप्नसंवेदनस्य प्रमाणताव्यैकल्यात्। उभयविकलो यथा, नास्ति सर्वज्ञः प्रत्यक्षाद्यनुपलब्धत्वात घटवत, घटस्य सत्वात् प्रत्यक्षादिभिरुपलब्धत्वाच्च। संदिग्धसाध्यधर्मो यथा, वीतरागोऽयं मरणधर्मत्वात् रथ्यापुरुषवत्, रथ्यापुरुषे वीतरागस्य संदिग्धत्वात्। संदिग्धसाधनधर्मो यथा, मरणधर्मोऽयं पुरुषो रागादिमत्वात्, रथ्यापुरुषवत् द्रष्टव्यः, पुरुषे रागादिमत्वस्य संदिग्धत्वात् वीतरागस्यापि तथा संभवात्। संदिग्धोभयधर्मो यथा असर्वज्ञोऽयं रागादिमत्वात् रथ्यापुरुषवत् इति रथ्यापुरुषे प्रदर्शितन्यायेन उभयस्यापि संदिग्धत्वात्।" Nyāyāvatāra-vivriti. Translation by Dr. S. C. Vidyābhūṣaṇa.

The fallacy of the heterogeneous example (Vaidharmya Driṣṭāntābhāsa) is of six kinds, thus :—

(1) Inference is invalid (major term) because it is a source of true knowledge (middle term) ; whatever is not invalid is not a source of true knowledge, as a dream (heterogeneous example). Here the example involves in the heterogeneous form a defect in the major term (Sādhya) for a dream is really invalid though it has been cited as not invalid.

(2) Perception is non-reflective or Nirvikalpaka (major term) because it is a source of true knowledge (middle term) ; whatever is reflective or Savikalpaka, is not a source of true knowledge, as inference (heterogeneous example). Here the example involves in the heterogeneous form a defect in the middle term (Sādhana) for inference is really a source of true knowledge, though it has been cited as not such.

(3) Sound is eternal and non-eternal (major term), because it is an existence (middle term) ; whatever is not eternal and non-eternal is not an existence, as a jar (heterogeneous example). Here the example involves in the heterogeneous form a defect in both the major and middle terms (Sādhya and Sādhana) for the jar is both 'eternal and non-eternal' and 'an existence'.

(4) Kapila is non-omniscient (major term) because he is a non-propounder of the four noble truths (middle term) ; whoever is not non-omniscient is not non-propounder of the four noble truths, as Buddha (heterogeneous example). Here the example involves in the negative form a doubt as to the validity of the major term (Sādhya) for it is doubtful whether Buddha was omniscient.

(5) This person is untrustworthy (major term) because he is full of passions (middle term) ; whoever is not untrustworthy is not full of passions, as Buddha (heterogeneous example) Here the example involves doubt as to the validity of the middle

term (Hetu) for it is doubtful whether Buddha is not full of passions.

(6) Kapila is not devoid of passions (major term) because he did not give his own flesh to the hungry (middle term) ; whoever is devoid of passions gives his own flesh to the hungry as Buddha (heterogeneous example). Here the example involves doubt as to the validity of both the major and middle terms (Sādhya and Sādhana) for it is doubtful whether Buddha was devoid of passions and gave his own flesh to the hungry".[1]

---

1. "तदनेन षड् दृष्टान्ताभासाः सूचिताः। तद् यथा साध्याव्यतिरेकी (१) साधनाव्यतिरेकी (२) साध्यसाधनाव्यतिरेकी (३) तथा संदिग्धसाध्याव्यतिरेकः (४) संदिग्धसाधनव्यतिरेकः (५) संदिग्धसाध्यसाधनव्यतिरेकश्च (६)। तत्र साध्याव्यतिरेकी यथा, भ्रान्तमनुमानं प्रमाणत्वात्, इत्यत्र वैधर्म्यदृष्टान्तो यत् पुनःभ्रान्तं न भवति न तत् प्रमाणं तद् यथा स्वप्नज्ञानमिति। स्वप्नज्ञानात् भ्रान्ततानिवृत्तेः साध्याव्यतिरेकित्वम्। साधनाव्यतिरेकी यथा, प्रत्यक्षं निर्विकल्पकं प्रमाणत्वात्। अत्र वैधर्म्यदृष्टान्तो, यत् पुनः सविकल्पकं न तत् प्रमाणं तद् यथानुमानमनुप्रमाणतानिवृत्तेः साधनाव्यतिरेकित्वम्। उभयाव्यतिरेकी यथा, नित्यानित्यः शब्दः सत्वात् इत्यत्र वैधर्म्यदृष्टान्तो यः पुनर्न नित्यानित्यः स न सन् तद् यथा घटः घटादुभयस्यापि अव्यावृत्तेरुभयाव्यतिरेकित्वम्। तथा संदिग्धसाध्यव्यतिरेकः, असर्वज्ञा अनाप्ता वा कपिलादयः आर्यसत्यचतुष्टयाप्रतिपादकत्वात्। अत्र वैधर्म्यदृष्टान्तः यः पुनः सर्वज्ञ आप्तो वा असौ आर्यसत्यचतुष्टयं प्रत्यपीपदत् तद् यथा शौद्धोदनिरिति। अयं च साध्यव्यतिरेकी वा आर्यसत्यचतुष्टयस्य दुःखसमुदयमार्गनिरोधलक्षणस्य प्रमाणवाधितत्वेन तद्भाषकस्य असर्वज्ञतानाप्ततोपपत्तः।...तस्मात् शौद्धोदनेः सकाशात् असर्वज्ञतानाप्ततालक्षणस्य साध्यस्य व्यावृत्तिः सन्दिग्धेति सन्दिग्धसाध्यव्यतिरेकित्वम्। सन्दिग्धसाधनव्यतिरेको यथा, अनादेयवाक्यः कश्चिद् विवक्षितः पुरुषो रागादिमत्वादित्यत्र वैधर्म्यदृष्टान्तो यः पुनः आदेयवाक्यो न स रागादिमान् तद्यथा सुगत इति।.... सुगतात् रागादिमत्वव्यावृत्तिसंशयात् संदिग्धसाधनव्यतिरेकित्वम्। संदिग्धसाध्यसाधनव्यतिरेको यथा, वीतरागाः कपिलादयः करुणास्पदेषु अपि अकरुणापरीतचित्ततया दत्तनिजमांसशकलत्वात्। अत्र वैधर्म्यदृष्टान्तो ये पुनर्वीतरागास्ते करुणापरीतचित्ततया दत्तनिजमांसशकलाः तद् यथा बोधिसत्वा इत्यत्र साधनसाध्यधर्मयोर्बोधिसत्वेभ्यो

Hemachandra in his Pramāṇa-mīmāṃsā lays down that there are eight varieties of Driṣṭāntābhāsa according to Sādharmya and Vaidharmya[1]. First, he defines and exemplifies the three varieties of Sādharmya Driṣṭāntābhāsa as given in the Parīkṣāmukhaṃ viz. Sādhya-vikala, Sādhana-vikala and Sādhyasādhanovaya-vikala[2]. Then he defines and illustrates the three varieties of Vaidharmya-Driṣṭāntābhāsa viz. Sādhya-vyatireki, Sādhana-vyatireki and Ubhaya-vyatireki[3]. Then he mentions the three varieties Sandigdha Sādhyānvaya, Sandigdha Sādhanānvaya and Sandigdha Ubhayānvaya and the three varieties Sandigdha Sādhya Vyatireka, Sandigdha Sādhana Vyatireka and Sandigdha Ubhaya Vyatireka[4]. Besides these he mentions two varieties Viparītānvaya and Viparīta Vyatireka and two varieties Apradarśita Anvaya and Apradarśita Vyatireka[5]. These last four varieties are not accepted by all.

व्यावृत्तिः सन्दिग्धा ततः प्रतिपादितप्रमाणवैकल्यात् न ज्ञायते किं ते रागादिमन्तः उत वीतरागास्तथानुकम्प्येषु किं स्वपिशितखण्डानि दत्तवन्तो नेति वा अतः सन्दिग्धसाध्य-साधनव्यतिरेकित्वमिति ।" Nyāyāvatāra-vivriti.

1. "साधर्म्यवैधर्म्याभ्यामष्टावष्टौ दृष्टान्ताभासाः ॥"

Pramāṇa-mīmāṃsā. II. 1. 22.

2. "अमूर्त्तत्वेन नित्ये शब्दे साध्ये कर्मपरमाणुघटाः साध्यसाधनोभय-विकलाः ॥" Ibid. II. 1. 23.

3. "वैधर्म्येण परमाणुकर्माकाशाः साध्याद्यव्यतिरेकिणः ॥"

Ibid II. 1. 24.

4. "वचनाद्रागे रागान्मरणधर्मत्वकिंचिज्ज्ञत्वयोः सन्दिग्धसाध्याद्यन्वय-व्यतिरेका रथ्यापुरुषादयः ॥" Ibid II. 1. 15.

5. "विपरीतान्वयव्यतिरेकौ ॥" Ibid II. 1. 26.

"अप्रदर्शितान्वयव्यतिरेकौ ॥" Ibid II. 1. 27.

The eight varieties of Sādharmya Driṣṭāntābhāsa are thus summed up by Hemachandra ;

For example, the author of the Nyāyāvatāra-vivriti refutes the view that there are three other varieties of Sādharmya Driṣṭāntābhāsa viz. Ananvaya, Apradarśitānvaya and Viparītānvaya and three other varieties of Vaidharmya Driṣṭāntābhāsa viz. Avyatireki, Apradarśita-vyatireka and Viparīta-vyatireka.

"Some unnecessarily lay down three other kinds of fallacy of the homogeneous example (Sādharmya Driṣṭāntābhāsa) viz. (1) Un-connected (Ananvaya) such as, this person is full of passions (major term), because he is a speaker (middle term) like a certain man in Magadha (example). Here though a certain man in Magadha is both a speaker and full of passions, yet there is no inseparable connection between "being a speaker" and "being full of passions".

(2) Of connection unshown (Apradarśitānvaya) such as, Sound is non-eternal (major term) because it is adventitious (middle term), as a jar (example). Here though there is an inseparable connection between 'adventitious' and 'non-eternal', yet it has not been shown in the proper form, as :—'Whatever is adventitious is non-eternal as a jar'. [Dignāga the Buddhist urged the necessity of converting the example into a universal proposition with a view to show the connection between the middle term and major term in the proper form].

(3) Of contrary connection (Viparītānvaya) such as :— Sound is non-eternal (major term) because it is adventitious,

---

"साध्यविकलः साधनविकलः उभयविकलः सन्दिग्धसाध्यान्वयः सन्दिग्धसाधनान्वयः, सन्दिग्धोभयान्वयः विपरीतान्वयः अप्रदर्शितान्वयः चेत्यष्टौ साधर्म्यदृष्टान्ताभासाः।"

The eight varieties of Vaidharmya Driṣṭāntābhāsa are mentioned by Hemachandra as follows :

"साध्याव्यावृत्तसाधनाव्यावृत्तोभयव्यावृत्ताः सन्दिग्धसाध्यव्यावृत्तिसन्दिग्धसाधनव्यावृत्तिसन्दिग्धोभयव्यावृत्तयो विपरीतव्यतिरेकोऽप्रदर्शितव्यतिरेकश्चेत्यष्टावेव वैधर्म्यदृष्टान्ताभासा भवन्ति।"

(middle term). Here if the inseparable connection (Vyāpti) is shown, thus 'whatever is non-eternal is adventitious as a jar' instead of thus : 'Whatever is adventitions, is non-eternal as a jar' the example would involve the fallacy of contrary connection"[1].

"Some unnecessarily lay down three other kinds of fallacy of the heterogeneous example (Vaidharmya Driṣṭāntābhāsa) viz. (1) Unseparated (Avyatireki) : This person is not *devoid of passions* (major term) because he is a *speaker* (middle term); whoever is devoid of passions is not a speaker as a *piece of stone* (heterogeneous example). Here though a piece of stone is both 'devoid of passions' and 'not a speaker', yet there is no unavoidable separation (Vyatireka Vyāpti) between 'devoid of passions' and 'a speaker'.

(2) Of separation unshown (Apradarśita Vyatireka) Sound is *non-eternal* (major term) because it is *adventitious* (middle term) just as *ether* (example). Here though there is an unavoidable separation between 'adventitious' and 'eternal', yet it has not been shown in the proper form such as 'whatever is not adventitious is eternal, just as ether'. [Dignāga the Buddhist urged the necessity of converting the heterogeneous example into a universal negative proposition, with a view to point out the connection of the middle term and major term].

(3) Of contrary separation (Viparīta Vyatireka) : Sound is not *eternal* (major term), because it is *adventitious* (middle

---

1. "ननु च परैरन्यदपि दृष्टान्ताभासत्रयमुक्तं तद् यथा अनन्वयोऽप्रदर्शितान्वयो विपरीतान्वयश्च। तत्र अनन्वयो यथा, रागादिमान् विवक्षितः पुरुषो वक्तृत्वाद् इष्टपुरुषवत् इति। यद्यपि किलेष्टपुरुषे रागादिमत्वं वक्तृत्वं च साध्यसाधनधर्मौ दृष्टौ तथापि यो यो वक्ता सो सो रागादिमानिति व्याप्त्यसिद्धेरनन्वयोऽयं दृष्टान्तः। तथाप्रदर्शितान्वयो यथा, अनित्यः शब्दः कृतकत्वात् घटवदिति। अत्र यद्यपि वास्तवोऽन्वयोऽस्ति तथापि वादिना वचनेन न प्रकाशित इति अप्रदर्शितान्वयो दृष्टान्तः। विपरीतान्वयो यथा, अनित्यः शब्दः कृतकत्वात्। हेतुमभिधाय यदनित्यं तत् कृतकं घटवदिति विपरीतव्याप्तिदर्शनात् विपरीतान्वयः ॥" Nyāyāvatāra-vivriti.

term); whatever is eternal, is not adventitious, just as *ether* (example). Here the example has been put in a contrary way, for the proper form should have been: 'Whatever is not adventitious is eternal just as *ether*'[1].

Hemachandra agrees that Ananvaya and Avyatireki might be excluded from varieties of Driṣṭāntābhāsa[2].

बालप्रयोगाभासः पंचावयवेषु कियद्धीनता ॥ ४६ ॥

46. Bālaprayogābhāsaḥ pañchāvayaveṣu kiyaddhīnatā.

अग्निमानयं देशो धूमवत्वात् यदित्थं तदित्थं यथा महानसः ॥४७॥

47. Agnimānayaṃ deśo dhūmavatvāt yadittham taditthaṃ yathā mahānasaḥ.

---

1. "परैः परेऽपि दृष्टान्ताभासास्त्रयो विमृश्यभाषितया दर्शितास्तद्यथा-ऽव्यतिरेकोऽप्रदर्शितव्यतिरेकोऽविपरीतव्यतिरेकश्च। ते अस्माभिः अयुक्तत्वात्तु दर्शयितव्याः। तथा हि अव्यतिरेकस्तैर्दर्शितो यथा, अवीतरागः कश्चिद् विवक्षितः पुरुषो वक्तृत्वादित्यत्र वैधर्म्यदृष्टान्तो यः पुनः वीतरागो न स वक्ता यथोपलखण्ड इति। यद्यपि किलोपलखण्डात् उभयं व्यावृत्तं तथापि व्याप्त्या व्यतिरेकासिद्धेः अव्यतिरेकित्वमिति।····तथाहि अप्रदर्शितव्यतिरेकस्तैरुक्तो यथा, अनित्यः शब्दः कृतकत्वात् आकाशवदित्यत्र विद्यमानोऽपि व्यतिरेको वादिना वचनेन उद्भावित इति दुष्टता। विपरीतव्यतिरेकः पुनरभिहितो यथा, अनित्यः शब्दः कृतकत्वात्, इत्यत्र वैधर्म्यदृष्टान्तो यदकृतकं तन्नित्यं भवति यथाकाशमिति इत्यत्र विपर्यस्तव्यतिरेकप्रदर्शनात् विपरीतव्यतिरेकित्वम्।" Nyāyāvatāra-vivriti.

2. "ननु अनन्वयाव्यतिरेकावपि कैश्चिद्दृष्टान्ताभासावुक्तौ, यथा रागादिमानयं वचनात् अत्र साधर्म्यदृष्टान्ते आत्मनि रागवचनयोः सत्यपि साहित्ये वैधर्म्यदृष्टान्ते चोपलखण्डे सत्यामपि सह निवृत्तौ प्रतिबन्धाभावेनान्वयव्यतिरेकयोरभाव इत्यनन्वयाव्यतिरेकौ तौ कस्मादिह नोक्तौ। उच्यते, ताभ्यां पूर्वे न भिद्यन्त इति साधर्म्यवैधर्म्याभ्यां प्रत्येकमष्टावेव दृष्टान्ताभासा भवन्ति यदाहुः—

लिंगस्यानन्वया अष्टावष्टावव्यतिरेकिणः।
नान्यथानुपपन्नत्वं कथंचित् ख्यापयन्त्यमी॥"

Bhāṣya to Aphorism II. 1. 27 in Pramāṇa-mīmāṃsā.

धूमवांश्चायमिति वा ॥ ४८ ॥

48. Dhūmavāñśchāyamiti vā.

तस्मादग्निमान् धूमवांश्चायं ॥ ४९ ॥

49. Tasmādagnimān dhūmavāñśchāyaṃ.

स्पष्टतया प्रकृत-प्रतिपत्तेरयोगात् ॥ ५० ॥

50. Spaṣṭatayā prakrita-pratipatterayogāt.

46. The fallacy of Bāla-prayoga consists of absence of one of the five limbs (of syllogism).

47. This place is full of fire as it is full of smoke. Where there is smoke there is fire. As for example, a kitchen.

48. Or, this is full of smoke.

49. So it is full of fire and it is full of smoke.

50. As clear understanding of the real thing is not established from it.

Commentary

In Chapter III, the five limbs of syllogism have been described. These are as follows :—

1. This hill is full of fire (Pratijñā).
2. Because it is full of smoke (Hetu).
3. Whatever is full of smoke is also full of fire, as a kitchen (Udāharaṇa).
4. So is this hill full of smoke (Upanaya).
5. Therefore, this hill is full of fire (Nigamana).

It has been mentioned in that Chapter, that only the first two are really necessary for inference, the last three being only used to convince children.

Fallacy in using syllogism to convince children arises if we do not mention all the five limbs of syllogism ; e. g. if we mention only the first three or the first four of these limbs. This fallacy also arises if we mention these in a wrong order i. e. if Nigamana be mentioned before Upanaya for this debars a clear understanding of the real thing.

रागद्वेषमोहाक्रान्तपुरुषवचनाज्जातमागमाभासम् ॥ ५१ ॥

51. Rāgadveṣamohākrāntapuruṣavachanājjātamāgamā-bhāsaṃ.

यथा नद्यास्तीरे मोदकराशयः सन्ति धावध्वं माणवकाः ॥५२॥

52. Yathā nadyāstire modakarāśayaḥ santi dhāvadhvaṃ māṇavakāḥ.

अंगुल्यग्रे हस्तियूथशतमास्त इति च ॥ ५३ ॥

53. Aṅgulyagre hastiyūthaśatamāsta iti cha.

विसंवादात् ॥ ५४ ॥

54. Visaṃvādāt.

51. Fallacy of Āgama arises from words of a person seized by attachment, hatred, mistake etc.

52. As for example, Run boys. There are a large quantity of sweetmeats on the river-bank.

53. Or, one hundred elephants are standing on the tip of the finger.

54. Because (these) want (the element of Pramāṇa) viz. true knowledge.

Commentary

Āgama has been defined in Aphorism 99, Samuddeśa III as the knowledge of objects got from words of reliable person etc. (viz. scripture). Now, the words of persons who are not reliable and who may be actuated to deceive people are examples of Āgamā-bhāsa. If one utters a falsehood urging that there are sweetmeats on the banks of a river and urges boys to run to the river side, this will be an example of fallacy of Āgama. Further, if one says what is impossible viz. one hundred elephants are standing on the tip of a finger, it will also be Āgamābhāsa. Jain logicians also say that when true scripture is mis-quoted to support a false proposition, we have an example of Āgamābhāsa.

प्रत्यक्षमेवैकं प्रमाणमित्यादि संख्याभासम् ॥ ५५ ॥

55. Pratyakṣamevaikaṃ pramāṇamityādi saṅkhyābhāsaṃ.

लौकायतिकस्य प्रत्यक्षतः परलोकादिनिषेधस्य परबुद्ध्यादेश्चासिद्धेरतद्विषयत्वात् ॥ ५६ ॥

56. Laukāyatikasya pratyakṣataḥ paralokādiniṣedhasya paravudhyādeśchāsiddheratadviṣayatvāt.

सौगत-सांख्ययौगप्राभाकर-जैमिनीयानां प्रत्यक्षानुमानागमोपमानार्थापत्त्यभावैरेकैकाधिकैर्व्याप्तिवत् ॥ ५७ ॥

57. Saugata-sāṅkhya-yauga-prābhākara-jaiminīyānāṃ pratyakṣānumānāgamopamānārthāpattyabhāvairekaikādhikairvyāptivat.

अनुमानादेस्तद्विषयत्वे प्रमाणान्तरत्वम् ॥ ५८ ॥

58. Anumānādestadviṣayatve pramāṇāntaratvaṃ.

तर्कस्येव व्याप्तिगोचरत्वे प्रमाणान्तरत्वम् अप्रमाणस्याव्यवस्थापकत्वात् ॥ ५९ ॥

59. Tarkasyeva vyāptigocharatve pramāṇāntaratvaṃ apramāṇasyāvyavasthāpakatvāt.

प्रतिभासभेदस्य च भेदकत्वात् ॥ ६० ॥

60. Pratibhāsa-bhedasya cha bhedakatvāt

55. Saṅkhyābhāsa (Fallacy of number) is maintaining 'Pratyakṣa is the only Pramāṇa' etc.

56. Because according to the view of the followers of Chārvāka philosophy the other world is denied from Pratyakṣa and

knowledge of others cannot be derived (from Pratyakṣa), so these cannot be the subject matter of it (Pratyakṣa).

57. Like Vyāpti in case of the followers of the Buddhist, Sāṅkhya, Nyāya, Prabhākara (school of Mīmāṃsa philosophy) and Jaimini (school of Mīmāṃsa philosophy) who accept Pratyakṣa, Anumāna, Āgama, Upamāna, Arthāpatti and Abhāva exceeding one by one (in their doctrines respectively).

58. Knowledge of others being the subject of Anumāna etc. will become another Pramāṇa.

59. Tarka also being understood from Vyāpti will become another Pramāṇa. For that which is not Pramāṇa cannot establish anything.

60. Because there is a difference according to difference of illumination.

Commentary

There is a great difference of opinion among Indian philosophers regarding the number of Pramāṇa. According to the Chārvāka view, there is only one Pramāṇa viz. Pratyakṣa. According to the Buddhist philosophy, there are two Pramāṇas viz. Pratyakṣa and Anumāna. In Vaiśeṣika philosophy, Pratyakṣa and Anumāna are accepted as Pramāṇas for according to this philosophy the Pramāṇas Śabda etc. are included within Anumāna.

In Sāṅkhya philosophy, three Pramāṇas viz. Pratyakṣa, Anumāna and Āgama have been accepted. In Nyāya philosophy, four kinds of Pramāṇa viz. Pratyakṣa, Anumāna, Upamāna and Śabda have been mentioned. In Mīmāṃsa philosophy those who follow the school of Prabhākara mention that there are five Pramāṇas : Pratyakṣa, Anumāna, Upamāna, Śabda and Arthāpatti, and those who follow the Bhatta school mention that there are six Pramāṇas viz. Pratyakṣa, Anumāna, Upamāna, Śabda, Arthāpatti and Abhāva.

In Parīkṣāmukhaṃ it is mentioned that denial of any kind of Pramāṇa as accepted in this work will lead to the fallacy of

Saṅkhyābhāsa (fallacy with reference to the number). It is urged that an example of this fallacy is the view of the Chārvāka philosophy that there is no other Pramāṇa except Pratyakṣa. For the other world or knowledge of others cannot be derived from Pratyakṣa Pramāṇa. That knowledge which cannot know an object cannot establish the existence or non-existence of that object. So the Chārvāka philosophy cannot establish the non-existence of the next world, or the existence of knowledge of others through Pratyakṣa.

Again the knowledge of Vyāpti has to be accepted separately. So the view of philosophers who accept two, three, four, five or six Pramāṇas commit the fallacy of Saṅkhyā (number). For example, if Chārvāka will say 'I will prove the other world by Anumāna (inference), he will have to accept a Pramāṇa other than Pratyakṣa. So the view of Chārvāka that there is only one Pramāṇa viz. Pratyakṣa, becomes vitiated by Saṅkhyābhāsa.

Again, some like the Buddhists accept Tarka to be a separate Pramāṇa to establish Vyāpti. The fallacy will be similar as shown in the acceptance of 'inference' by the Chārvākas for Tarka will increase the number of Pramāṇas as accepted by these philosophers. It cannot be said that though Tarka is accepted, it is not accepted as Pramāṇa. To hold such a view will lead to the failure of establishing Vyāpti for if Tarka be not accepted as Pramāṇa, Vyāpti will not be established by it. That which is not a Pramāṇa cannot establish an object. So if we accept establishment of Vyāpti by Tarka, we must accept Tarka to be a Pramāṇa.

There is a further reason for accepting Tarka etc. as Pramāṇas. Where illuminations are different, Pramāṇas must also be different. In Pratyakṣa, Tarka etc. the illumination is not the same. So these must be treated as different Pramāṇas.

विषयाभासः सामान्यं विशेषो द्वयं वा स्वतंत्रम् ॥ ६१ ॥

61. Viṣayābhāsaḥ sāmānyaṃ viśeṣo dvayaṃ vā svatantraṃ.

तथा प्रतिभासनात् कार्याकरणाच्च ॥ ६२ ॥

62. Tathā pratibhāsanāt kāryākaraṇāchcha.

समर्थस्य करणे सर्वदोत्पत्तिरनपेक्षत्वात् ॥ ६३ ॥

63. Samarthasya karaṇe sarvadotpattiranapekṣatvāt.

परापेक्षणे परिणामित्वमन्यथा तदभावात् ॥ ६४ ॥

64. Parāpekṣaṇe pariṇāmitvamanyathā tadabhāvāt.

स्वयमसमर्थस्य अकारकत्वात् पूर्ववत् ॥ ६५ ॥

65. Svayamasamarthasya akārakatvāt pūrvavat.

61. Viṣayābhāsa (fallacy of object) (happens) where Sāmānya or Viśeṣa or both of them (are) separately (accepted).

62. As it appears like the same, and as it does not do any work.

63. Accepting it to be Samartha (effective) will lead to creation (of result) at all times, being independant.

64. On accepting dependency on other (causes), the quality of being modified will have to be accepted as otherwise, this does not exist.

65. Because, that which is ineffective in itself cannot cause anything as the former.

Commentary

Fallacy of Viṣaya (object) arises when we say that the object of Pramāṇa is only Sāmānya or only Viśeṣa or that Sāmānya and Viśeṣa are separate objects of Pramāṇa. In objects only Sāmānya etc. are not seen and only Sāmānya etc. cannot produce any result. On accepting that Sāmānya etc. can effect something we are led to two stand-points viz. whether Sāmānya etc. effect anything being Samartha (effective cause) or Asamartha (non-effective cause). If we accept that Sāmānya etc. effect things being Samartha, we will be led to the inevitable conclusion that effects will always arise for no other thing than Sāmānya etc. will be required to produce effects. If we maintain that Sāmānya etc. require other accessories, we must maintain that it consists of modification. Whenever we accept accessory causes for production of an effect, the conclusion is inevitable that modification will occur. To accept the second view viz. that Sāmānya etc. produce effect being Asamartha will not be proper. A cause which is Asamartha cannot produce anything either before or after combination with accessory causes. So Sāmānya etc. if taken as Asamartha will not be able to produce any result.

फलाभासं प्रमाणादभिन्नं भिन्नमेव वा ॥ ६६ ॥

66. Phalābhāsaṃ pramāṇādabhinnaṃ bhinnameva vā.

अभेदे तद्व्यवहारानुपपत्तेः ॥ ६७ ॥

67. Abhede tadvyavahārānupapatteḥ.

व्यावृत्त्यापि न तत्कल्पना फलान्तराद्व्यावृत्त्याफलत्वप्रसंगात् ॥ ६८ ॥

68. Vyāvrittyāpi na tatkalpanā phalāntarādvyāvrittyāphalatvaprasaṅgāt.

प्रमाणाद्व्यावृत्त्येवाप्रमाणत्वस्य ॥ ६९ ॥

69. Pramāṇādvyāvrittyevāpramāṇatvasya.

तस्माद्वास्तवोऽभेदः ॥ ७० ॥

70. Tasmādvāstavo'bhedaḥ.

भेदे त्वात्मान्तरवत्तदनुपपत्तेः ॥ ७१ ॥

71. Bhede tvātmāntaravattadanupapatteḥ.

समवायेऽतिप्रसंगः ॥ ७२ ॥

72. Samavāye'tiprasaṅgaḥ.

66. Phalābhāsa (fallacy of result) is either separate or not separate from Pramāṇa.

67. If we accept inseparableness, its (separate) use cannot happen.

68. Its imagination by its opposite cannot (be accepted) for (we) shall have to assume (then) non-result by its opposite (e. g.) another result.

69. Just as Apramāṇa is derived from Pramāṇa by holding the opposite.

70. So, really there is no difference.

71. (If) difference (be accepted), it will not be derived as in the case of another soul.

72. There will be Atiprasaṅga (if we urge) Samavāya.

Commentary

Phalābhāsa (fallacy of the result of Pramāṇa) is either separate from Pramāṇa or inseparable from it. If we accept that the result is always inseparable from Pramāṇa, we cannot say as usual that this is the Pramāṇa and this is the result. If it is mentioned as is done by the Buddhists, that the result will be understood by absence of non-result, it will not be correct. For non-result can then in a similar manner be understood by result of a like nature just as the Buddhists agree to Apramāṇa by absence of Pramāṇa of a like nature. If non-result is taken to be imagined in all cases, there will be nothing as result in this world. So it must be accepted that there is a real difference between Pramāṇa and its result. But it cannot be said that the difference is absolute. For in that case there will be the following difficulty. The result of Pramāṇa in a being other than myself is separate from me. If the difference of Pramāṇa and its result is taken as absolute the result of Pramāṇa of my own soul will also be different from me. It will therefore become impossible to say "this result is the result of my Pramāṇa". If you urge that though Pramāṇa and its result are separate, still according to the relation-ship of Samavāya (co-inherence), wherever there will be Pramāṇa in a soul, there will also be the result by relationship of co-inherence, we will reply that there will be the fault of Atiprasaṅga viz. as Samavāya has been accepted as Nitya (eternal) and Vyāpaka (pervasive), all souls will have the quality of equal co-inherence, and it cannot be that in a particular soul Pramāṇa and the result will exist in relationship of Samavāya.

प्रमाणतदाभासौ दुष्टतयोद्भावितौ परिहृतापरिहृतदोषौ वादिनः साधनतदाभासौ प्रतिवादिनो दूषणभूषणे च ॥७३॥

73. Pramāṇatadābhāsau duṣṭatayodbhāvitau parihritāparihritadoṣau vādinaḥ sādhanatadābhāsau prativādino dūṣaṇabhūṣaṇe cha.

73. Pramāna and its Ābhāsa being shown as faulty and being made free from or connected with fault will be Sādhana or its Ābhāsa in case of the Vādi and Duṣaṇa (fault) or Bhūsaṇa (adornment) respectively of Prativādi (opponent).

Commentary

In a discussion between two persons, one uses Pramāṇa first. He is called the Vādi. His opponent is known as Prativādi. When the Vādi uses a Pramāṇa his Prativādi may say that this is faulty. If the Vādi can show that the fault urged is really non-existent, he wins in the argument and the Pramāṇa becomes Sādhana in case of the Vādi and Dusaṇa in case of the Prativādi. If again, at the outset the Vādi uses Sādhanābhāsa and the Prativādi points out the fault which the Vādi fails to refute, then this Sādhanābhāsa becomes Duṣaṇa to the Vādi and Bhūṣaṇa to the Prativādi.

Hemachandra defines Dūṣaṇa as the words by which faults like Asiddha, Viruddha etc. are shown in propositions[1]. There can also be Dūṣaṇābhāsa viz. an apparent Dūṣaṇa though really it can be proved to be non-existent[2]. Vāda is laying down of a

---

1. "साधनदोषोद्भावनं दूषणम् ॥" Pramāṇa-mīmāṃsā, II. 1. 28.
2. "अभूतदोषोद्भावनानि दूषणाभासा जात्युत्तराणि ॥"

Pramāṇa-mīmāṃsā II. 1. 29.

proposition and its faults in the presence of members of a council and others to prove the real thing[1]. When the Vādi lays down a proposition, the Prativādi finds out its fault. Again when the Prativādi lays down anything, the Vādi finds out its fault. The utterances of the Vādi and Prativādi in this manner are vāda[2].

संभवदन्यद्विचारणीयम् ॥ ७४ ॥

74. Sambhavadanyadvichāraṇīyaṃ.

74. Other (varieties) which exist, are to be understood by reasoning (from other works).

Commentary

In Parīkṣāmukhaṃ, Pramāṇa only is described in detail. But it has been laid down that Pramāṇa as well as Naya are means of instruction ("प्रमाणनयैरधिगमः" Tattvārtha Sūtra I. 6) by which right faith is established. In this aphorism it is mentioned that Nayas are not described in detail in this work but may be learnt from other works[3].

---

1. "तत्वसंरक्षणार्थं प्राश्निकादिसमक्षं साधनदूषणवदनं वादः ॥"

Pramāṇa-mīmāṃsā II. 1. 30.

2. "स्वपक्षसिद्धये वादिनः साधनं, तत्प्रतिषेधाय प्रतिवादिनो दूषणं, प्रतिवादिनोऽपि स्वपक्षसिद्धये साधनं तत्प्रतिषेधाय वादिनो दूषणं, तदेवं वादिनः साधनदूषणे प्रतिवादिनोऽपि साधनदूषणे तयोर्वादिप्रतिवादिभ्यां वदनमभिधानं वादः ॥" Bhāṣya to Pramāṇa-mīmāṃsā. II. 1. 30. Hemachandra says that Vādi, Prativādi, Sabhāpati (the president or umpire) and members of the Council—these four are limbs of a discussion. The members of the Council must be impartial, learned, efficient in discussions and capable of balancing the arguments like a scale "स्वसमयपरसमयज्ञाः कुलजाः पक्षद्वयेप्सिताः क्षमिणः । वादपथेष्वभियुक्तास्तुलासमाः प्राश्निकाः प्रोक्ताः ॥"

3. "संभवद्विद्यमानं अन्यत् प्रमाणतत्वात् नयस्वरूपं शास्त्रान्तरप्रसिद्धं विचारणीयमिह युक्त्या प्रतिपत्तव्यम् ।" Prameya-ratnamālā.

Nayas are mainly divided into two classes : (i) Dravyārthika Naya and (ii) Paryāyārthika Naya. Dravyārthika Naya is subdivided into (a) Naigama (b) Saṅgraha and (c) Vyavahāra and Paryāyārthika Naya is subdivided into (a) Riju-sūtra (b) Śabda (c) Samabhiruḍha and (d) Evambhūta[1].

Siddhasena mentions : "Since things have many characters (that is, may be conceived from many points of view) they are the objects of all-sided knowledge (omniscience) ; but a thing conceived from one particular point of view is the object of Naya (or one-sided knowledge)"[2].

"Objects whether intrinsic or extrinsic, possess many different characteristics, and may be taken from different stand-points. They are understood in their entire character by omniscience alone, while to take them from a certain stand-point is the scope of Naya (the one sided method of comprehension)"[3].

To be more clear, All that exists is capable of being known and as such is an object of knowledge and each substance is possessed of innumerable attributes. We sometimes take a partial view of reality and sometimes we apprehend the whole reality. The former view is known as the Naya or the theory of stand-points, whereas the latter is called the Pramāṇa or complete comprehension[4].

A Naya deals with only the particular aspect in view of the speaker but it does not deny the existence of the remaining attri-

---

1. 'तत्र मूलनयौ द्वौ द्रव्यार्थिकपर्यायार्थिकभेदात्। तत्र द्रव्यार्थिकस्त्रेधा नैगम-संग्रहव्यवहारभेदात्। पर्यायार्थिकश्चतुर्धा ऋजुसूत्रसमभिरूढैवम्भूतभेदात् ॥" Prameya-ratnamālā.

2. "अनेकान्तात्मकं वस्तु गोचरः सर्वसंविदाम्।
एकदेशविशिष्टोऽर्थो नयस्य विषयो मतः ॥" Nyāyāvatāra 29.

3. Ibid. Note to the above by Dr. S. C. Vidyābhūṣaṇa.

4. "सकलादेशः प्रमाणाधीनः, विकलादेशो नयाधीनः।" Quotation in Tattvārtharājavārttika,

butes. When we speak of the colour of gold, we make no mention of its weight, touch, taste, smell and other attributes but our statement does not mean that gold is devoid of all the other attributes besides colour. When speaking from a limited point of view, Jain scholars prefix the word Syāt to every such predication to signify that the object is of a particular type from a particular stand point but it is not so from other points of view. 'Syāt' suggests the existence of other attributes but does not give primary importance to them. This is the differentiating point which helps in accuracy of expression by a scholar of the Jain school of thought. One school of philosophy might say that all that exists is momentary and another school might say that reality is permanent. Jainism reconciles both these seemingly contradictory statements by pointing out that the first view is true from the stand point of modifications only which are subject to change every moment and the second view is also correct from the standpoint of elements of which the thing is composed. One sided systems of philosophy deny the existence of attributes other than what they adopt, whereas the Jain point of view admits their existence though these are not described being not of primary importance. This Nayavāda or Syādvāda system is the distinctive feature of Jain philosophy and logic[1].

The Nayas have broadly been classified as Dravyārthika i. e. statements which refer only to the general attributes of a substance and not to the modifications which the substance is constantly undergoing and (2) Paryāyārthika i. e. statements which refer to the constantly changing conditions of a substance.

The Nayas are further classified into (1) Artha-naya and (2) Śabda-naya. The former deals with the objects and the latter

---

1. A detailed description of Nayas and Saptabhaṅgi (seven modes of predication) has been given in Pages LII—LXXXV of the Introduction to Pañchāstikāya-samayasāra Vol. III of The Sacred Books of the Jainas.

lays emphasis on the words and their grammatical significance.

The Nayas have again been classified as (1) Naigama, (2) Saṅgraha, (3) Vyavahāra, (4) Riju-sūtra, (5) Śabda, (6) Samabhirūḍha and (7) Evambhūta. The first three are subdivisions of Dravyārthika because they deal with objects and the last four are the same of Paryāyārthika Naya because they are concerned with the modifications of substances.

I. Naigama (Not literal or figurative). When we speak of a past or future event as a present one, we have an illustration of this Naya. It is of three kinds relating to past, present and future. If we say on the Diwali day "Lord Mahāvīra attained liberation to-day" we mean that this day is the anniversary day of the past event. Again, we see a man booking his passage and on our query, he says "I am going to England." This is a figurative way of speaking about a present event. Further, when we see a man making a fire and on our questioning him, he says "I am cooking", he really speaks of a future event for which he is making only a preparation.

II. Saṃgraha (common or general). When we use a word denoting a class to mean the whole, we have an example of this Naya. By using the word Dravya we take the six kinds of Dravyas, taking only the general attributes of Dravya (substance) and not considering the distinguishing features.

III. Vyavahāra (distributive). When we divide or separate a general term into its classes, orders, kinds or species, we have an example of this Naya. For example when we speak of Dravya (substance) implying its six subdivisions soul, matter, space, time, media of motion and rest, we have an example of this Naya.

By Saṅgraha Naya the generic properties alone are taken into consideration without any cognizance of the particular properties and by Vyavahāra Naya the particular properties alone are considered.

IV. Riju-sūtra (the straight expression). This Naya takes into account of (1) the actual condition at a particular moment and (2) the actual condition for a long time. The first variety is called Sūkṣma (fine) and the second Sthūla (gross). A soul with a momentary good thought is an example of the former while a man with a human condition for a life time is an example of the latter.

By this Naya a thing as it exists at present is considered without any reference to the past or future. The followers of this Naya say that it is useless to ponder over things as they were in the past or will become in the future. All practical purposes are served by the thing itself as it exists at the present moment.

V. Śabda (descriptive). This Naya includes grammatical correctness and propriety of expression. From this point of view we can use the present for the past tense, plural for the singular number, faminine for the masculine gender etc. An example of the first is when we speak "In 1066 A. D. we see the Normans attack the Anglo-Saxons". The second is illustrated by the use of "you" for one man. The third is exemplified by the use of a masculine name e. g. Lord Nelson for a vessel which is used in feminine gender.

VI. Samabhirūḍha (specific). This Naya is employed when we give a word a fixed meaning out of several which it has. This is exemplified by the use of the word 'Nut' to denote an extra smart man or "Dread nought" to denote a particular kind of warship.

VII. Evambhūta (active). When we restrict the name to the very activity which is connoted by the name we have an example of this Naya e. g. when we call Stratford on Avon by that name only so long as the town stands on the banks of the river Avon[1].

---

1. "नैगम-संग्रह व्यवहारजु सूत्रशब्दसमभिरूढैवम्भूता नयाः ।" Tattvārthādhigama Sutra I. 33. See The Sacred Books of the Jainas Vol. II. P. 45.

Amongst these Nayas, the range of each becomes more and more fine according to their position in the list as mentioned above[1].

These Nayas deal with the various aspects of reality from their particular angles of vision, but they do not predicate the non-existence of other points of views. When one point of view becomes primary, the others become of secondary importance. It is incorrect to suppose that only a particular Naya is correct and others are erroneous. As a matter of fact all these stand points are equally true and valid and lead to correct knowledge, provided that they do not deny the existence of the other points of view, for

---

"अनभिनिवृत्तार्थसंकल्पमात्रग्राही नैगमः। सजात्यविरोधेनैकध्यमुपनीय पर्यायानाक्रान्तभेदानविशेषेण समस्तग्रहणात् संग्रहः। संग्रहनयाक्षिप्तानामर्थानां विधिपूर्वकमवहरणं व्यवहारः। ऋजुं प्रगुणं सूत्रयति तन्त्रयत इति ऋजुसूत्रः। लिंगसंख्यासाधनादिव्यभिचारनिवृत्तिपरः शब्दनयः। नानार्थसमभिरोहणात् समभिरूढः। येनात्मना भूतस्तेनैवाध्यवसाययतीति एवंभूतः।" Sarvārtha-siddhiḥ.

The definition of Nayas with Nayābhāsas is thus given in Prameya-ratna-mālā :

"अन्योऽन्यगुणप्रधानभूतभेदाभेदप्ररूपणो नैगमः। नैकं गमो नैगम इति निरुक्तेः। सर्वथाभेदवादस्तदाभासः। प्रतिपक्षव्यपेक्षः सन्मात्रग्राही संग्रहः। ब्रह्मवादस्तदाभासः। संग्रहगृहीतभेदको व्यवहारः। काल्पनिको भेदस्तदाभासः। शुद्धपर्यायग्राही प्रतिपक्षसापेक्ष ऋजुसूत्रः। क्षणिकैकान्तनयस्तदाभासः। कालकारकलिंगानां भेदाच्छब्दस्य कथंचिदर्थभेदकथनं शब्दनयः। अर्थभेदं विना शब्दानामेव नानात्वैकान्तस्तदाभासः। पर्यायभेदात् पदार्थनानात्वनिरूपकः समभिरूढः। पर्यायनानात्वमन्तरेणापीन्द्रादिभेदकथनं तदाभासः। क्रियाश्रयेण भेदप्ररूपणमित्थंभावः। क्रियानिरपेक्षत्वेन क्रियावाचकेषु काल्पनिको व्यवहारस्तदाभासः। इति नयस्तदाभासलक्षणं संक्षेपेणोक्तं विस्तरेण 'नय-चक्रा'त् प्रतिपत्तव्यम् ॥" Prameya-ratnamālā.

1. "नैगमादयो नया उत्तरोत्तर-सूक्ष्मविषयत्वादेषां क्रमः, पूर्वपूर्वहेतुकत्वाच्च। एवमेते नयाः पूर्वपूर्वविरुद्धमहाविषया उत्तरोत्तरानुकूलाल्पविषयाः।"

Tattvārtha-rāja-vārttika,

one will be wholly untrue without the existence of others. In other words, the valid Nayas are inter-dependent and when they become independent, the result is that their very nature is annihilated. For example, the inter-dependence of cotton threads is possessed of the potentiality of warding off cold and providing comfort to the body, but if each of these threads become independent of others, these will not be able to serve the aforesaid purpose. This pinciple is applied to the doctrine of Nayas. Āchārya Amritachandra Sūri has mentioned that as a milk-maid draws part of the rope of the churning rod by one hand loosening the other part to get butter out of curd, so the Jain doctrine of Naya gives prominence to a particular attribute leaving aside the other views and by this means churns the nectar of reality (Tattva)[1].

The harmonious combination of these co-ordinating Nayas paves the way to right faith (Saṃyog-darśana)[2].

This aphorism of Parikṣāmukhaṃ has been given an alternative explanation by Anantavīrya. He says that besides being explained as above, we may take this aphorism to mean "Vāda-lakṣmaṇa or Patra-lakṣmaṇa which are mentioned elsewhere should be noted here"[3].

Vāda has been defined as words which establish their import[4]. Patra is defined as a sentence the limbs of which are well-known and which establish the import which it desires to convey

---

1. "एकेनाकर्षयन्ती श्लथयन्ती वस्तुतत्वमितरेण ।
अंतेन जयति जैनी नीतिर्मंथाननेत्रमिव गोपी ।।"

Purusārtha-siddhyupāya, Verse 225.

2. "एते गुणप्रधानतया परस्परतंत्राः सम्यग्दर्शनहेतवः ।"

Tattvārtha-rāja-vārttika.

3. "अथवा संभवद् विद्यमानं, अन्यद् वादलक्षणं पत्रलक्षणं वान्यत्रोक्तमिह द्रष्टव्यम् ।" Prameya-ratna-mālā.

4. "समर्थवचनं वादः ।" Ibid.

and which consists of correct and unambiguous words having a deep significance[1].

According to this interpretation the Aphorism will mean that Vāda and Patra have not been described in this work, but these should be studied from other works where the same have been treated in detail.

परीक्षामुखमादर्शं हेयोपादेयतत्त्वयोः ।
संविदे मादृशो बालः परीक्षादक्षवद् व्यधाम् ॥

Parīkṣāmukhamādarśaṃ heyopādeyatattvayoḥ.
Saṅvide mādriśo vālaḥ parīkṣādakṣavad vyadhāṃ.

I, having little knowledge (like a child) have written as one who is conversant with Parīkṣā, (this work) Parīkṣāmukhaṃ (resembling) a mirror for understanding of realities to be accepted or discarded.

Commentary

The author Māṇikyanandī in this concluding verse of his work shows humility by describing himself as a child having little knowledge. This work is compared to a mirror. As good or bad looks of a person adorned with ornaments are seen in a mirror so things to be accepted or discarded will be determined by this work by means of Pramāṇa[2]. As a man conversant with Parīkṣā[3]

---

1. "प्रसिद्धावयवं वाक्यं स्येष्टस्यार्थस्य साधकम् ।
साधुगूढपदप्रायं पत्रमाहुरनाकुलम् ॥" Ibid.

2. "यथैवादर्श आत्मनोऽलंकारमंडितस्य सौरूप्यं वैरूप्यं वा प्रतिविंवोपदर्शनद्वारेण सूचयति तथेदमपि हेयोपादेयतत्त्वं साधनदूषणोपदर्शनद्वारेण निश्चाययतीत्यादर्शत्वेन निरूप्यते ।"

3. Parīkṣā is a full discussion used in finding out the strength and weakness of various arguments which are opposed to one another. 'Pari' means 'full' and 'Īkṣaṇaṃ' means discussion of of subjects. Vide :

completes the work undertaken by him, so the author also has completed this book[1].

End of Samuddeśa VI.

Finis.

—:*:—

"अन्योन्यविरुद्ध-नानायुक्ति-प्रावल्यदौर्वल्यावधारणाय प्रवर्त्तमानो विचारः परीक्षा तर्क इति यावत्। परि समन्तादशेषनिःशेषत ईक्षणं विचारणं यन्न अर्थानामिति व्युत्पत्तेः।" Nyāyamaṇi-dīpikā.

1. "यथा परीक्षादक्षः स्वप्रारब्धशास्त्रं निरुढवांस्तथाहमपि।"

Prameya-ratna-mālā.

TABLE OF CONTENTS

Introduction

SAMUDDEŚA I.

SAMUDDEŚA II.

SAMUDDEŚA III.

SAMUDDEŚA IV.

SAMUDDEŚA V.

SAMUDDEŚA VI.

LIST OF CHARTS

Alphabetical List of Works Quoted and Consulted

Abhidharmakoṣa (Vasubandhu). Kāśī Vidyāpīṭha Granthmālā, Benares.

Āchārāṅga-Sūtra (Commentary on; by Sīlāṅkāchārya) Āgamodaya Samiti, Surat.

Ādipurāṇa (Jinasena)

Akalaṅka-charitra

Annals of the Bhāndārkar Oriental Research Institute Vols. II, XIII.

Āpta-mīmāṃsā (Samantabhadra) Jain Siddhānta Prakāśinī Saṃsthā, Calcutta, 1914.

Āpta-parīkṣā (Vidyānanda) Jain Siddhānta Prakāśinī Saṃsthā. Calcutta, 1913.

Arādhanā-Kathā-Koṣa

Aṣṭādhyāyī (Pāṇini) Nirṇaya Sāgar Press, Bombay.

Aṣṭaśati (Akalaṅka) Nirṇaya Sāgar Press, Bombay.

Aṣṭasahasrī (Vidyānanda) Do

Bhāmatī (Vāchaspati Miśra) Nirnaya Sāgar Press, Bombay.

Bhāṣya on Nyāya Sūtras of Gautama (Vātsyāyana) Bangīya Sāhitya Pāriṣat, Calcutta.

Bhāṣya on Vaiśeṣika Sūtras (Praśastapāda) Chowkhamba Sanskrit Series, Benares.

Bhāṣya on Vedānta Sūtras (Śankarāchārya) Nirnaya Sāgar Press, Bombay.

Brahmavidyābharaṇa

Brihadāraṇyak Upaniṣad Nirnaya Sāgar Press, Bombay.

Catalogue of Sanskrit and Prakrit Mss. in the Central Provinces and Berar (R. B. Hiralal, B. A.)

Chandraprabhacharitaṃ (Vīranandi) Ed. by Pandit Durgaprasad and V. L. Sastri, Nirnaya Sāgar Press, Bombay 1912.

Chhāndogya Upaniṣād Nirnaya Sāgar Press, Bombay.

Devapratiṣṭhātattva (Raghunandana)

Dharmaśarmâbhyudayaṃ Edited by Pandit Durgaprasad, Bombay, 1894.

Dravya-Saṃgraha. Edited by S. C. Ghoshal. Sacred Books of the Jainas Vol. I.

Dravya-saṃgraha-Vritti (Brahmaveva) Do

Dvātriṃśikā (Hemachandra)

Dvātriṃśikā (Siddhasena) Bhavanagar.

Early History of India (Vincent Smith) Oxford 1914.

Encyclopædia Brittannica Vol. XII.

Ephigraphia Carnatica (Lewis Rice) Vol. II. Bangalore 1889.

Epitome of Jainism, An (Nahar and Ghosh) Calcutta.
Guṇakiraṇāvali.
History of the Medieval School of Indian Logic (S. C. Vidyabhusana)
Harivaṃśapurāṇa (Jinasena)
Harṣa-charitaṃ (Bāṇabhatta). Nirnaya Sāgar Press, Bombay.
Hayaśīrṣapañcharātra.
Introduction to the Science of Language (Sayce) London 1900,
Jaina-tarka-bhāṣā. Sindhi Jain Series. Calcutta.
Jaina-tarka-vārttika. Lazarus and Company, Benares.
Jainendra Vyākaraṇa (Devanandi alias Pūyapāda) Srilal Jain, Benares, 1914.
Jainism (Herbert Warren) Madras 1912 ; Arrah 1916.
Kādambarī (Bāṇa-bhatta) Nirnaya Sāgar Press, Bombay.
Karma-mīmāṃsā (A. B. Keith) Heritage of India Series. London, 1921.
Kāśikā (Vāmana and Jayāditya) Lazarus & Co., Benares.
Kāvya-mīmāṃsā (Rājaśekhar) Gaekwad Oriental Series, Baroda.
Kusumāñjali (Udayanāchārya)
Laghīyastraya (Akalaṅka) Sindhi Jain Series, Calcutta.
Mahābhārataṃ. Bangabasi Press, Calcutta.
Mahābhāṣya (Patañjali) Nirnaya Sāgar Press, Bombay.
Manusaṃhitā. Nirnaya Sāgar Press, Bombay.
Meghadūtaṃ (Kālidāsa) Nirnaya Sāgar Press, Bombay.
Miliṅda Pañha. Pali Text Society.
Mīmāṃsā Sūtras. (Jaimini).
Muktāvali. Nirnaya Sāgar Press, Bombay.
Nayachakraṃ. Manikchandra Granthamālā, Bombay.
Nayakarṇikā (Ed. by M. D. Desai) Arrah, 1915.
Nayapradīpa. Jaina-dharma-prasārak Sabhā, Bhāvanagar.
Naya-rahasyaṃ. Jain-dharma-prasārak Sabhā, Bhāvanagar.
Nayopadeśaḥ. Jain-dharma-prasārak Sabhā, Bhāvanagar.
Nemi-nirvāṇaṃ (Ed. by Pandit Sivadatta) Bombay, 1896.
Niśītha-sūtra-chūrṇi (Jinadas Gaṇi Mahottar)
Niyama-sāra (Kundakunda)
Nyāya-darśana Edited by Mahamahopadhyaya Phnibhusan Tarkabagis Bangīya Sāhitya Parisat, Calcutta.
Nyāya-dīpikā (Dharmabhūṣaṇa) Srilal Jain, Calcutta. 1915
Nyāya-koṣa.
Nyāyakumudachandrodaya (Prabhāchandra)
Nyāyamañjarī (Jayanta Bhatta) Vijaynagaram Series, Benares.
Nyāya-praveśa (Dharmakīrti) Gaekwad Oriental Series, Baroda.
Nyāya-Sāra (Bhāsarvajña)

Nyāya-sūtras (Gautama) Chowkhamba Sanskrit Series, Benares.

Nyāya-vārttika (Udyotkara) Chowkhamba Sanskrit Series, Benares.

Nyāyāvatāra (Siddhasena Divākara) Ed. by S. C. Vidyabhusan. Central Jain Publishing House, Arrah 1915.

Nyāyāvatāra-vivriti (Chandraprabha Sūri) Do

Nyāya-vindu (Dharmakīrti) Chowkhamba Sanskrit Series, Benares.

Nyāya-viniśchaya (Akalaṅka) Sindhi Jain Series, Calcutta.

Nyāya-viniśchaya-vivaraṇa (Vādirāja Sūri) Syadvādavidyālaya Benares, (Mss.)

Pañchāstikāya-samaya-sāra (Kundakunda) Rāyachandra Śāstramālā, Bombay.

Pārśvābhyudayaṃ (Jinasena) Bombay, Vira Nirvāna 1913.

Patraparīkṣā (Vidyānanda) Jaina Siddhanta Prakāśinī Saṃsthā, Calcutta.

Pramālakṣma (Vidyānandi)

Pramāṇa-mīmāṃsā (Hemachadra) Sindhi Jain Series, Calcutta.

Pramāṇa-naya-tattvālokālaṅkāra (Deva-sūri) Jaśovijaya Granthamālā, Benares.

Pramāṇa-nirṇayaḥ. Manikchandra Granthmālā, Bombay.

Pramāṇa-parīkṣā (Vidyānanda) Jain Siddhanta Prakāśinī Saṃsthā, Calcutta.

Pramāṇa-saṃgraha (Akalaṅka) Sindhi Jain Series, Calcutta.

Pramāṇa-samuchchaya (Dignāga) Mysore University Series.

Pramāṇa-vārttika (Dharma-kīrti) Ed. by Bhikṣu Rāhula Sāṅkrityāyana (Proofs)

Pramāṇa-viniśchaya (Dharma-kīrti)

Prameyakamala-mārtaṇḍa (Prabhāchandra) Nirṇaya Sāgar Press, Bombay.

Pravachana-sāra (Kundakunda) Edited by Barrend Faddegon.

Principal results of my last two years studies in Sanskrit Mss. Literature (R. G. Bhandarkar) Weir 1889.

Puruṣārthasiddhyupāyaḥ (Amritachandra) Ed. by Ajitprasāda.

Rāmāyaṇa (Vālmīki) Nirnaya Sagar Press. Bombay.

Ratnakarāvatārikā. Yaśovijaya Granthamala, Benares.

Ratnakaraṇḍa-śrāvakāchāraḥ (Samantabhadra) Tr. by C. R. Jain. Central Jaina Publishing House, Arrah 1917.

Śabdaśaktiprakāśika (Jagadis) Jivananda Vidyasagar, Calcutta.

Sacred Books of the East Edited by Max Muller. Vol. XXXIV.

Sacred Books of the Jainas Edited by S. C. Ghoshal Vols. II and III.

Saḍdarśanasamuchchyaya (Haribhadra) Yaśovijaya Granthamālā, Benares.

Sādhanamālā Edited by B. Bhattacharya. Gaekwad's Oriental Series, Baroda.

Śaktisaṅgama Tantra. Do

Samaya sāra (Kundakunda) Brahmachari Sitalprasad, Surat.
Sammati Tarka (Siddhasena) Purātattvamandir, Ahmedabad.
Sanjīvanī (on Meghadūtaṃ) (Mallinātha) Nirnaya Sagar Press, Bombay.
Śaṅkaravijaya (Mādhava)
Sānkhyakārikā (Īśvarakriṣṇa) Chaukhamba Sanskrit Series, Benares.
Sānkhyapravachana Sūtra. Jivananda Vidyasāgar, Calcntta.
Saptabhangitaranginī (Vimaladāsa) Rayachandra Sastramala, Bombay.
Sarvadarśanasaṃgraha (Mādhavāchārya) Ed. by V. S. Abhayankar.
Sarvārtha-siddhiḥ (Pūjyapāda Devanandi) Kalāpa Sarmā, Kolhapur, 1903.
Science of Thought, (C. R. Jain) Central Jain Publishing House. Arrah, 1916.
Siddhi-viniśchaya (Akalaṅka)
Śloka-vārttika (Kumārila Bhatta) Lazarus & Co., Benares.
Śrīmadbhagavadgītā. Nirnaya Sagar Press, Bombay.
Svayambhū-stotra (Samanta-bhadra) Brahmachāri Sitalprasad, Surat.
Suvalopaniṣad. Nirṇaya Sagar Press, Bombay.
Syādvādaratnākara (Devasūri) Ārhat Prabhākara Kāryālaya, Poona.
Syādvādaratnākarāvatārikā (Ranaprabhasūri)
Tārkika-rakṣā (Varadarāja) Ed. by V. P. Dvivedi. Lazarus & Co., Benares.
Tarkakaumudī (Laugākṣi Bhāskara) Nirnaya Sagar Press, Bombay.
Tattva-chintāmaṇi (Gangeśa)
Tattvārthādhigama Sūtra (Umāsvāmi) Sacred Books of the Jainas Vol. II.
Ta-Tang-Hsi-Yu-Chi (Yuan Chwang) Tr. by T. Watters.
Tattvārtha-rāja-vārttika (Akalaṅka) Pandit Gajadharlal, Benares, 1915.
Tattvārtha-sāra. Sanatan Jain Granthamala, Bombay, 1905.
Tattvārtha-śloka-vārttika (Vidyānandi) Nirnaya Sagar Press, Bombay.
Vaiśeṣika Sūtras (Kaṇāda) Lazarus & Co. Benares.
Vākyapadīya (Bhartihari)
Vāsavadattā (Subandhu) Ed. by Jibananda Vidyasagar, Calcutta.
Vedānta-paribhāṣā Ed. by S. C. Ghoshal. White Lotus Publishing House, Calcutta.
Vedānta-Sūtras. Nirṇaya Sāgar Press, Bombay.
Viśvakoṣa (First Edition) Ed. by Nagendranath Basu, Calcutta.
Vivekavilāsa (Jinadatta Sūri)
Yājñavalkya saṃhitā. Anandasram Series, Poona.
Yaśodharacharitaṃ.
Yoga-Sūtras (Patañjali) Ānandasram Series, Poona.
Yogavāśiṣṭha Rāmāyaṇa, Nirnaya Sagar Press, Bombay.

Journals.

Anekānta (Hindi)
Annals of the Bhandarkar Oriental Research Institute Vols. II, XIII.
Jain Gazette, The
Jain Hitaisi (Hindi) Bhag II.
Jain Jagat (Hindi) Year IX, Vol. 15.
Jain Sāhitya Saṃśodhaka (Hindi) Bhag 1 Anka 1.
Jain Siddhānta Bhāskar (Hindi) Bhag 2 Nos. 1, 4 Bhag 3. No. 4 Bhag 4 Nos. 1 and 3.
Journal of the American Oriental Society Vol. 31.

Manuscripts.

[Preserved in Jain Siddhānta Bhavan, Arrah]

Arthaprakāśikā (Panditāchārya ?)
Nyāyamaṇidīpikā (Ajitasenāchārya)
Prameyakaṇṭhikā (Sāntivarṇi)
Prameya-ratnamālaṅkāra (Chāru-kīrti).

ALPHABETICAL INDEX OF THE APHORiSMS.

GENERAL INDEX.